# NELSON'S ANNUAL
# Youth Ministry
# SOURCEBOOK

## 2008 EDITION

# NELSON'S ANNUAL
# Youth Ministry
# SOURCEBOOK

## 2008 EDITION

THOMAS NELSON
*Since 1798*

NASHVILLE   DALLAS   MEXICO CITY   RIO DE JANEIRO   BEIJING

Published in Nashville, TN, by Thomas Nelson. Thomas Nelson is a trademark of Thomas Nelson, Inc.

Thomas Nelson, Inc. titles may be purchased in bulk for educational, business, fund-raising, or sales promotional use. For information, please email SpecialMarkets@Thomas Nelson.com.

Unless otherwise indicated, Scripture quotations are from the NEW KING JAMES VERSION of the Bible, © 1979, 1980, 1982, 1990, 1992 by Thomas Nelson, Inc., Publishers.

Verses marked NASB are from the NEW AMERICAN STANDARD BIBLE®, © 1960, 1962, 1963, 1968, 1971, 1972, 1973, 1975, 1977, 1995 by The Lockman Foundation. Used by permission.

Verses marked NIV are taken from the HOLY BIBLE, NEW INTERNATIONAL VERSION®, © 1973, 1978, 1984 by the International Bible Society. Used by permission of Zondervan Publishing House. All rights reserved.

Verses marked NRSV are from the New Revised Standard Version Bible, © 1989, Division of Christian Education of the National Council of the Churches of Christ in the United States of America. Used by permission. All rights reserved.

Verses marked MSG are taken from The Message, © 1993, 1994, 1995, 1996, 2000, 2001, 2002. Used by permission of NavPress Publishing Group.

Verses marked NLT are taken from the Holy Bible, New Living Translation, © 1996. Used by permission of Tyndale House Publishers, Inc., Wheaton, Illinois 60189. All rights reserved.

*Book design by Kristy L. Morrell, Smyrna, Tennessee. Typesetting by ProtoType Graphics, Inc., Nashville, Tennessee.*

ISBN 10: 1-4185-2752-1
ISBN 13: 978-1-4185-2752-5

Printed in the United States of America

07 08 09 10 11 — 7 6 5 4 3 2 1

# Contents

117392

# Introduction

There are dozens of ways to say it—"You can't give what you don't have"; "Give out of the overflow of what the Lord has given to you"; "When you are on empty, you can't fill others"—you get the picture.

A question that has been guiding my thoughts lately is, *What if I were as physically healthy as I am spiritually healthy?* In other words, what if my physical body mirrored the health of my spiritual life? Would I be limping? Relying on pain killers? Achey and tired? Running a 10K? We spend a great deal of time thinking about the food we eat, what we drink, how much and when to exercise, and too little time thinking about our souls. (Granted some of us need to pay a little more attention to our physical bodies!) As a leader, you must take care of yourself in order to set an example for your students. God teaches that we are to treat our bodies as temples. This includes body, mind, and soul. We must spend time in prayer and study, eat healthy, and exercise to keep our bodies and minds in good condition.

The first place for you as a leader to begin is in prayer. Slow down; spend time with the Lord, and prepare yourself spiritually for your leadership role. Seek God's face. Praise Him for who He is, thank Him for what He has done in your life, and confess your needs. Ask God to minister through you to the youth in your church.

My youth group meetings begin with two minutes of prayer. This prayer consists of four parts of thirty seconds each: Praising God, Thanking God, Confessing needs or sins, and Requests. This isn't a lot of time, but it gets your mind focused on God and prayer and gets the meeting off to an uplifted start.

We offer this book as a guide for leaders to use in Youth Ministry Services. We have filled it with ideas for worship, prayer, games, activities, and teaching tools. There are many choices available to make your youth meetings educational, fun, exciting, and interesting. The lessons are broken into sections including *Memory Verse, Scripture, The Big Picture, Focus, Discovery, Life Application, Making It Personal, Options,* and *Songs.* There are lessons for Sunday services and for Wednesday night services.

You will be introduced to the lesson by a short summary of what the *students will learn,* accompanied by a list of *items you will need* to use in the lessons. The *Memory Verse* and *Scripture* are for study. The *Focus* section gets the attention of the students. It introduces a topic or concept to make them think. Usually including a game, this gets the group interacting with each other. *Discovery* is the core of the lesson. It delivers information to challenge the thoughts and beliefs of the students, encouraging them to ask questions and seek answers for themselves. *Life Application* is for Christians in general and is a great avenue for group discussion and application to situations in our world today. *Making It Personal* focuses on the individual. It allows the students to find ways to grow in their faith as they face life's challenges and struggles. The information in this book is designed as a guideline and can easily be adjusted to suit your particular group's needs.

Teach from the overflow of your own life. Make the illustrations yours. Spend time with your students and get to know them. Listen to their ideas and offer them a place of security, peace, and comfort. Encourage them to share their fears and concerns with each other in an atmosphere of caring and love. Give them principles to apply to their lives today. Allow this book to be a useful tool as you share Christ with your students. May God bless each step of your ministry and fill you to overflowing!!

Grace and peace,
*Amy Elizabeth Jacober*

# Contributors

**Rick Bennett** is a church consultant in Tampa, Florida. He and his wife, Kristi, planted a church in Boston, assisted in church planting in Houston, and ministered to youth in Virginia, Florida, and Georgia. They have three beautiful children.

**Janelle Comfort** is the youth pastor at Baseline Community Church in Glendora, California.

**Joyce del Rosario** is a graduate of Princeton Theological Seminary and is currently an Area Director for Young Life in San Francisco. While concerned with many issues, her area of interest includes ministry to and with Asian American adolescents.

**Ben Donley** is a wordsmith and lover of music. He is Associate Pastor of Agape Christian Church of Pasadena. He and his wife, Stephanie, work for affordable housing and issues of homelessness in the local community.

**Pamela Erwin** is a veteran youth worker beginning in the south and currently serving in Minnesota. She is Professor of Youth Ministry and Practical Theology at Bethel University in St. Paul. She is also the President of the Association of Youth Ministry Educators.

**Rev. Chuck Hunt** is a long-time youth worker and even longer California beach lover. He serves as the Pastor of Student Ministries and Church Life at St. Peter's by the Sea Presbyterian Church in Rancho Pales Verdes, California.

**Amy Jacober** has made youth ministry her life's work. She serves as the Youth Pastor at Agape Christian Church and Associate Professor of Practical Theology and Youth Ministry at Truett Theological Seminary. She is passionate about marginalized people, urban issues, securing time with her community, and most importantly, her husband.

**Sharon Koh** is the Director of Young Adult and College Ministries at Evergreen Baptist Church of Los Angeles, California. She is a graduate of Fuller Seminary with youth ministry experience.

**Jim Krill** has a deep passion for Jesus and His justice in the world. He serves along with his wife, Robin, in Thousand Oaks, California. Jim is the Youth Pastor at Christian Church of Thousand Oaks.

**Captains Matthew and Dianne Madsen,** both Salvation Army officers, have had many opportunities serving youth populations in several communities, including heading up the Salvation Army's youth programs for San Diego and Los Angeles (Diane) and serving as a youth pastor in El Cajon, California (Matthew). The Madsens are Pastors for the Salvation Army's Corps Community Center in Puyallup, Washington.

**James W. Mohler, Ph.D.,** is a veteran youth worker serving as Chair of the Department of Theology at Talbot School of Theology. In very magical ways, he has been a youth pastor, camp director, church leader, and dedicated husband and father.

**R. Scott Okamoto** is first a writer and then a fisherman. He teaches English at Azusa Pacific University while raising three beautiful children with his wife, Geri, in Pasadena, California. In his spare time, he is writing his latest novel.

**Randy and Whitney Prosperi** make their home in Tyler, Texas, with their two daughters. Whitney contributes to numerous devotionals and magazines and is the author of *Lifestyle: Real Perspectives from Radical Women in the Bible.* She is a former Girls' Minister and is currently working on a book about girls' ministry.

**Carina Schubert** has been the Associate Youth Director for Sierra Madre Congregational Church since June, 2006, after graduating with a Youth Ministry degree from Azusa Pacific University. She enjoys exploring Los Angeles with her new husband, Scott, and is excited about their future ministry adventures together!

**Scott Schubert** is a recent graduate of Azusa Pacific University. Scott founded and runs a home church in Rowland Heights, California, for high school boys. He is excited to begin married life with his new wife, Carina.

**David Upchurch** serves young married adults on the Maturity and Ministry staff at Champion Forest Baptist Church. He has been in ministry since 1990 and worked with students for over fifteen years in churches of various styles and sizes in Texas and Georgia. David is married to Kendra, his high school sweetheart, and they have three children. David has a Communications degree from Baylor University and a Masters of Divinity from Southwestern Baptist Theological Seminary.

**Bryan Whiteside** is the Director of Student Ministries at Bethlehem Lutheran Church in Auburn, California. He loves baseball, God, and teenagers, and will enroll at Fuller Seminary in the fall.

**Ivan Wild** has been an Officer/Minister in The Salvation Army for fifteen years, including service as Divisional Youth Secretary in the Southwest states and Southern California. Ivan and his wife are Majors serving as Pastors of The Salvation Army Church in Torrance, California. Ivan received a Masters degree in Theology from Fuller Seminary in 2004. He has been married for eighteen years and has three children.

**Angela Williams** is a lover of hip hop and ministry with teens. When not dancing, she serves as the Youth Director at Brentwood Presbyterian Church in Los Angeles, California.

# 2008 Calendar

| | |
|---|---|
| January 1 | New Year's Day |
| **January 6** | **Epiphany** |
| **January 13** | |
| **January 20** | **Sanctity of Human Life Sunday** |
| January 21 | Martin Luther King, Jr. Day |
| January 26 | Australia Day |
| **January 27** | |
| February 1–29 | Black History Month |
| **February 3** | **Transfiguration Sunday; Super Bowl Sunday** |
| February 6 | Ash Wednesday |
| **February 10** | **First Sunday of Lent** |
| February 12 | Lincoln's Birthday |
| February 14 | Valentine's Day |
| **February 17** | **Second Sunday of Lent** |
| February 18 | Presidents' Day |
| February 22 | Washington's Birthday |
| **February 24** | **Third Sunday of Lent** |
| February 29 | Leap Day |
| **March 2** | **Fourth Sunday of Lent** |
| **March 9** | **Fifth Sunday of Lent; Daylight Saving Time Begins** |
| **March 16** | **Palm Sunday** |
| March 17 | St. Patrick's Day |
| March 20 | Maundy Thursday; First Day of Spring |
| March 21 | Good Friday; Purim |
| **March 23** | **Easter Sunday** |

| | |
|---|---|
| **March 30** | |
| **April 6** | |
| **April 13** | **Jefferson's Birthday** |
| **April 20** | **Passover** |
| April 22 | Earth Day |
| April 23 | Administrative Professionals Day |
| **April 27** | |
| May 1 | Ascension Day; National Day of Prayer |
| **May 4** | |
| **May 11** | **Mother's Day; Pentecost** |
| May 17 | Armed Forces Day |
| **May 18** | **Trinity Sunday** |
| **May 25** | |
| May 26 | Memorial Day |
| **June 1** | |
| **June 8** | |
| June 14 | Flag Day |
| **June 15** | **Father's Day** |
| June 20 | First Day of Summer |
| **June 22** | |
| **June 29** | |
| July 4 | Independence Day |
| **July 6** | |
| **July 13** | |
| **July 20** | |
| **July 27** | **Parent's Day** |
| **August 3** | **Friendship Day** |
| August 6 | Transfiguration Day |

| | |
|---|---|
| **August 10** | |
| **August 17** | |
| **August 24** | |
| **August 31** | |
| September 1 | Labor Day |
| **September 7** | **Grandparent's Day** |
| **September 14** | |
| **September 21** | |
| September 22 | First Day of Autumn |
| September 26 | Native American Day |
| **September 28** | |
| September 30 | Rosh Hashanah |
| October 1–31 | Pastor Appreciation Month |
| **October 5** | |
| October 9 | Yom Kippur |
| **October 12** | |
| October 13 | Columbus Day |
| **October 19** | |
| **October 26** | **Reformation Day; Mother-in-Law Day** |
| October 31 | Halloween |
| November 1 | All Saints' Day |
| **November 2** | **Daylight Saving Time Ends** |
| **November 9** | **International Day of Prayer for the Persecuted Church** |
| November 11 | Veterans Day |
| **November 16** | |
| **November 23** | |
| November 27 | Thanksgiving Day |

| | |
|---|---|
| **November 30** | **First Sunday of Advent** |
| **December 7** | **Second Sunday of Advent; National Pearl Harbor Remembrance Day** |
| **December 14** | **Third Sunday of Advent** |
| **December 21** | **Fourth Sunday of Advent; First Day of Winter** |
| December 22 | Hanukkah Begins |
| December 24 | Christmas Eve |
| December 25 | Christmas Day |
| December 26 | Kwanzaa Begins |
| **December 28** | |
| December 31 | New Year's Eve |

**Boldface dates are Sundays**

# Weekly Suggestions for 52 Weeks

# Wise Men

*By Sharon Koh*

**In this lesson, students will:**
- ✔ Have an opportunity to explore a few of the different ways that God reveals Himself to humanity.
- ✔ Recognize that God is not limited to these methods of revelation, but that He, in His wisdom, chooses when and how to reveal Himself to us.

**Stuff you'll need:**
- ❑ A large blanket or bed sheet

## Epiphany

The Christian feast commemorating the revelation of Jesus to humanity, specifically the visit of the Magi: "I once was blind . . ."—Mark 8:22–26

## Memory Verse

If any of you lacks wisdom, he should ask God, who gives generously to all without finding fault, and it will be given to him.—James 1:5 NIV

## Scripture

Mark 8:22–25

## Lesson in a Sentence

God reveals Himself to us in different ways and, usually, over a period of time.

## The Big Picture

When Jesus heals the blind man in Mark 8, it is a gradual process. The man does not regain his sight all at once. Instead, Jesus allows the healing to take place over a period of time, in two stages. God sometimes reveals Himself to us in a gradual manner.

# Focus

### Who Am I?

This game allows students to have fun familiarizing themselves with each other's names. Split the students into two groups and ask the groups to sit on opposite sides of a blanket held up like a curtain. Each side has to silently choose a representative to sit directly in front of the blanket. Make sure the other team cannot see any movement or hear any communication taking place on your side of the blanket.

When the blanket is dropped and the other team revealed, the first of the two representatives to call the other's name wins. When one side wins, the loser has to join the winning team. This makes the team slightly larger. The object of the game is to gain the membership of all present.

This is a particularly good game for groups in which not all students know each other well. However, if your group is very familiar with each other, you can let them choose fictional names. Another good variation of this game involves students picking adjectives that describe themselves. For example, sweet or smart or funny are words that people can choose to have people on the opposing team yell out once they are spotted.

# Discovery

God has many attributes. Ask students to list as many of the attributes of God as they can think of (holy, wise, loving, fatherly, gentle, just, strong, powerful). If the question arises as to what an attribute is, refer to the adjectives used in the game. They are characteristics a person possesses that describe that person.

After the students have had the opportunity to brainstorm for a while, ask them how they would feel if God revealed Himself to them in all of these capacities *at once.* Would they feel overwhelmed?

Read Mark 8:22–25. Could Jesus have healed the man instantly? Could Jesus have healed the man without touching him? Yes, but He chooses to touch the man instead. Why do you think the Lord chose to heal in this manner?

Furthermore, the recovery of sight takes place in two stages: First, the man sees people who look like walking trees. A forest scene from *The Lord of the Rings* comes to mind. Then, he sees everything clearly. Jesus, in His wisdom, chose to restore the man's sight to him *gradually.* Why might this have been?

## Life Application

Some of us are impatient for God to reveal Himself in our lives. We plead with Him to "Show me your face!" But, we don't really know what we are asking for. If God were to reveal Himself to us in the fullness of His glory, it would blow us away and completely overwhelm us. Instead, God has to reveal Himself to us gradually—one step at a time.

Just like Jesus seemed to know that the blind man needed to feel His touch, Jesus also knew that the man's sight needed to be restored in stages. Perhaps instant clarity of vision would have been too much for the man to receive at once. We don't really know exactly why Jesus decided to heal in this manner, but it is illustrative of the way that God needs to reveal Himself to us—gradually.

## Making It Personal

As we remember the revelation that the Magi received, we also remember that the package was simple—a Baby in a manger was the Incarnation of God Himself. They understood Him just *a little*—enough to journey far and to offer Him precious gifts—but they would come to understand Jesus a whole lot more as He grew up and began to teach and perform miracles.

Likewise, God allows us to understand Him one step at a time. Each day that we hear a little more from His Word or about His work around the world, we learn a little more about who He is and what He cares about. It is not a full revelation in one instant, but it is a gradual revelation that allows us to grow in our understanding of Him. He knows what we need.

## TEACHER'S NOTE:

The story of Epiphany can be found in Matthew 2:1–12. The gifts that the magi brought to the infant Jesus are frequently of great interest. Gold, frankincense, and myrrh are all significant gifts that demonstrate the wise men's understanding of Jesus' identity. Gold is a gift fit for a king. Frankincense is a gift that would be offered to a deity. Myrrh is what would be used to preserve a dead body—for someone who would die.

# Wise Men

*By Sharon Koh*

## Epiphany

". . . but now I see."—Mark 8:22–26

## Memory Verse

They asked each other, "Were not our hearts burning within us while he talked with us on the road and opened the Scriptures to us?"—Luke 24:32 NIV

## Scripture

Luke 24:13–35

## Lesson in a Sentence

The full revelation of God is available to us in the Bible.

# Focus

Students sometimes ask how they can come to know more about God: Who is He and how are we to know about Him? Let students list all the questions they have about who God is. What is He like? What does He care about? What is His nature?

# Discovery

Read Luke 24:13–35.

1. What were the two men discussing as they were walking along? What emotions were they feeling as they conversed?
2. They did not immediately recognize Jesus. Instead, they proceeded to tell Him about the things that hurt and confused them, ". . . we had hoped that He was the One who was going to redeem Israel . . ." What was Jesus' response to their question?
3. How did Jesus substantiate His answer? Where were the teachings that would prove His statements about the Christ?
4. The phrase "Moses and all the prophets" (v. 27) was the way they referred to the Scriptures at the time. Today, we refer to the Word of God as the Bible. So, what did Jesus refer them to when they did not understand who He was?

## Application

Soon after referring the two men to the Scriptures, their eyes were opened to who He was—it was Jesus Himself. Then, in hindsight, they realized that their hearts had been burning within them when He was talking to them. Invite students to share about times when something was taking place and they did not know that God was behind it. Later, what was the trigger that allowed them to see that God's hand was in the occurrence all along?

# Complacency in Times of Prosperity

*By Amy Jacober*

## In this lesson, students will:

✔ Learn that God warns us not to forget what He has done.
✔ Recognize God's provision in our own lives.
✔ Understand that money and fame are not the ultimate goals in life.
✔ Realize that God is important to us in good times and difficult times.

## Stuff you'll need:

❑ Five lunch bags
❑ Index cards
❑ Pens or pencils
❑ Clip from *MTV cribs* found on www.MTV.com

## Memory Verse

The rich and the poor have this in common, the Lord is the maker of them all.
—Proverbs 22:2

## Scripture

Amos 6:1–7

## Lesson in a Sentence

It is too easy to rely on yourself, forgetting God, when life is going well.

## The Big Picture

God does not like to be forgotten. He is the One who provides, protects, and gives all that we have. The sad part is that most of us don't recognize this on a daily basis. I think of a saying I only heard from mothers in the south when I read the book of Amos: "I brought you into this world and Lord knows I can take you out!" Now that may not be quite the way Amos would have put it but the point gets across. God provided and is angry His people are now thinking they no longer need Him. In His continuous generosity and patience, God offers warning long before action comes. Make no mistake; He is patient but if we ignore His warnings, change will come.

# Focus

## Option 1

### What's in Your Future?

There is nothing scientific or guaranteed about this exercise. It is purely for fun.

Have five lunch bags and enough index cards for each student to have five.

Ask the students to write one of each of the following items on a separate index card: a vehicle, a job, a country, a pet, and a home. For example, a VW bug, Sri Lanka, a bicycle repairman, an iguana, and a trailer. Be certain they write only one car on a card and one job on a card—not all five items on the same card. What they write really does not matter. Once they are done, toss all of the car cards in one bag, all of the job cards in another, all of the country cards in a third, and so on. Take turns drawing one card from each bag to *see your future*. How many students ended up with great wealth? How many ended in great poverty? What were the funniest jobs listed? Whose life improved? Whose life got worse? This should be a fun activity to get people thinking about what they have now and how their future can change.

If the students wrote Hummers and mansions on their cards, ask them how many think they will really end up with these kinds of possessions? If they wrote items like bicycles and tents, ask what they really need to survive and how many of them have more than this now?

## Option 2

Show a clip from *MTV cribs*. You can download this from www.MTV.com and look under shows.

Watch a few clips to see how the celebrities live. What is so great about having a house like this? Are these homes over the top? Why do shows like this do so well? In other words, why do so many of us like to see how the rich and famous live? Would living in a house like this guarantee happiness?

# Discovery

How much could you eat right after Thanksgiving dinner? How much more do you need right after opening presents from Christmas or your birthday? Are any of you in serious need of clothes right now? I'm not talking about the latest trends. I mean, are you covered and warm?

Amos was a prophet during a most difficult time for people to listen—when Israel was doing well! They were at peace; no more running or hanging out in the wilderness. Cities were established; trade was good; money was coming in; and no one was invading their land and setting them to war. Life was GOOD!

Check out what Amos has to say to Israel during this time of peace and prosperity.

Break into groups of four and read Amos 6:1–7. After each group has finished reading, ask them to listen and follow along as the same passage is read from *The Message*.

Ask each group to write a summary of what Amos is saying such as, "When you think you have it all, guess again," or "God is not impressed by wealth."

## Teacher's Note:

The book of Amos was written by a shepherd from south of Jerusalem named Amos. God called him out of Judah, the southern kingdom, to head north. His time of prophecy was relatively short, about ten years. His was a prophetic voice to Israel during a time of peace and prosperity. Israel had a history of struggle but at this time they were at rest and doing quite well.

## Life Application

Ask each group of four to split into pairs. Ask them to list every expense they have each week: food, Internet, cell phone, gasoline, clothes, books, CDs (even if they are using their parents' money). Total those expenses for a week, a month, and then the year. You may need to help them by offering an amount for phone (roughly $25/month for their portion of the family plan on the cell phone, at least $150/month for food, $100 each month for their portion of rent, and so on.

Notice anything? We are a culture filled with prosperity. At war or peace, the last few generations have been able to spend regardless of the circumstances in our world. Amos was clear that people in Jerusalem and Samaria thought they were it because they were wealthy and powerful. Amos knew otherwise and cried out to these people to not get so comfortable in their lives. He wanted them to rely on God, not their possessions that would surely disappear in time.

Lead in a discussion linking Amos' words for Israel with our world today.

- How are we alike or different from the culture Amos was describing?
- Is our response the same as that of the Israelites? How are the responses different?
- How easy or hard is it to seek God when our needs are met everywhere else?
- Why do we so easily forget that it was God who provided in the first place?
- How can we try to remember all He has done in the past?

Sadly, the news today is full of stories of famous teen idols who have it all yet throw it all away by messing up their lives. Check out the Web or magazine stand for examples of singers, actors, or athletes who have money and fame and are still unhappy and struggling. Money and fame do not equal happiness. Many of our current celebrities are proof of this!

## Making It Personal

What dreams do you have for the future? Are they dreams to help others? Build a house? Solve a crime? Or are they dreams of money and fame? Of power and lots of material things?

It is human nature to want more than we have. The problem comes when we lose perspective and become jealous of others who have more than we do. We have to realize there will always be someone with more than us and there will always be someone with less.

Invite each student to thank God for what they have in their lives right now. Remind them of Amos' warning not to get too comfortable relying on their own material goods and possessions.

# Complacency in Times of Prosperity

By Amy Jacober

## Memory Verse
The rich and the poor have this in common, the LORD is the maker of them all.
—Proverbs 22:2

## Scripture
Deuteronomy 6:10–25

## Lesson in a Sentence
It is too easy to rely on yourself, forgetting God, when life is going well.

# Focus

**Who Done It? Trivia**
Begin with the following list and build it to match the interests of your students. The Internet has a great collection of trivia on all sorts of topics.

Q: Where is the Empire State Building?
A: New York

Q: Who built it?
A: Sterret Brothers and Eken

Q: Who gave the Statue of Liberty to the United States?
A: France

Q: Who won the Super Bowl last year?
A: Indianapolis Colts

Q: Oscar winner for movie of the year last year?
A: *The Departed*

Q: Who invented peanut butter?
A: George Washington Carver

Q: Who invented PlayStation?
A: Ken Kutaragi

After the game, score the answers and offer a small prize to the person who had the most correct answers. If you want a treat for your whole group, offer them individually wrapped LifeSavers—you know, the ones invented by Clarence Crane.

# Discovery

God does not mess around. The same truths that were present in the Old Testament apply today. He provides and does not want us to take Him for granted.

Set the scene for your students. The Israelites were delivered out of Egypt and are currently wandering in the wilderness. They have been promised a land flowing with milk and honey and are currently experiencing freedom. They are beginning to complain.

Turn to Deuteronomy 6:10–25. Make two lists. On one side of a paper or your dry-erase board, list what God has done for His people. On the other side, list what God is requiring of them.

## Life Application

What does God require of us today?

Reread verse 12. How is it that we still forget the Lord, even with all of His warnings?

Give each student a piece of paper, pencil, and a tea light. Invite each person to light their candle as they write a letter to God thanking Him for what He has given to them in their lives. Realize that some of your students may be in very difficult places at this time in their life. They may have just learned their parents are divorcing or they know the family is struggling with money issues. Don't negate the worries they have. Encourage them to take their concerns to the Lord and recognize that God still provides exactly what they need. The secret is in remembering this.

At the end of the meeting, be sure to blow out the tea lights. Close in prayer by thanking God that He has brought you together as a group. Tell each student to take their tea light home and light it for the night as a reminder of all they offered to the Lord in their letter.

## Song Connect

"To the Only God" by Dave Crowder and Shane & Shane on *Glory Revealed*

## Quotable Quotes

*Happiness is not in the mere possession of money; it lies in the joy of achievement, in the thrill of creative effort.*—Franklin D. Roosevelt

*Ordinary riches can be stolen; real riches cannot. In your soul are infinitely precious things that cannot be taken from you.*—Oscar Wilde

## Service Option

It's been a few weeks since Christmas. By this time, some of those gifts you received are sitting on their shelves. Other items that have been replaced are collecting dust. There are still plenty of people who have needs. Giving decreases after the holidays. Suggest a closet clean out of good used clothing and shoes, toys and books that you will collect as a group and donate to a local shelter. Winter has just begun and life is about to get much harder for many people. You may even want to consider volunteering at a shelter or a soup kitchen.

# Who's Got Your Back?

JANUARY 20 2008

*By Amy Jacober*

In this lesson, students will:
- ✔ Identify the vulnerable people in their world.
- ✔ Consider the cost they may incur for helping others.
- ✔ Understand we all need one another as we walk through life, some more than others.
- ✔ Recognize that God values all people, including the vulnerable.
- ✔ Discuss what it means to follow God when it goes against earthly authority.

Stuff you'll need:
- ❏ Headlines made by you about your students (see Option 2)
- ❏ Index cards
- ❏ Pens or pencils

## Memory Verse

I have shown you in every way, by laboring like this, that you must support the weak. And remember the words of the Lord Jesus, that He said, "It is more blessed to give than to receive."—Acts 20:35

## TEACHER'S NOTE:

For the more curious of you and your students, you may try to find where in Scripture Jesus said this particular phrase. You will be looking for a very long time. Realize that only a fraction of what Jesus ever said and did was actually recorded. Just look at the large absence of information we have from His early teen years to age thirty! John 20:30–31 and John 21:25 tell us that the Bible acknowledges this very fact. Do not let this be a reason to detract from this verse. While this exact phrase is not recorded elsewhere, His entire life and teachings echo this sentiment, giving it credibility.

## Scripture

Exodus 1:15–20

## Lesson in a Sentence

God calls each of us to take care of one another.

## The Big Picture

We were never meant to try to walk this life alone. In fact, before we were able to walk, we literally could not do this alone! Somewhere along the way we lose this insight. We lose the wisdom that says, "I need you." One of the fun parts of life is that just as much as we need others, someone somewhere needs us. You have *something* to offer, no matter how little you may think that something is. Teenagers sometimes feel they have no power. They feel they have to "grow up" before they can make a difference. We read stories every day of teenagers who decided they *could* make a difference now and they go right ahead and succeed.

The midwives in this story were not women of status and power. In fact, they never would be powerful but they chose to help those who were even more vulnerable than themselves. Remind the students that they are to help those more vulnerable than themselves and to accept help from those who are more fortunate. Most people err too much on one side or the other. You will have students who are great at helping others but refuse to accept help when they need it. You may have students who are *help vampires*. They not only accept help, but they seek it out until everyone around them is sucked dry of energy and compassion. The key is balance. At times we all need help. At times we may all offer help. God set up the system and we have to learn how to live within it.

# Focus

## Option 1

### Freeze Tag

If you have a large space somewhere inside, all the better. If not, the *freeze* in this game may take on a whole new meaning.

Choose one or two people to be *it*. Designate specific boundaries within which the players must remain (if not, they could end up running all around the building). The object of the game is to have *it* tag each person. Once a person has been tagged, they must stop where they are and freeze. A player may become unfrozen by another free player stopping, touching them on the shoulder, and yelling "melt, melt, melt!" If melt is not said three times, the original player remains frozen and *it* can get them, too! If all the players become frozen, declare winners and play again.

## Option 2

This game will take a little work ahead of time but it is worth it! You are going to investigate who in your youth group is helping others or has helped someone else in the past. This can be something big (organizing a blood drive or volunteering weekly with an after-school program) or something less spectacular (the day they helped an elderly neighbor clean out her kitchen or volunteered one day at a soup kitchen). It doesn't even matter if it was for school credit (some schools require community service); they did it and followed through! Talk to the parents, siblings, grandparents, aunts, and uncles of your students. Ask their best friends or their cousins, if you need to do so. When your students arrive, have headlines posted all over the walls in the room stating all of the things they have done. Don't place a name next to the headline; rather focus on what was done. You can ask them to guess who belongs to which headline.

Way too often teenagers hear negative talk about what they do wrong rather than positive feedback on things they do right. This exercise is a good way to bring some positive influence into their lives.

Now comes the flip side of this. Give each student paper and a marker to write their own *headline* of a time someone has helped them. It can be huge (someone sitting at the hospital with them when they were sick) or an everyday event (like being given a ride to school every day.) Help your students recognize how they have been helped by many people throughout their lives.

# Discovery

Before your students arrive, print out the passage, one verse at a time with a break in between each verse large enough to cut them apart. Do this several times so that you have the entire passage in sets to hand out to your students.

Break your students into groups of three to five. Give each group a stack of verses and tell them their job is to put them in order. With only five verses this will not be a difficult task, but it will force them to read the Bible. After a few moments, tell them they can check their accuracy with Exodus 1:15–20.

Ask your students if there are any questions.

If they stare at you saying nothing, don't worry, you are not alone. The temptation is to rush to fill the silence. To prevent talking too quickly, count to sixty in your mind while waiting. If still no one has asked a question, you ask them a few questions.

- What is a midwife?
- Why did the King of Egypt get to tell Hebrew midwives what to do?
- Was it okay that the midwives lied?
- Why did God bless the lying midwives?
- Does this seem consistent with the God you know?
- Why were only the boys to be thrown in the Nile and not the girls?

## Life Application

There are many directions the conversation could go from this one passage. As best you can, try to keep the focus on helping those in need.

The midwives risked everything by choosing to lie to the Pharaoh. They knew the babies would have no chance at life if they did as he asked. Realize that at this time in history, the Pharaoh could just as easily have ordered their deaths as well.

While chances are none of you will be in the place of being a midwife any time soon, you can look to help others. Ask your students to list people they consider to be vulnerable in this world. Write this list on a dry-erase board for all to see.

In small groups, ask your students to consider this list.

- What could they do to help others?
- What keeps us from helping others?

- What specifically could your youth group do to help just one person or group on the list you created?
- What kind of risk are you willing to face to help someone more vulnerable than you?
- If this makes you vulnerable, would you still be willing to help?

## TEACHER'S NOTE:

Once you have covered the focus of helping those more vulnerable, consider unpacking the issue that God blessed the midwives who lied. Scripture says to let your yes be yes and your no be no. This seems to contradict. How do you reconcile that God blessed liars, yet we typically encourage our students to not lie about anything?

## Making It Personal

While there are things that we can only do in groups to help others, there are plenty of things we may do individually.

Give your students a few moments to reread this passage on their own. The story is about two women. In fact it is about two women who had little power in their society. They did not lead a revolution or ensure that everyone had all they needed to eat. What they did was pay attention to what God had placed before them and were faithful right where they were.

Each of your students is in school. Some are on sports teams, in band, hold a job, or help out their families in a variety of ways. There may come a day when they are able to help those who are vulnerable on a large scale but right now, today, in the places where they live and interact, they can make a difference.

Ask the students to spend a few moments asking the Lord to guide them to one concrete thing they can do this week. Give each student two index cards to write down what they choose to do this week. They will take one card and the other you will keep in order to be able to follow up next week. Share with the entire group, if you have enough time for each person to share. If not, share in groups of three what specific thing they have chosen to do. Remind them to take their card home and place it where they will see it as a reminder.

## Song Connect

"Give It All Away" by Aaron Shust on *Anything Worth Saying*

## Quotable Quotes

*How wonderful it is that nobody need wait a single moment before starting to improve the world.*—Anne Frank

*Do not wait for leaders; do it alone, person to person.*—Mother Teresa

*Find out how much God has given you and from it take what you need; the remainder is needed by others.*—Saint Augustine

## Service Option

**World Vision** has a campaign that focuses on one life—one that can be saved and one that can help do the saving. It is only when individuals decide they can make a difference that change comes. The AIDS crisis in Africa continues and we are a part of a global world. One of your students could be the one to save the life of a child on the far side of the world. Go to www.oneliferevolution.org to learn more.

# Who's Got Your Back?

*By Amy Jacober*

## Memory Verse

I have shown you in every way, by laboring like this, that you must support the weak. And remember the words of the Lord Jesus, that He said, "It is more blessed to give than to receive."—Acts 20:35

## Scripture

Mark 10:13–16

## Lesson in a Sentence

God calls each of us to take care of one another.

# Focus

Tape two large pieces of butcher paper on the wall. On one piece, ask your students to write things the world says about teenagers, both negative and positive. What messages do they get from the media and marketers? What ways do they feel that the world takes advantage of teenagers in general? Where do they feel they lack power? There is no right or wrong answer to this. Encourage each student to offer at least one.

Lead your students in a discussion about where they feel empowered and where they feel powerless. The daily news is a great source of where teenagers are being targeted by many who wish them harm or do not want to listen to their voices. At the time of this writing, *Dateline* has had several shows entitled "To Catch a Predator" which shows adults looking for underage teenagers on the Internet to have sex. Every day there is talk of teenagers struggling to have their voices heard. In many cases, they do get through. Unfortunately, in many they do not.

# Discovery

Tell your students that you are going to take them through an experience of Scripture instead of reading it this week. Invite them to get comfortable in a place where they can hear you well and not be distracted.

Read loudly and clearly Mark 10:13–16. Read the passage at least three times. Remind your students that while they may feel vulnerable or powerless at times, Jesus not only pays attention to the most vulnerable in society but He rebukes those who try to keep the vulnerable silent. He goes even further to bless those who are vulnerable.

What blessing might Jesus speak to you? Allow a few moments of silence to allow your students to focus. Encourage them to set aside their to-do list, homework, phone calls they want to make, and any other distractions they may have, and think about the blessings God might want to bestow upon them.

## Life Application
- What did they experience?
- What was it like to take a few moments and listen to God?
- Ask if anyone is willing to share what they believe Jesus was saying to them. What blessing was He giving?

There are studies that show for every negative comment said to a person, anywhere from three to eight positive ones are required to undo the damage inflicted. If people hear negative comments all day long, they begin to believe them.

In whatever way suits your group best, spend some time offering blessings to each person. If your group is large, assign a leader to every group of five to six, go around the circle, and ask the group to offer something positive about each person present. Remind your leaders they will need to set the tone. If your group is smaller, you may do this with the entire group. Remind students that only positive, appropriate remarks are to be stated.

There is a reason the children's song "Jesus Loves Me" has endured. Depending on your group, either close by reading the words or singing this song together. If you have one person particularly skilled, ask him or her to sing over your students exchanging the word "me" for "you."

## Extra! Extra!
**Youth Service America** is an incredible resource for learning about other teenagers around the country and opportunities for your own students. The Web site can be a little overwhelming so set aside enough time to browse. The site offers stories of amazing teenage accomplishments, encourages future success, and has connections to many grant and scholarship opportunities. The Web site is www.ysa.org. While many sites lament the current state of adolescent life, this Web site focuses on what teens do well and encourages positive contributions in their lives.

# The Problem with Power

By Joyce del Rosario and Amy Jacober

In this lesson, students will:
- ✔ Identify leadership styles of leaders in their school, church, and government.
- ✔ Find the source of strength/support for those leaders.
- ✔ Determine their own personal leadership skills and gifts.
- ✔ Discuss the leadership of well-known Christian leaders and how the students might apply these leadership styles to their own situations.

Stuff you'll need:
- ❏ News articles and Youtube video clips on famous Christian and non-Christian leaders (school principal, George W. Bush, Billy Graham, Oprah, Arnold Shwarzenegger, Pat Robertson, T. D. Jakes, Martin Luther King, Jr., Ted Haggard, Jr., Jesse Jackson, etc.)

## Memory Verse

I can do all things through Christ who strengthens me.—Philippians 4:13

## Scripture

Micah 3:1–4, 11

## Lesson in a Sentence

There are many temptations as leaders of the church to make things all about us. But we must keep our eyes on Christ, and keep things all about Him.

## The Big Picture

When God calls us to leadership, our role comes with much responsibility. In order to handle the responsibilities and temptations that come with leadership, we must keep our eyes set on Christ. Peter was able to walk on water as long as he kept his eyes on Jesus who was enabling him to do so. But the minute he took his eyes off Jesus, he was subject to his human limitations and began to drown.

# Focus

Watch Youtube clips on "leadership."

Discuss the various reactions to the clips. What are people saying about leadership? What examples do we have today?

# Discovery

Have students look up Scripture on *power* such as Matthew 21:22, Acts 10:44, Acts 16:25–26, 2 Corinthians 12:7–10, and Philippians 4:13. Be certain the last passage discussed is Micah 3:1–4, 11.

There are many more verses from which to choose. This is a great time to teach your students about a concordance and how to use it to study the Bible.

- What does God have to say about power?
- What kind of power is acceptable to God?
- What kind of power is not acceptable to God?
- What did leaders who abused their power do to make God/Jesus angry?

## Life Application

In the book of Micah, we find that God is very angry with the leaders of Israel. They had turned their focus and efforts away from God to themselves. In the name of serving God, these leaders were actually doing things that served themselves. In the name of serving God, they also caused destruction of God's people by misusing them. These leaders based their decisions on how much money they could gain. Whether it's money, popularity, or other idols, we often mistake what we do in the name of Jesus by serving ourselves instead.

After abusing their power and leadership roles, the leaders would then ask God for help when they found themselves in trouble. They assumed that God would always take care of them since they were *serving* Him. But Micah 3:4 states, ". . . He will not hear them; He will even hide His face from them at that time . . ."

How can we use the gifts that God has given us as leaders of the church without being tempted to abuse the gifts? We keep our eyes fixed on Christ daily. We evaluate decisions by asking ourselves, "Who will gain from this? Is this about me or is it about the Lord? Can I set aside my own desires to lead the way Christ would want me to lead?"

When God calls us to leadership, He wants us to be a part of something greater than ourselves. But leadership also means becoming a greater *target* for the enemy. The enemy knows our weaknesses and will use his power to keep us from using our gift for God's purposes. We must always keep our focus on Christ, the Source of our leadership abilities.

## Making It Personal

On a dry-erase board, make two lists. The first list header is *Leading for Personal Gain*. The second list header is *Leading for God and Others*. Explain to the students that the first list should contain ways leaders have led for their own personal gain or have been tempted to do so. The second list should reflect ways that leadership was related to helping others or advancing God's work and persons who used leadership in this way. Ask for student participation in adding to the lists.

Circle any attributes from both sides of the list that most closely resemble you. Pray over those attributes. Ask God to guard you from any temptations that you circled. Pray also that God will help you develop the qualities and characteristics that He has given you to become a leader.

## TEACHER'S NOTE:

Depending on your church's history, this may be a good time to bring up leadership issues and examples within the church. We often try to save our young people from the darker issues of church leadership, but in the right time and setting, it is good for us to engage the youth in discussions that could affect their understanding of what it means to lead in the name of Christ. Pray about the timing and tact for how to bring up sensitive issues involving church leadership.

## Quotable Quote

*Keep yourself steadily faced by the judgment seat of Christ, walk now in the light of the holiest you know . . . No struggling or praying will enable you to stop doing some things, and the penalty of sin is that gradually you get used to it and do not know that it is sin. No power, save the incoming of the Holy Ghost, can alter the inherent consequences of sin. "But if we walk in the light as He is in the light" Walking in the light means for many of us walking according to our standard for another person. The deadliest Pharisaism to-day is not hypocrisy, but unconscious unreality.*
—Oswald Chambers March 16

## Web Connect

www.YouTube.com, search "Brett Keane—Fallen from Grace" or similar videos that pose the question of Christian leadership and how it affects others.

Other searches on Youtube about Christian leadership may include Ted Haggard, Jim Bakker, Billy Graham, etc.

Discuss how a leader could be helpful/destructive in these instances.

## Service Options

Identify some people in the community that could benefit from being helped. Maybe it's an elderly couple who could use help cleaning out their backyard, or a person with a disability who could use help painting their house. Maybe it's walking up and down a mile of city street picking up garbage. Maybe it's a short-term mission project to a neighborhood where your students wouldn't normally visit. Whatever the case is, make sure it is someone the group can serve.

After the project, talk to the students about how it felt to work for others without monetary compensation. Did they experience satisfaction and a sense of accomplishment? Was it hard to give unconditionally? Were there moments where they wanted to complain or take a break? What temptations might have come up to change their focus away from God and onto themselves. What does it take to keep their mind focused on Him?

# The Problem with Power

*By Joyce del Rosario and Amy Jacober*

Memory Verse

I can do all things through Christ who strengthens me.—Philippians 4:13

Scripture

2 Corinthians 12:7–10

Lesson in a Sentence

As leaders of the church there are many temptations to make it all about Us. But we must keep our eyes on Christ, and keep things all about Him.

# Focus

Option 1

Think you have a strong student? Bring in an old phone book and ask for a volunteer to rip it in half.

Ask a second person with whom you have already talked to take another phone book and begin ripping it in half by small sections.

What is the difference in the two? One is trying to do the entire thing all at once getting nowhere. The second person knows his or her limitations and is able to accomplish much by taking it in small, manageable steps.

Jesus never said we have to do all, all at once. In fact, He asks us to take up our cross daily and follow Him. Each and every day we must make small choices that lead to a lifetime of honoring the Lord.

Option 2

Ask your students to stand and raise their arms. Let them know that there is a prize for the person who can keep his or her hands raised above their head for the longest amount of time. This will seem easy at first but quickly the weight of their own arms begins to take a toll.

As each student drops out, turn to those who are able to maintain. You have said nothing about whether they are able to get help from any others. If someone comes up with that idea and asks, simply repeat that there is a prize for the one who can hold his or her hands above their head for the longest amount of time.

When you are down to the last person, debrief with your group. If someone came to their aide (Just like Moses with Hur and Aaron) talk about needing others and more importantly needing God when we grow weak or encounter a place in our lives where we are weak. If they go it alone, ask your group why no one considered helping someone else? We tend to be competitive and individualistic. Once a person is out of the game, for him or her it tends to be not about encouraging or helping someone else to go further but about walking away. God is not about to walk away. In fact, it is when we finally stop moving in our own strength that God is able to work through us and we are able to accomplish far more than we ever dreamed on our own.

# Discovery

Ask your students to create a list of things teenagers struggle with: body image, grades, anger, the pressure to be perfect, money, time management, lust, etc. There is no right or wrong answer.

Remind your students that everyone struggles. Even people who seem to have it all together—if you really knew them—have insecurities and places where they feel out of control. This is normal. It is when these struggles begin to control your life that a problem arises.

In small groups, read 2 Corinthians 12:7–10.

- What do you think this passage means?
- What do you like about this Scripture?
- What do you dislike?
- Do you really believe God's grace is sufficient for all weaknesses? Are there exceptions?
- What would it look like for God's grace to be present in a weakness?
- What keeps us from boasting in weaknesses today?

## Life Application

This is a tough passage on many levels. Some students have a deeply ingrained belief that perfection is the only acceptable path. Others are so consumed with awareness of their own weakness, they can't imagine God being able to see anything of value in them or that He may be able to work through them. Most land somewhere in the middle.

Regardless of where your students are, this is a difficult passage. It is asking them to get real, to admit that they have deep struggles. You will know your group best. If it is appropriate, ask them to share in their small groups at least one real point of weakness they need to hand over to God. Ideally, have a leader in each group.

Consider the great powers that have collapsed over the course of history. Nothing apart from Christ has eternal staying power. What seems powerful today will be gone in a few short years. Seeking power is not all it is cracked up to be. The world tells individuals to be powerful, to get the best grades, have the best clothes, and to find the most influential friends and adults you can to have in your life. Jesus sought out the outcasts, the poor, the prostitutes, and the rejected. This is not to suggest to your students that they should aim low—rather that they should shift their own focus as to who and what they think is important.

Give your students five minutes of time with the Lord. Ask them to consider the two following questions. First, what weakness do they need to admit so that the Lord may begin to work in that area? And secondly, what shift do they need to make in their own way of thinking about what or who is powerful?

## Extra! Extra!

This is an excellent time to teach or remind your students about the power of prayer. We as a community are called to pray for one another. Consider setting up a prayer bulletin board either in your room or virtually on the Web. Remind your students that this is not to be a guise for gossip, but rather a legitimate way to share concerns and issues about which you as a group need to be crying out to the Lord. These requests may be for individual concerns or for things in your community or world. For a teenager to learn early that seeking God in all things is more effective than doing it on his or her own is a gift that will last a lifetime!

# Prayer for a Rainy Day

*By Ben Donley*

What can I say about prayer to you very brave and underappreciated youth workers out there? Probably nothing new, but maybe some reminders will help refocus you and get you some much needed refreshment. Check out the following:

> Therefore confess your sins to each other and pray for each other so that you may be healed. The prayer of a righteous man is powerful and effective. Elijah was a man just like us. He prayed earnestly that it would not rain, and it did not rain on the land for three and a half years. Again he prayed, and the heavens gave rain, and the earth produced its crops (James 5:16–18).

In these passages, the writer encourages all of us to pray like Elijah—earnestly, powerfully, and effectively. To pray for change and see it through until it happens. To come from a place of Christ's righteousness as a confessing, healed, and knee-bent servant of God, who has the faith to know that God will hear you and the knowledge that without His movement, an unnecessary rain or unending drought will kill your ministry.

All of this is key to anyone in youth ministry, because youth ministry is tough. You've got teenagers facing some of the most difficult life shifts and going head-on hormonally toward temptations that might wreck the rest of their existences. And you—YOU—have been placed in their midst as a change agent—the person chosen by God to go to their gaps and grab hold of their struggles and tell the current weather to change. That's right—a change agent. Not an entertainer or a puppet for the parents—not a numbers person or a travel agent—not the bottom of the staff totem pole. No, you are the leader of lives which are searching for real encounters with God and for an escape from the ridiculous cultural conformity within which they have been placed.

And if you pray—yes—drop down and in a humble soul pose, speak out with authority to the winds and hailstones beating down on these lives—doing it over and over and over until you see the clouds separate, your ministry will be real ministry. There will be healing and victory and change. This is your only hope of doing anything good.

If you don't pray like this—if you instead choose to be a youth programmer and an entertaining circus clown whose only tools are games and tight, little morality lessons on abstinence, you will watch helplessly as the storms come and ruin your kids' lives. You will have no power to offer and you will be ineffective.

Prayer is the act of turning everything over to God. It is relational submission to our water-walking Lord and Savior. And how badly do our teenagers need to be in His hands rather than ours. If you are anything like me, your hands will be well-meaning but not so helpful. Good intentions will not cut it. Talent and ability will not cut it. It all comes down to getting down to prayer. Enhance this part of your personal spirituality and increase the amount of prayer that goes into your professional dealings with your group.

If you do this, you will see sudden miracles appearing on the horizon and be given reason to praise your God for real hope.

Then once you've got it flowing out of you, you must teach your teenagers to pray the same way. You will show them that prayer is done for more than a checklist. You will change them by showing them that prayer is a power tool that can be applied to their circumstances. And they will come to know God, not as a gray, old man dishing out boredom from the skies, but as a weather changer and a life alterer.

What I'm calling you to here is radical, because so few Christian leaders make this sort of earnest prayer a priority. Most leaders have been overtrained in "successful" youth group growth models and thus they ignore the only thing that can infuse their group with strength.

You have to be different, and being different is a choice only you can make. You can choose to stop right now and begin praying like Elijah for amazing things to happen and they will. You can pull your kids to the floor and challenge them to give God a chance to show Himself. Or not.

If you decide to go for this solution, I recommend that you begin by taking out thirty minutes to an hour a day and handing it to God. That's only one episode of "The Office" or one confusing episode of "Lost" a day. Spend this time recalling and proclaiming that you are the one who is lost and that you are weak and unable to do anything on your own about anyone in your group. Then ask for Jesus to empty you of your pride, of your programs, and of your ambitions. Ask for Jesus to fill these spaces with His blood, His favor, His wisdom, His success and more than anything, the Holy Spirit. Then cry out against the situations that are hitting your kids. Cry out and then be quiet over and over until you get a confirmation that it is all taken care of. Start the rain or stop it—whatever is needed—and then praise God that He is on the move for you.

This is the best advice I can give and it really works. I have tried other stuff and none of it does much for anyone. Believe me now and act accordingly or barely pray those opening and closing prayers and be a witness to nothing but trouble.

May God bless you brave change agents and may the skies turn with your uplifted voices!

# Doing a 180

*By Amy Jacober*

---

In this lesson, students will:
- ✔ Realize that being with Jesus causes change.
- ✔ Discuss the principle learned from Zacchaeus and how it pertains to our lives.
- ✔ Wrestle with the idea that Jesus really does call us to a radical counter-culture.
- ✔ Find out that struggles are a part of realizing that our lives need to change.

Stuff you'll need:
- ❏ Index cards
- ❏ Markers or pens

---

## Memory Verse

Therefore if anyone is in Christ, he is a new creation; old things have passed away; behold all things have become new.—2 Corinthians 5:17

## Scripture

Luke 19:1–10

## Lesson in a Sentence

When we really meet Jesus, we can't help but change!

## The Big Picture

Power, fame, and money are all the rage! Somehow, these three things follow each other and become entwined. There is an old saying, "Money can't buy happiness, but it sure can help!" In our world today, the pursuit of money has replaced the pursuit of happiness in far too many cases. Seldom do we hear of someone who has achieved wealth and status giving it all up and walking away. However, it does happen once in a while. The lesson we learn from Zacchaeus is that getting finances in order is just a part of what we need to do to get our lives in order. He knew that he had wronged many people and he chose to make it right. His entire life needed to change and he took dramatic steps to make this happen. In response to Jesus' love and the salvation He offered Zacchaeus, he made a complete turnaround with his life. He gave half of his goods to the poor and made fourfold restitution to anyone from whom he had unlawfully taken money.

# Focus

## Option 1

Ever been around someone so much that you begin to use the same words? What about dressing alike? Have fun with this one. If you like, ask each leader to choose one person in your group to imitate! (Be certain it is someone who will find this funny or flattering and not feel like you are putting him or her down.)

After presentations from your leaders, ask the students if they would like a crack at imitating the leaders. How close (or far) from what you are really like do they get?

How easy or hard was it to do the imitations? What if you had to keep it up for an entire day? A week? Longer? When does it stop being imitation and become an actual change in yourself?

## Option 2

### Opposites Attract

This is a variation on an ice breaker. Write the following list of words (or your own variations) on small pieces of paper. Then tape them to the backs of your students. They must find their opposite and are only able to ask yes or no questions to discover what word is on their own back. Here are some examples:

- Black/White
- Hot/Cold
- Up/Down
- Front/Back
- Open/Close
- On/Off
- Big/Small
- Loud/Quiet
- Soft/Hard
- Smooth/Rough

Once they have found their partner, have each of them share the most difficult thing they ever had to change about themselves in the past. Give examples such as a haircut or biting nails.

# Discovery

What jobs or positions in life are considered to be held by wealthy people who gained their wealth at the expense of other people? Most of these jobs are necessary to the economy and the people who hold these positions are not always bad or unjust. Some examples to consider would be lawyers, doctors, music icons, models, landlords, business owners, politicians, and so on. Make a list and discuss the pros and cons of the positions.

In biblical times, tax collectors were a symbol of the wealthy but were highly disliked by the masses. They collected the actual taxes and handed the money over to the Romans. Above and beyond the actual tax, it was common practice for tax collectors to take a little extra for their own pockets. They were considered cheats and bullies. Even the honest ones were not trusted since the position as a whole was considered to be untrustworthy.

Read Luke 19:1–10.

Ask your students to retell the story without looking at their Bibles.

What really stands out to you?

## Life Application
Reread verses 8–9.

Zacchaeus offered to give away half of what he owned and to pay back four times what he owed to others. Can you imagine anyone today doing that?

Money had been the center of Zacchaeus' life. What things today consume teenagers? What things take a teenager's focus off God and onto something else? Some examples could be sports, personal looks, material possessions, family drama, getting into the right college, and so on.

Can you describe an average teenager who is interested in all of his or her favorite things, yet places God first, above the other things?

Do you personally know anyone who lives this way?

What would have to happen in your life for you to live this way? Is this already a priority in your life?

## Making It Personal
Shift from thinking about teenage life in general to the lives of your students and each individual.

Zacchaeus made a complete 180-degree change in his life. He had been wealthy and in pursuit of even more money. Upon meeting and spending time with Jesus, he started giving it all away. The thing that had been the center of his world lost its value, and Jesus became his focus. The crazy part is that Jesus never said to Zacchaeus, "you must get rid of your possessions." He did this of his own free will in response to encountering Jesus.

Chances are, most of your students are not rolling in money nor have they cheated lots of people out of money. They probably do, however, have things that are the center of their lives, far more than Jesus. Ask them to discuss their lives and what they need to do to make Jesus the main focus of their lives. Are they willing to make changes the way Zacchaeus did when he encountered Jesus?

## Memory Verse Activity
Hand out an index card with the verse written on it to each student. Allow ten minutes of quiet time for your students to read and meditate on the verse. If they are not accustomed to doing this, let them know meditation simply means reading and then slowing down long enough to think about what something means. Encourage them to consider what it means to be a new creation.

**TEACHER'S NOTE:**

Change will come as a result of time spent with Christ. You cannot force this kind of change. If you do, it will look like change on the outside but not be a reflection of what Christ is actually calling you to do. This is essential when trying to talk with your students about change in their lives. It is a delicate balance between introducing them to the concept and allowing the Holy Spirit to work in God's timing, not ours.

Close in prayer asking the Lord to make Himself known in the lives of your students. Pray for your students to recognize Jesus as they go about their week.

## Song Connect

"You Know My Name" by Detour 180 on *Fighting for You*

## Quotable Quotes

*If you don't like something, change it; if you can't change it, change the way you think about it.*—Mary Engelbreit

*When we are no longer able to change a situation, we are challenged to change ourselves.*
—Victor Frankl

**TEACHER'S NOTE:**

Don't forget! February 6th is Ash Wednesday. This is a great opportunity to teach your students about the greater church calendar and the true meaning of Mardi Gras. If this is not a part of your church tradition, feel free to spend a little time learning about this as we begin to transition toward the Passion.

# Doing a 180

*By Amy Jacober*

## Memory Verse

Therefore if anyone is in Christ, he is a new creation; old things have passed away; behold all things have become new.—2 Corinthians 5:17

## Scripture

Exodus 34:29–35; Psalm 34:4–7; 2 Corinthians 3:11–18

## Lesson in a Sentence

When we really meet Jesus, we can't help but change!

# Focus

### After Image

Divide a large sheet of white paper in half. Turn the paper horizontal to have enough room. On half of the paper, draw a blue circle at least the size of a golf ball, a plus sign in black equal in size, and a green circle equal in size to the blue. (Imagine a math problem, only it looks like you are trying to add blue and green!) Draw a plus sign alone on the other half of the paper.

Ask your students to stare at the plus sign surrounded by the blue and green circles for at least thirty seconds. Now tell them to shift their gaze to the plus sign with only white paper around it. What do they see? What will most likely appear is an after image of reddish and yellow circles in the place of the blue and green. If you want the scientific explanation including rods and cones, look up *After Image* on the Internet.

Every day our minds subliminally absorb things while we are totally unaware. We think we know what is going on around us, but there are so many layers of information in various forms, we simply don't notice.

A great example of a similar concept is when you see a friend who has just been around the guy or girl they like. Ever notice what a good mood they are in or how dreamy they can look? We've all seen that *look* on someone's face. Being around God produces a similar reaction. When someone has been with Him, really face to face in worship and relationship, people around notice the difference in his or her demeanor.

# Discovery

In groups of three, read Exodus 34:29–35. And no, the following are not trick questions. They are just to show what a simple concept this is!

- With whom was Moses speaking?
- What happened to him (Moses)?
- Did he know this happened?
- How could everyone else tell?
- What did Moses do once he knew?

Ask half of your students to read Psalm 34:4–7.

- What do these two passages have in common?

Let the other half of your students read 2 Corinthians 3:11–18.

- What do these two passages have in common?

Invite your students to share with one another what they have learned from reading these passages. Moses was with God and his demeanor could not hide this fact! He was undeniably altered and it was obvious to everyone around.

## Life Application

Have you ever been around someone you knew without a doubt was a devout Christian and spent time worshiping the Lord? This could be a youth leader when you were in high school, a neighbor, a pastor, a friend, or whomever. What was it about that person that made you know they had been in the presence of God?

Ask your students to share any of their own stories.

- What about them? What are they like when they have been in the presence of God?
- If they have been, ask them to describe what it was like afterward.
- If they have not, what do they imagine it to be like?

Lead an open and honest discussion about being with God.

- What fears do they have?
- What do they wish would change? What do they hope doesn't have to change?
- How much time do they spend worshiping God? Do they feel they could spend more time?

## Ancient Practice

Give each of your students a chance to be with God right now. While most of us don't have Moses' experience of literally getting to talk face to face, God is still interested in listening to us and hearing from us every day.

Encourage the students to meditate on Psalm 34:4–7. Allow at least ten minutes asking your students to refrain from talking or bothering anyone else. If you need to, play a CD quietly in the background to block outside noise.

Close in prayer by thanking God for His impression on the students during this quiet time of meditating and communing with Him.

# Ancient Friends

*By David Upchurch*

In this lesson, students will:
- ✔ Learn lessons from the friendship of David and Jonathan.
- ✔ Relate the characteristics of this friendship to their friends.

Stuff you'll need:
- ❏ Marker board
- ❏ PowerPoint

## Memory Verse

Greater love has no one than this, that he lay down his life for his friends.
—John 15:13 NIV

## Scripture

1 Samuel 18:1–4

## Lesson in a Sentence

In order to be a real and true friend, character must determine the direction of your relationships.

## The Big Picture

Friends with character are important to one's success and joy in life. As teenagers go through their lives, their friends have the biggest impact on them—sometimes even more so than God. The friends who accept them first become the influencers in their life. Often teenagers give those friends the power to define who they are by category such as jocks, computer geeks, band guys, and skaters. Students need to know and be aware of that concept, and also the temptation to use friendships to influence others. Our closest friends should be those who have the same spiritual values we do, as defined by God. Always be careful in choosing friends so that you have support and relationships that will glorify God and ensure success in your life.

# Focus

Friends . . . do you know or have friends who remind you of the following animals?

| Porcupine | Turtle | Skunk | Squirrel | Fox | Fish |
| Shark | Lion | Snake | Cat | Dog | Beaver |

What qualities do some of these animals represent when you think of your friends?

Some examples are loyal, laid back, painful to be around, friendly, industrious, shy, loud, sneaky, busy, lots of chatter/talk, cunning, or having a powerful bite.

Which animal would your friends choose to describe you?

How would you describe yourself?

Which Bible characters come to mind when you think of these animals?

# Discovery

Read 1 Samuel 18:1–4.

What makes Jonathan and David's friendship so strong? What does it mean to be "one in spirit" with a friend? How does the way you feel about yourself impact your friendships? What are some qualities that are important in strong friendships?

These verses describe certain details of David and Jonathan's instant friendship. There are key words and phrases in the Scripture that provide some insight into this initial meeting. Their friendship was based on at least three things that we should take note of and attempt to find in our closest friends. The same way Jonathan observed David and his actions, you can observe and discern things about the friends in your life.

The first quality one finds in verse 1 is "one in spirit." The spiritual aspect of friendship is vitally important to your life and your relationship with Jesus. The deepest bond between friends is essentially a spiritual one. Those who connect on this level connect in a way that is hard to put into words. This type of connection allows for the many ups and downs of typical friendships and involves honesty on all levels. Think about it from a "higher" perspective. "Do you believe your friendships are important to God?" "Yes," has to be the answer since God has a plan for your life and has given you a mission. Don't forget that God has chosen you as a friend. John 15:13–16 speaks about this spiritual connection in that they were "bound" or "knit" together. Imagine two pieces of cloth sewn together or glued together. It was not easy to separate them. That is the result of a strong spiritual bond.

For a friend to be a true best friend, he/she needs to be someone who shares the same spiritual foundation with you. *The Message* translation of these verses finishes verse 1 with, "From that point on he [Jonathan] would be David's number-one advocate." You can have other friends and acquaintances who don't share your commitment to Christ, but your closest friend should be a believer who can encourage you, stand by you, and challenge you in your faith. We are not too sure what drew Jonathan to David, but in chapter 17, David had demonstrated incredible faith in his God by taking on the giant, Goliath. The way David spoke as if he were defending God showed a deep, daily relationship with God. Even though Jonathan had experienced a lot while in the Israelite army, seeing a teenager speak that way in the face of huge odds was quite remarkable. Jonathan probably thought this act was pretty awesome and from then on, he wanted to be around the courageous David. When you act on your commitment and convictions, others will notice and people who are spiritually awake will be drawn to you. The spirit makes a powerful connector!

The second quality that marks a unique friendship is that of love. When there is a spiritual foundation, showing love is easy to do. In verses 1 and 3, the phrase is repeated,

"Jonathan loved him [David] as himself." Love like that creates a deep, strong friendship because it continually puts the friend first, not self as seen in Philippians 2:3. Various Scriptures speak about loving others such as 1 Corinthians 13, John 13:35, 1 Peter 4:8, and 1 John. Right after the Great Commandment, Jesus says we are to love our neighbors as ourselves. This type of love is marked by *sacrifice*. Notice the sacrifice of Jonathan. He gives David his robe, tunic (possibly a layer of armor), and even his belt and sword. Not everyone had several changes of clothes in this day and time, so the value of these items is quite large. But that wasn't what was important to Jonathan. His friendship to David meant more than the monetary value of things. Imagine giving up your favorite label shirt or jeans, your Ipod or accessory of choice. Would you be willing to give any of those items to someone? If so, who? Why? Why not?

Not only did Jonathan sacrifice things of monetary value, but consider the status Jonathan is giving up, too. In chapter 16, David has already been anointed as the next king of Israel. Here Jonathan is giving up the very things that identify him as Saul's son, prince, and soldier, and he is giving them to the one who will succeed his father on the throne.

The other side of sacrifice in friendships is the aspect of receiving. Sometimes we don't want to accept help or to be given handouts because we might appear weak. David accepts these things as tokens of his friendship with Jonathan. Quite possibly the articles were things he didn't have. (Remember the story of Saul letting David try on his armor and sword.) Jonathan made David feel comfortable with some of his best possessions. In healthy friendships, there exists a *give and receive* that is not based on anything other than the bond of friendship. Some people will try to make everything equal. They may say, "I owe you or you owe me." But that is not truly giving and receiving. David didn't have anything to give to Jonathan; he simply received and was grateful.

The final quality is the action of covenant making. Generally, this quality happens over time in a friendship. Verse 3 states that Jonathan made a covenant with David. Those words mark a unique characteristic of good friends because the stakes of the friendship are raised and it creates another purpose for the relationship. Nowadays, students sometimes only know the first names or screen names of their friends. Knowing someone's name doesn't automatically make you friends. In order to become friends on a deeper level, students must take steps to get to know each other by finding out spiritual beliefs, personality, family history, and interests. The action of a covenant reminds us to be authentic and accountable. The purpose of the friendship takes on a bonding of spirits and a desire to care for and protect each other. Jonathan and David, in this covenant, look out for each other and even risk their lives for one another. Read chapter 19:1–2. Jonathan saves David's life by warning him of his father's (Saul) order. When David becomes king, he finds Jonathan's son, Mephibosheth, and takes care of him by restoring all his land and allowing him to eat at David's table. He did all this because of his friendship with Jonathan as stated in 2 Samuel 9:1–7.

As a friendship matures and deepens, so does the attitude of spiritual closeness. Take time to get to know someone and when appropriate, take steps toward accountability. Ask for prayer, share your story, be a good listener, and whatever else is necessary to have an incredible lasting friendship. Who knows, someday you may actually save someone's life when you place his or her best interests ahead of your own.

## Life Application

Evaluate your friendships and discuss the reasons you have chosen your specific friends. Then compare your friendships with the friendship of Jonathan and David.

## Making It Personal

What kind of friend are you? What are the values of your heart? Take some time and answer these questions honestly. Write your answers down and remember them so that as you look for true friends, you'll be one.

What if I recognize now that I have some *bad* friends? Do I break off all of those friendships?

Students should always be honest, because that is what friends do. Tell the person what changed your mind and let them know that you want to live the best life possible because of Jesus and the Bible. Explain to them that the qualities of a real friend should always include being honest, uplifting, caring, and not harmful to the other person. Let them know that while you have not always made the best choices for your life, you are striving to live a life for God. It could be the most influential moment in your friendship and one that has eternal significance.

## Quotable Quotes

*Friends are people with whom you dare to be yourself*—Unknown author

*In a survey of more than 40,000 Americans these qualities were most valued in a friend: (1) The ability to keep confidences, (2) Loyalty, and (3) Warmth and affection—Psychology Today,* quoted in June, 1982

*Once I told my old man, "Nobody likes me." He said, "Don't say that—everybody hasn't met you yet."*—Rodney Dangerfield, *I Don't Get No Respect*

# Ancient Friends

*By David Upchurch*

## Memory Verse

Greater love has no one than this, that he lay down his life for his friends.
—John 15:13 NIV

## Scripture

Mark 2:1–5

## Lesson in a Sentence

Pick your friends with wisdom and you will experience lifelong compassion, accountability, adventure, and joy.

# Focus

Make a list of your top ten possessions. Include things like clothes, car, computer,
stereo, or Ipod. "What items would you sacrifice for your best friend?" "Would anyone
sacrifice their intangibles such as time or reputation by being seen with the un-cool,
new kid?" "Have you ever sacrificed something to make someone else's life better?"

# Discovery

The story of four friends lowering their friend through the roof, highlights several
facets of true friendship. These four friends cared deeply and compassionately for
another friend who couldn't walk. Their faith put him in the path of Jesus who healed
him physically and spiritually. That should be one of the goals of every true friend—
to always seek the best for each other and especially for the ones who are unable to
take care of themselves.

These friends wouldn't accept anything less than getting their paralytic friend to
Jesus. They did everything they could to the point of inconveniencing someone else. If
four of them could walk on the roof, it must have been substantially thick and strong.
Digging through the roof must have taken time. How long do you think it took to dig
through? These four were willing to use time, energy, and a certain amount of emotion
to get help for this friend. They didn't just talk about helping him, they took action to
make it happen.

This kind of friend is one to keep for a lifetime. They ignore public opinion and
criticism to do the right thing and get the best for you. They have the faith to believe
that Jesus has a great plan for you and for them.

Think about this: The crowd did nothing. They didn't make a path for the friends to get to Jesus. When the four got near the house, you know someone noticed them but no one moved. Their last resort was to go to the roof. The people probably stared in disbelief at the measures these four were willing to take to get their friend to Jesus. More importantly, they didn't even understand who Jesus was. Several of the Pharisees were even mad at Jesus afterward for forgiving the paralytic. Talk about no compassion! No one will move to let them in and then when Jesus demonstrates the grace of a lifetime, they grumble.

Check out these other Scriptures for some personal applications that deal with friendships.

## John 13:34–35

These Scriptures highlight the importance of the relationships of people within a church. If the Christians demonstrate love for each other then the witness and power of their friendships will affect everyone they come in contact with. This is a part of Jesus' plan for every Christian and His design for great friendships. How are your relationships with your entire youth group?

Read the following verses and then think about your communication with your friends.

Read Proverbs 16:24; 28. A part of all our relationships is communication which we carry out by phone, e-mail, text messaging, writing, talking, and even nonverbally. What do these verses say about the importance of good communication? Actually, one of the biggest destroyers of healthy friendships is bad communication. It tears at the actual heart of the friend, as you read in Psalm 55:20–21. If you let your mom or dad, youth minister, or a teacher listen in to any conversation with your friends during the past week, would they hear anything that would be considered harmful?

The writer of Proverbs 12:26 says to be "cautious in friendship." Why?

Proverbs 13:20 talks about the mutual growth friends experience as they challenge each other. Do you have friends like that? Have you ever suffered harm because your friends got in trouble, even though you didn't participate?

Read Proverbs 17:17. The Hebrew word for love has a broad definition that includes the ties of emotion and spirit between friends like Jonathan and David. Notice how the parallel part of the verse includes a family *love* and ties it to a circumstance when fair-weather friends might not stick around. Has there been a rough time in your life when a friend—teenager or adult—was a big help?

Proverbs 18:24 states, "a friend sticks closer than a brother." Put into your own words what this kind of friend does.

# Lifted Up with Something to Say!

*By Amy Jacober*

---

In this lesson, students will:
- ✔ Discuss what it means to be created by God.
- ✔ Learn that age is not the deciding factor in who can by used by God.
- ✔ Recognize God created each of us with unique talents.
- ✔ Understand that God will provide if we fall short in His calling.

Stuff you'll need:
- ❏ A collection of random items (see Option 1 under Focus)
- ❏ Paper
- ❏ Pencils or pens

---

## Memory Verse
I can do all things through Christ who strengthens me.—Philippians 4:13

## Scripture
Jeremiah 1:4–10

## Lesson in a Sentence
When God calls us to do something, He gives us everything we need to carry it through.

## The Big Picture
Teenagers have so much to offer. Too often, their amazing thoughts, ideas, projects, and activities are overlooked as being *just a kid thing*. God knew well that age was not the only factor in the effectiveness of a leader. Jeremiah serves as encouragement that God not only can, but has, and will continue to work through teenagers. This is an opportunity to remind your students that now is the time to consider their choices of who they are and what they can do in the world. There are so many opportunities in the world today for teenagers to make a difference if they will be accepting when Jesus calls on them. Jeremiah did not make this choice on his own. He was available and willing when God called and he chose obedience. Are your students listening? Are you?

# Focus

## Option 1
### What Is It?

The point of the game is to find creative uses for everyday items. Gather a variety of items such as a tutu, a traffic cone, a pool floatie, a tablecloth, an exercise ball, etc. The actual object does not matter, just grab a variety and have at least fifteen, more if your group is larger.

Assign one of the leaders as the rules official and timekeeper. This person will determine when a player has paused too long or when their creative use for an item is too farfetched and doesn't count.

Split your group into two teams. Each team will send a volunteer to the front of the room. Hand each volunteer one of the items. The object of the game is to improvise a new use for that item. They will take turns until they can no longer think of a creative use of their object or they have paused too long at their turn. A creative use of an item might be something like declaring a traffic cone as a dunce cap or giant ice cream cone.

Give 10,000 points to the team whose member was able to come up with the greatest number of creative uses for their item in each round. Play at least five rounds using different volunteers each time. Play for either highest points or the team that gets to 50,000 first.

Many items will find new uses thanks to the creativity of your students. We are often asked to do things for which we have no prior experience or training. Interestingly enough, this seems to be one of God's favorite ways to choose people to do amazing things.

## Option 2
### Taboo Password

Assign one person as the facilitator. Divide into at least two teams. Have each team create a list of words that the other team will have to try to guess. In turns, each team will choose a person as the passer. The facilitator will tell each passer what their word is from the other team's list. The passer tries to pass their word to their team without ever saying the word or any part of the word. For example, if the word is shoelace, they can say string, grommet, tighten, or tie but not Velcro. If you want to make it a little more difficult, require them to use only one-word clues.

Play for points until each list is done. You determine how long your list should be. At least six words per list is a good place to start. Add more if your students really like to play.

Anyone frustrated about not being able to identify the word? Why is it so hard to get your point across sometimes?

# Discovery

Ask each student to share a time when they accomplished something for which they thought they had no ability. Being the coach for their little sister's soccer team or climbing over the wall at camp would be two examples. It doesn't have to be a major task, just something they feel they were not equipped to do. The point is to get them thinking about accomplishing something beyond what they think they are able.

Turn to Jeremiah 1:4–10 and read this passage in pairs. Have one of your leaders reread the same passage nice and loud, inserting the names of some of your students. If you have a small group, insert the name of each student.

Ask your students which parts of the passage they have a hard time believing or accepting.

What do they think of God calling a youth to discipline and build up an entire nation?

## Life Application

God clearly had big plans for Jeremiah. Just as men in the past who were called by God, he immediately began telling God why he should not be the leader (as if God would make a mistake!). Moses seemed to have started the whole "I'm not good enough" excuse, stating he could not speak well. God didn't buy that either.

Ask your students to think of all the things they know have been done by teenagers to help this world. (The temptation at this point could be to focus on those who are famous, not those who have actually done something. Guide your students to stay on track as they brainstorm.) If you think they will struggle, bring a few examples of your own. Check www.amazing-kids.org for some examples.

What things do your students dream of doing or being? This doesn't mean they have to do it tomorrow. Some of their dreams will take years of preparation. This is fine! In fact, what a blessing that they have a dream to move toward!

## Making It Personal

Play a song like "Made to Worship" by Chris Tomlin on *See the Morning* or some other encouraging song in the background. Hand out stationary and an envelope to each student. Invite each person to pray for the duration of the song and then spend a few moments writing a short note to themselves about their future dreams. If they don't have a specific dream yet, this may be a time to ask God to guide them. If they already have a dream, this is a good time to ask God to help them move now toward what they want to accomplish. Remind your students that God does work through all people, some right now as teenagers and some a little later in life, but choices made now will pave the way for dreams to come true in the future. Close by reading together Psalm 139:13–16.

## Song Connect

"Let It Rise" by Big Daddy Weave on *Every Time I Breathe*

## Quotable Quote

*Young people need models, not critics . . .*—John Wooden

# Lifted Up with Something to Say!

*By Amy Jacober*

## Memory Verse
I can do all things through Christ who strengthens me.—Philippians 4:13

## Scripture
John 15:12–17; Psalm 139:13–16

## Lesson in a Sentence
When God calls us to do something, He gives us everything we need to carry it through.

## Focus

### World's Worst
Place five chairs up front and ask for five volunteers to take those seats.

Once they are seated, tell them you are going to give a scenario and their job is to think of the worst things you could possibly say. For example: You are at a fancy dinner party. Comments might be: "Oh, I see the fur around your neck; I was wondering where my dog went!" Another could be: "I'd prefer not to eat anything I can't pronounce." The rest of the group gets to vote on the funniest response.

Ask for new volunteers and give a new scenario at least two more times. After three rounds, have the winner of each round go for an all-star winner.

Feel free to make up your own scenarios. For a few options, consider the following:

- You are in a doctor's waiting room.
- You are behind home plate at a baseball game.
- You are in line at airport security.
- You are on a job interview.

Make a big deal out of the winner. Tell them they have been chosen, above all others! While this might not be the most prestigious thing anyone has ever been chosen for, there is something good about being chosen. Some of you weren't so good at this. Perhaps you don't perform well on spur of the moment thinking. God created each of us with individual talents and abilities. We discover the things we are good at and the things we are not so good at as we go through life.

# Discovery

Ask your students to sit in a circle. Hand out a sheet of construction paper to each person with a marker or crayon. Ask them to write their name in large letters on one side of the paper. Once they are finished, they should pass their paper to the left. Tell them to write one word that describes the person whose name is on that paper. Pass the papers at least four more times. (It is important to pass these in a circle to ensure that each person has several words written on their paper. If not, there is the risk of more popular students having many comments and others having few to none.)

Once this gets to the sixth person, ask your students to turn to Psalm 139:13–16. Read this to your group. Ask each of them to write this on the back of the paper they have in front of them.

God knew you when you were in the womb. You are not a mistake!

Whether you fully accept this or not, it is true. This has all kinds of implications for life! Keeping Psalm 139 in mind, check out John 15:12–17.

Decide what is best for your group, to continue in a large group or to break into smaller groups. Be certain one person facilitates the discussion. Use the following questions as guides:

- What stands out to you?
- How would this change your life if you really lived this way?

Reread verse 16 out loud.

- How does it feel to not be chosen?
- What does it mean to be chosen by God?

## Life Application

Have you ever felt you couldn't do something because of the way you are made?

Basketball may be frustrating in school if you are less than five feet tall. You know you are good in English but can't figure out why Math gives you a headache and takes three times as long to do. We all have things we are good at and things that are not our strong suit.

Psalm 139 affirms that the way you were created was not a mistake. We can't all be good at the same things! God is much more creative than that!! He wants His children to be able to accomplish many different things in life. He has designed a variety of abilities and talents into the human race. We just have to determine where we fit in the pattern He has created.

John 15:16 states that we are chosen and chosen with a purpose. We are to bear fruit. This is a really weird analogy for many students today. Spend a few moments discussing this with them. Fruit doesn't happen overnight. It is slow. It takes a number of things to grow (the right tree, sunlight, rain, and a whole lot of time). Once all of these things are in place, fruit happens. It is the natural outpouring of the purpose for that particular tree.

Jesus calls us to be like the tree. What we do with our lives is the natural outpouring of who we are. Unlike the tree, we do have choices about who we are to be and how we are to make this happen.

Shift the conversation away from a self-focus for a few moments.

We have established that we in this room were created with a purpose and God chose us.

Who in our society do many still consider to be less than worthy in life? Why do we do this? How can we be an example to others to help change this attitude?

If we think about the passages of Psalm 139 and John 15, how does this shift the way we see other people as well? How is God calling you to help change these prejudices?

## Service Option

The outcome of this lesson should be that students realize they are created special and unique with talents and abilities that no one else possesses. These talents are to be used to offer praise and worship to God in whatever way the students choose to use them. It is also about getting them to open their eyes and consider that *all people* are created by God. It is a sad but true fact that some teens who are faithful in church are sometimes the most judgmental and hurtful to others. They may not have noticed others who are left out or teased. Brainstorm an experiment for the next two weeks. How can each student in your group encourage those who are overlooked, ignored, teased, or worse? Have a conversation with a disabled teenager at their school? Consider taking a homeless person for a cup of coffee or a meal? Visit an assisted living home during game night? The opportunities are limitless. Let wisdom and God guide any plans you choose.

Close the meeting with a prayer that God will lead the students to opportunities to witness their faith and help others who are less fortunate.

# Rising Boats

*By Amy Jacober*

## In this lesson, students will:
✔ Understand that we all need encouragement.
✔ Consider the relationship between being encouraged and being an encourager.
✔ Learn the process of encouraging one another.

## Stuff you'll need:
❏ Equipment for whichever game you choose
❏ Dry-erase board with questions written before you begin
❏ Name and contact information for missionaries connected to your church (see Focus in the Midweek lesson)

## Memory Verse
And let us consider one another in order to stir up love and good works, not forsaking the assembling of ourselves together, as is the manner of some, but exhorting one another, and so much the more as you see the Day approaching.—Hebrews 10:24–25

## Scripture
1 Thessalonians 3:1–10

## Lesson in a Sentence
Christians need to encourage and be encouraged.

## The Big Picture
We were never meant to live alone or to just hang out with each other. When we are struggling, we need encouragement so we should seek people who are positive and upbeat to help us gain perspective on our struggles. The cliché "when burdens are shared they are halved and when joys are shared they are doubled" is true. The passage for today offers an important but not often discussed lesson. All the people are encouraged when one person is doing well. This is so counter to our world today. We are taught to be happy for another's success but not that it is actually good for everyone. We are a competitive society with each person or company looking out for ourselves. Other cultures have a better understanding of the theory of cheering for others. While I was in seminary, I met people from all over the world. Some villages would pool money and save for ten years or more just so one person could go to school and succeed. When that student spoke of getting the education, he or she talked of a desire to honor their community by going back to serve and help others. Their success was

good for their village. I have also seen the other side having traveled to remote areas in Ghana. When their pastor did well in school, the entire village was encouraged. Being encouraged and encouraging others should be a major part of our lives.

# Focus

## Option 1

Pick a team sport your group likes to play. If you have not been very athletic in the past, it's always easy to put together a quick game of kickball. Divide into teams and go for it! It's summer and some of the best lessons are learned through experience. Don't be afraid to use up to half of your meeting time during this activity. Sports activities are an obvious example of the concept of competition. Win the game at any cost. Work hard, train, play well, but at the end of the day there is just one winner.

Have drinks and snacks available after the game such as water, juice, oranges, granola bars, apples cut up and soaked in lemon to avoid discoloration, celery with peanut butter and any other energizing snack you choose. While this may not have been the most competitive game, what is good about competition? What can be bad? How could we all benefit when anyone wins? Sports have changed over the years. With each new generation, there are new games and new rules. We continue to move forward. But games and sports will always have the competitive atmosphere. Learning to win or lose with a positive attitude will help you in the real world where competition is an everyday occurrence.

## Extra! Extra!

There are athletes who are known as much for their character as their talent in sports. Check out the following two Web sites to share with your students: **Athletes in Action,** www.aia.com, is a ministry of Campus Crusade for Christ. **Beyond the Ultimate,** www. Beyondtheultimate.com, takes a look at professional football in particular. Started by the coaches of the Baltimore Colts and the Chicago Bears (think Super Bowl 2007!). This is a great site that does not deny competition but puts it in perspective.

# Discovery

There is a phrase that says, "When one boat rises, so do all the others." This shifts the focus of an individual success to be something that reflects well on all those around.

Paul considers life in much the same way. He is quick to ask for encouragement when he is down and quick to give encouragement so that others do not remain discouraged.

**TEACHER'S NOTE:**

This passage will have a greater impact if you cover the background with your students. Acts 17:1–14 tells of the first time Paul, Silas, and Timothy went to Thessalonica. While their trip was a tremendous success on one hand, some in the town were not so thrilled.

People were skipping synagogue to listen to the gospel. Not surprisingly, the leaders of the day became angry and were not about to let the three get away with causing this disruption. A man named Jason was hosting Paul and his companions. Jason was arrested for causing trouble and Paul, Silas, and Timothy had to get out of town. Paul was worried about leaving the immature church under bad circumstances without a strong leader. First Thessalonians 3 is a letter written to the church in Thessalonica giving Timothy's report after visiting the church there.

Turn to 1 Thessalonians 3:1–10 to learn what happens next in the story.

Write the following questions on a dry-erase board so your students can look for the answers as they read. Having questions to guide will ensure that your students pay attention to the details of the story rather than skimming it quickly and missing the point. You may want to go through and answer each of these as a group.

- Why was Timothy sent?
- What did Paul tell them would happen when he was with them previously?
- What has Paul been afraid of?
- What did Timothy report that the church in Thessalonica was doing?
- What encouraged Paul in the midst of his own persecution?
- What is the cause of Paul's joy?
- Why does Paul hope he can see these people again?

## Life Application

Just in case you missed it, Paul, Timothy, and Silas went to Thessalonica and were chased out. Paul was no stranger to struggle. They made it to Athens where Paul couldn't stand to think the church in Thessalonica was not doing well. A combination of concern and curiosity caused him to send Timothy back to Thessalonica.

What is the point of this passage for us today? Paul went to help and encourage, and having been chased out, he was now worried. He longed both to be relieved of his distress and to encourage those left behind despite his awkward departure.

In small groups, ask your students to recall a time when someone was a great encourager to them. What were the circumstances? What was the impact on them? Do you think we need one another for encouragement on a regular basis? Why or why not?

## Making It Personal

Transition the conversation at this point. Ask each group to discuss any areas of their life where they could use encouragement right now. Many responses will be rather trite but be prepared because you never know who may be going through a deep struggle. Play something from Chris Tomlin's *See the Morning* or any other worship CD you have. Ask your students to pray for one another around their circle.

Once they have finished prayer, ask them to consider how they may encourage others this week. Have them set a goal to encourage at least one person in some way before your next meeting and be prepared to share with the class how doing this made them feel about themselves. Brainstorm a few options with your entire group. Close in prayer by asking the Lord to equip the students to be encouragers.

If texting or e-mailing is a part of your student ministry culture, consider sending a reminder to your students about their commitment to encourage someone this week.

## Song Connect
"Share the Well" by Caedmon's Call on *Share the Well*

## Quotable Quote
*If I regarded my life from the point of view of the pessimist, I should be undone. I should seek in vain for the light that does not visit my eyes and the music that does not ring in my ears. I should beg night and day and never be satisfied. I should sit apart in awful solitude, a prey to fear and despair. But since I consider it a duty to myself and to others to be happy, I escape a misery worse than any physical deprivation.*—Helen Keller

# Rising Boats

*By Amy Jacober*

## Memory Verse

And let us consider one another in order to stir up love and good works, not forsaking the assembling of ourselves together, as is the manner of some, but exhorting one another, and so much the more as you see the Day approaching.—Hebrews 10:24–25

## Scripture

Hebrews 10:19–25

## Lesson in a Sentence

Christians need to encourage and be encouraged.

# Focus

Ask your students to recall what your topic was the last time you were together. Do not be disappointed if they cannot. The major theme was encouragement—giving and receiving encouragement. Discuss with the students their commitment to encourage someone this week. Did they follow through? How did they feel after being an encourager? Did they receive encouragement from someone this week? If so, how did they respond?

## Service Option

Before you gather as a group, talk with your pastor about any missionaries your church or denomination may be sponsoring. Get a little info. It would be great if you could have e-mailed that person or family before your youth meeting as well. Ask for a little information to share with your group on their mission and what kind of prayers or encouragement they would like to receive.

You are getting a chance right now to be an encourager! Hand out stationary to each student. Depending on the missionaries you have, either assign one to each student or have your students write more than one note to each. Ask your students to share their name, grade, and at least one personal thing about themselves. Explain to them that they are to send a note of encouragement letting that missionary know they are not forgotten and that people back home are praying for them. You may even ask your students to write a prayer to be included in the note.

BE CERTAIN TO ACTUALLY SEND ALL THESE NOTES WHEN YOU ARE THROUGH!

A letter may not seem like a big deal but when you are far from home and constantly battling spiritual issues, this simple act can make a person's day!

# Discovery

- What gives you the confidence to approach God?
- Have you ever thought about not being able to approach God or not feeling worthy of approaching God? The Israelites had to go through the high priest to reach God. At the Crucifixion of Christ, the veil was torn and all could approach the throne of grace.

Read through Hebrews 10:19–25.

- What specifically were they being encouraged to do?
- Why were they to assemble together?

## TEACHER'S NOTE:

There is some question about the intended addressee of this book. It is commonly accepted that the audience was primarily comprised of believers. This was a letter instructing those who chose to follow Jesus how to live and interact with one another. They were reminded of the ones who came before and were faithful, being encouraged to do the same (see Heb. 11). Bitterness, strife, and dissension were creeping into the church. Cooperation and encouragement were badly needed.

This passage has a great deal of information that can be discussed. If you can, cover the breadth of the passage but if not, consider studying carefully verses 24–25.

## Life Application

Brainstorm ways that people receive encouragement. Notes, spoken words, grades, by spending time together and so on. There are many ways to give and receive encouragement. Let your students know that what works for them may or may not work for their family and friends.

All Christians struggle with doubts and frustrations at times. Some events in life can really challenge our faith. Ask your students what they have been through already that has caused them to question or struggle with their faith.

What kinds of things do all teenagers struggle with? Some possibilities are: Christians trying to honor God by practicing abstinence and being ridiculed or not getting asked out on dates, divorce, being taunted for not being willing to cheat, being teased for befriending an unpopular student, and money problems. There is no right or wrong answer on this subject. Let them offer as many as they can.

Are you beginning to realize why God considers it important to come together as a group? He never intended for us to go through difficult times alone.

How can we in this group encourage each other? This could be out of the frame of reference for some in your group. You may need to guide them in some specific ideas.

# Extra! Extra!

### *An Encouragement Board!*

Hang a corkboard up in your meeting room. If you share space and cannot do this permanently, a corkboard is a great way to personalize a space temporarily! Tell your students this is an encouragement board. As leaders, you will need to set the example. Each week, have a leader write an encouraging note to two or three students. Stick these on the board with the name of the student in a prominent place on the note. When your students arrive, they check for their note! Imagine building a culture of encouragement. Tell your students they are welcome, in fact encouraged, to write notes to one another and the leaders as well. Display these each week and watch the atmosphere change to one of positive reinforcement.

# Get Your Praise On!

*By Amy Jacober*

## In this lesson, students will:
- ✔ Learn that praising God is more important than anything else.
- ✔ Know that all people, regardless of status or image, are to worship God.
- ✔ Be able to spend time with God corporately and be encouraged to do so individually.

## Stuff you'll need:
- ❏ Sidewalk chalk
- ❏ Deep, intense colors of chalk
- ❏ Sheets of butcher paper for posters
- ❏ Markers

## Memory Verse
For a day in Your courts is better than a thousand outside. I would rather stand at the threshold of the house of my God than dwell in the tents of wickedness.
—Psalm 84:10 NASB

## Scripture
2 Samuel 6:12–22

## Lesson in a Sentence
Worshiping God is more important than impressing anyone on earth.

## The Big Picture
Have you ever gazed into the eyes of someone else so intently that it was like the world melted away? Now imagine doing that with God! There are also times when that kind of focus is not so quiet. We go crazy at ball games, when we are at a concert of one of our favorite artists, and happily shout out when we are excited to see a friend after a long absence. People were made to be emotional and expressive. There is not a formula for being expressive. When you are really trying to honor Jesus with your entire life, some people will misunderstand you. Even more confusing, some of the very people who are believers and have walked on this path with you will be among the ones who put you down when you focus too much on Jesus. The idea of being totally focused on worshiping God above yourself and all others is not a new concept. This passage reveals the way David honored God. There were heavy expectations placed on David for the way he was to behave, dress, speak, and with whom he could spend time. None of this mattered to David as long as he was honoring God!

# Focus

## Option 1
### Voiceover
This is a great game that will get everyone laughing! Ask for six volunteers. Three of these will be your actors; the other three will be their voices. Suggest the beginning of a scenario such as planting a garden or making dinner. Anything simple is best. The actors act out the scene while their voices are offstage giving the dialogue. Actors are to respond to the words being said and the voices are to respond to the actions as they interpret them.

Call time after two or three minutes and offer another scene for a different group of students. Does anyone feel silly doing this? Did you enjoy just letting go and having fun? Did you worry about what the other students might think of you? Can you imagine worshiping God with this kind of abandon? If not, why not?

## Option 2
Worship can take place in many, many ways—even in art.

An easy and affordable way to offer art is by creating some great chalk drawings. Get a bucket of sidewalk chalk and a few boxes of the higher quality, darker colors for details. Adjust the amounts to suit the number of students you have.

Gather your students in a group outside. Read Psalm 96:1–6. Let them know you are about to set them free to do just what the psalmist talked about—to praise the Lord! Tell them they will have twenty to thirty minutes to draw what they would like to say to God. It can be as simple or fancy as they would like and there is no right or wrong expression of praise. Encourage them to sincerely focus on what they want to say to God. Read Psalm 96:1–6 once again and then set them free.

# Discovery

If you have some animated leaders, this makes a great presentation as a narrated skit.

Be certain you have someone to play the part of David, ark carriers, Michal, and a few townspeople.

Read through 2 Samuel 6:12–22 while it is acted out. If you have someone who is really over the top and gets everyone laughing, you may need to read it a second time to be certain they heard the whole thing. Don't forget to tell your students where the story is found in the Bible.

## TEACHER'S NOTE:
It would be easy to get the idea that David was running around naked or close to it if you didn't know what an *ephod* was. An *ephod* is a sleeveless tunic or apron that comes down to the hips and was worn primarily by the priests when performing their priestly duties. The scandal was not in what he *was* wearing, rather in what he *was not*. Michal

viewed this attire as scandalous for David to wear, believing he should not be seen in anything other than his royal robes.

## Life Application

Create five teams. Give each a large sheet of butcher paper and some markers. Each team is going to create a separate poster of what is expected of a person who is educated, powerful, royalty, strong, and famous.

When they have finished, have each team present their poster.

We all live with expectations. Some have greater expectations placed on them than others. David was the KING! This was a big deal. It would take all five of the posters just presented to even come close to what was expected of him. And yet, he blew off all these expectations to praise God the way he felt he should!

Ask your teams to discuss what keeps us from praising God the way we should.

What would change in *your* lives if *you* lived in a way that declared praise for God?

Be certain to point out that not everyone would have to dance and be crazy like David (though if that's your thing, go for it!). If it is necessary, restate the question reminding them that you are not asking them what would change in their lives if they danced down the street in an ephod. This is how David felt he should praise God. The students should come up with their own ideas of worship.

## Making It Personal

Close by giving your students five minutes or so to be alone with God. What would they personally change in order to praise God with their lives? What would they like to say to God right now?

Use the final five minutes to ask your students to do a *popcorn* praise. This simply means that there is no set person to pray for the group. Rather, as they feel led, they are to call out a word or a short phrase that expresses the praise they are feeling.

## Connection

Typically only a priest was allowed to sacrifice offerings of any kind. First Kings 8:62–65 lets us know that an exception came in the allowance of a king to perform such duties as well.

## Song Connect

"Everything Glorious" by David Crowder Band/Passion Band on *Everything Glorious*

# Get Your Praise On!

*By Amy Jacober*

## Memory Verse

For a day in Your courts is better than a thousand outside. I would rather stand at the threshold of the house of my God than dwell in the tents of wickedness.
—Psalm 84:10 NASB

## Scripture

Psalm 100

## Lesson in a Sentence

Worshiping God is more important than impressing anyone on earth.

# Focus

Most of us have busy days that sometimes become crazy! Teenagers' lives are no exception to this. In fact, with all the activities available to them today, their days are usually quite full.

Let this meeting be a relaxed space for praising God together and individually. The meeting should be a lot less about what they have to learn and much more about what they can experience together. Do not fret about teaching as much as creating an environment that allows your students to enter into quiet fellowship with God and each other.

You might consider having an extended time of worship through singing. If you don't feel like you can pull this off, ask your worship leader from church to join you as a guest for the night.

Set the tone. Create a space that is comfortable and not distracting. If you can, dim the lights. If not, turn them out and bring in a few candles and lamps with low-wattage bulbs. This creates an atmosphere of intimacy and focus on the Lord.

Feel free to add prayers and Scriptures throughout your time praising together. Close the meeting with a prayer.

# Discovery

Invite your students to read Psalm 100 together. If you have PowerPoint, Media Shout, or an overhead projector, type the words so all students are reading from the same Bible translation. If you don't have any of those, you are like most churches! Go old school; type it on paper and make a copy for each person. Read this together at least twice.

There are two major sections to this Psalm. Verses 1–3 speak of praise before you are in His presence. Verses 4–5 speak of praise while in His presence.

Tonight, you have been together praising the Lord. Continue with your time of worship through song, prayer, and Scripture reading.

## Life Application

Tape a large sheet of butcher paper on an unobstructed wall. Throw several markers on the floor in front of this paper. After having read Psalm 100, invite your students to write their responses tonight on a Graffiti wall.

## Memory Verse Activity

During the time of worship, have a space set up with blank index cards and a Bible open to Psalm 84:10 with written instructions next to them. Students are to take an index card and write the verse on one side. On the other side, they should write one thing of the world that is distracting them from being in His court. Let your students take this card home and tape it in their room so they can memorize it.

# When a Weakness Is Not a Weakness

*By Amy Jacober*

## In this lesson, students will:
- ✔ Understand that all people have weaknesses.
- ✔ Learn that God can be glorified in our weaknesses.
- ✔ Realize that we are to rely on God in all circumstances for all things.

## Stuff you'll need:
- ❏ *Dust*, from Nooma Videos, www.nooma.com
- ❏ Cookie jar from a thrift store
- ❏ Flashlight
- ❏ Butcher paper
- ❏ Markers or crayons
- ❏ Chenille sticks or pipe cleaners

## Memory Verse
And He said to me, "My grace is sufficient for you, for My strength is made perfect in weakness." Therefore most gladly I will rather boast in my infirmities, that the power of Christ may rest upon me.—2 Corinthians 12:9

## Scripture
2 Corinthians 12:7–10

## Lesson in a Sentence
In strength *and* weakness, God gives us what we need.

## The Big Picture
It is a mature concept to realize that our weaknesses can actually be blessings. This is not to be taken lightly. When put in perspective, weaknesses can help grow our faith. They can also be crushing if we let them take over or define us. Weakness for some people is a public one such as anger, drugs, or drinking. For others, an internal battle about how they look or how they perceive themselves could be the problem. As adults, we know that everyone has weaknesses but we don't like to admit that we have one. For a teenager, the idea of admitting weakness is both frightening and liberating. Letting them know that God is sufficient to meet their needs is a huge gift for those who are desperately trying to live by their own strength. Both lessons this week focus on relying on God. In the first lesson, God reminds us that He is glorified and shines in our

weakness. The other lesson shows us that we have nothing that did not come from God in the first place. God provides for us lavishly and loves us without exception.

## Song Connect
"Only a Man" by Jonny Lang on *Turn Around*

# Focus

## Option 1
Show the video *Dust* from Nooma videos. If you have not heard of these or do not have this one, go to www.nooma.com. These short videos are designed to drive home a single point in very unique ways often using life observation but with a twist.

*Dust* offers a look at how much faith God has in us to be able to accomplish more than we think is possible. In particular it shows how God believes we can be people of love, compassion, forgiveness, peace, and hope.

This video can bring about many directions of conversation. Try to focus the conversation around that which God believes we are able to do.

## Option 2
Go to a thrift store and pick up a large ceramic cookie jar. Break the jar and glue it back together. As best you can, break it in large pieces so that it is easier to glue back together. It is just fine if there are still cracks and small holes all the way through as long as the basic shape is present.

Show the jar to your students. Ask them what they think of your jar. If you want, create a story around the jar to really drag this out. After a few minutes, tell how this jar looks perfect. Turn out the lights and shine a flashlight inside of it to allow the cracks to show. Everyone see this? Did anyone notice the cracks before? (If it is truly pitch black in your room, turn the lights back on for the rest of the conversation. If it is simply dim lighting, this is a great conversation to have with the jar lit the entire time.)

While this jar looked perfect, it was not! But that does not mean it is useless. Far from it! It can still be used for cookies or a whole host of other storage needs. For some people, the cracks mean it is no longer good and should be thrown away. Interestingly enough, without the cracks you could not see the light shining through. Most of us try to look like the perfect, flawless jar that you originally thought this to be. Reality is, we all have cracks and broken places in our lives. Instead of working so hard to cover these up or pretend that they do not exist, realize that it is most often in these places of our lives that Jesus is able to shine through.

# Discovery

In small groups, read 2 Corinthians 12:7–10. Use the following questions as a guide for this passage:

- How does Paul view what he calls "a thorn in his flesh"?
- What do you think was meant when Jesus said, "My grace is sufficient for you"?
- What about "My (Jesus') power was perfected in weakness"?
- Do you really think Paul was content with weakness, insults, distress, persecutions, and difficulties?

## Life Application

For each group, roll out a sheet of butcher paper roughly six feet long. Ask one student to lie down on the paper and trace around his or her body. Give markers or crayons to the students so they can create their own person to explain the temptations faced by teenagers today. Weaknesses come from the temptations we cannot resist. They can be big or small but they are there and we all have them. On your outline drawing, label every part of the person and temptations that teenagers face in general. For example, point to the eyes and write, "porn on the Internet"; point to the mouth and write "lying or cursing." Encourage them to be brutally honest.

Tell your students to look back over their drawing. Jesus says, "His grace is sufficient." What does this mean for you today with the temptations listed?

Can Jesus really make a difference in the places where we are weak? If no, why not? If yes, how?

Paul says that he is content with his weaknesses, insults, distresses, persecutions, and difficulties *for Christ's sake*. Paul is very clear that even he has difficulties.

Reread verse 7.

- What was the reason for the thorn in his flesh?
- Have you ever considered any of your struggles as being ways to drive you to God?
- How is God exalted when we submit our weakness?

## Making It Personal

No one wants to be seen as weak but we all have areas of life where we struggle. A weakness could be low self-esteem or the other end of the spectrum when one thinks too highly of himself. Weaknesses are deeply personal and as much a part of who we are as our strengths.

Paul reminds us that a weakness is nothing to be ashamed of. In fact, it is in our weakness that we may boast in Christ acknowledging that we cannot make it without Him.

Give each person a Chenille stick or pipe cleaner. Tell them to create a symbolic shape to take home to remind themselves of their weakness. Jesus' grace is sufficient but only if they allow Him to work in their lives.

Play the song "Only a Man" by Jonny Lang that tells the story of his journey to faith. He has been hailed as one of the most talented and respected guitarists, playing with some of the best artists in the music industry. Still, he knew that in his own strength, he could not continue.

Invite your students to listen and consider their own lives. What area of life do they need to hand over to God? What is the weakness that they need to ask for God's help on every single day? Give a few moments for silent prayer for the close of your meeting.

Let your students know that confession and accountability go a long way in being able to change some of the places where we are weak. Remind them that there are leaders available who would be happy to pray with them tonight or any time they are ready.

Close by asking the Lord to give each person the courage and strength to face their weakness. Ask that this weakness does not define them, but rather defines God's greatness in their lives.

## Song Connect
"Psalm 73 (My God's Enough)" by Barlow Girl on *Another Journal Entry*

# When a Weakness Is Not a Weakness

*By Amy Jacober*

## Memory Verse

And He said to me, "My grace is sufficient for you, for My strength is made perfect in weakness." Therefore most gladly I will rather boast in my infirmities, that the power of Christ may rest upon me.—2 Corinthians 12:9

## Scripture

Psalm 127:1–2; John 3:27; 2 Corinthians 3:5–6; James 1:17

## Lesson in a Sentence

In strength *and* weakness, God gives us everything we need.

# Focus

### Who's the Leader?

Ask the group to form a circle. Choose one person to start the game. The first person makes a statement such as, "I like to kick box" but snaps his fingers. The second person says, "I like to surf," but acts out kick boxing. Get the pattern? Whatever the person before him or her says, the next person must do. Play until you have gone around the circle at least once—the crazier the better!

Often we see or hear someone doing something and think we should do that, too. God requires us to be different. He says that everything we say and do is to be based on our love and worship of Him. Even when we think it is an impossible task, we are to trust God for everything.

# Discovery

Divide into at least four groups, eight if you prefer. Tell each group their assignment is to create a billboard, pop-up, or magazine ad that will get the point of their assigned Bible passage across. Give Psalm 127:1–2 to group one; John 3:27 to group two; 2 Corinthians 3:5–6 to group three; and James 1:17 to group four. If you choose eight groups, double up these passages or find others that convey the same concept.

Hand out paper and markers, crayons, or colored pencils to each group to create their advertisement.

Set a time limit. Call out a ten-minute and five-minute warning to ensure that they will be finished in time to share their advertisement with the entire group. Once they are through, ask each group to show the concept they designed from their verse. After each group has shared, ask if they see a theme? According to all of these verses, is there anything we have, material or immaterial, that did not come from God?

This runs through the Old Testament, the Gospels, and on to the New Testament and Epistles. Everything we have comes from God. We are to rely completely on God and not on our own abilities.

## Life Application

In the same small groups, discuss what it means to have everything we have come from God.

- What does this mean for those who are weak and let Him down all the time?
- What does this mean for those who are lacking a strong family, clothing, or a roof over their head?

Look back over the advertisements that have been created. Which one seems really hard to believe? Why? Which one would you most like to believe? Why?

In the previous lesson, pipe cleaners were handed out and each person was invited to create a symbol of something that would remind them of their weakness and their need for God's help. Today, hand out a new pipe cleaner to each person. Some of us rely too much on our own abilities and possessions without trusting God for our strength. With this pipe cleaner, create a symbol that will remind you of instances where you rely too much on yourself. It may be your intelligence, popularity, money, or athletic talent. It may be none of these but something entirely different. Be honest and search your heart for the answer.

Give each person a few moments in their groups to share, if they feel comfortable doing so. Each group should close in prayer asking that they may recognize their need for God daily more now than ever before.

# A Crowd for a King

*By Bryan Whiteside*

## In this lesson, students will:

✔ Learn the meaning of the tradition of Palm Sunday.
✔ Be able to retell the story of Jesus' entrance into Jerusalem.
✔ Recognize how persuasive a crowd can be.
✔ Consider what it means to worship Jesus with our whole life and be encouraged to do so.

## Stuff you'll need:

❏ The movie *Rudy*
❏ A TV and DVD player or VCR
❏ One piece of paper, pen, envelope, and stamp for each student

## Memory Verse

Hosanna! Blessed is he who comes in the name of the Lord! Blessed is the coming kingdom of our father David! Hosanna in the Highest!—Mark 11:9b–10 NIV

## Scripture

Mark 11:1–11

## Lesson in a Sentence

One week before Jesus was crucified, the crowds hailed Him as King.

## The Big Picture

By this time Jesus has been in public ministry for three years. The people have heard the rumors of His healings, teachings, and miracles. One week before Jesus was crucified, a crowd gathered outside Jerusalem and hailed Him as King as He rode into town. Jesus finally receives the recognition that He deserves. He enters on a donkey while a line of people wave palm branches (signifying royalty), line his paths with coats, and chant "Hosanna" (which means "save us now").

It is important to point out that Jesus was coming to Jerusalem for the Passover feast along with many other Jews in Palestine. There would have been a lot more people in Jerusalem so the crowd would have been huge. This Sunday has been celebrated throughout church history as Palm Sunday so that we may never forget that Jesus was hailed as a King one week before the crowd chanted, "crucify Him."

The people that gathered in front of Jerusalem were awaiting a savior. They were looking to be saved from the Roman government (temporary), not from their sins (eternal). This story shows how easy it is to worship Jesus for the wrong reasons if everyone else is doing it. We are forced to ask ourselves if we are willing to worship our King when it is not the popular thing to do.

Just as Jesus was hailed as King on Palm Sunday, we need to hail Him as King in our hearts and in our life. He deserves proper worship for all to see, and we are called to worship Him in a crowd (community), with our coats (resources), and in our individual shouts of praise. Just as the crowd cried out "Hosanna," we must also cry out for Jesus to save us from our sins.

# Focus

Show the last scene of the film *Rudy* (1:44:00 or chapter 15 through the end of the film).

Introduce the film by relating the background. Rudy had to overcome many incredible obstacles to play football for the University of Notre Dame. It was his dream since childhood to attend and play football there. After barely getting accepted into the University as a junior, Rudy tries out for the team. He is placed on the practice team for two years without ever getting on the sidelines (let alone a game). So, in the last game of his senior year, Rudy's teammates petition to the coach to allow Rudy to stand on the sidelines.

Listen to the announcer. He will talk about how Rudy's story had been published in the school paper that week and how the audience had an idea of Rudy's accomplishments. Point out how Rudy is finally given recognition at the end of the movie.

Do you think everyone in the stadium knew who Rudy was? Then why were all of them chanting his name?

# Discovery

Who knows the story of Jesus' entrance into Jerusalem? Once you have a volunteer, before he or she tells the story, ask the students, "Why are we discussing this story one week before Easter?" If anyone knows, let him explain. If not, then you can explain that the Sunday before Easter is the Sunday that Jesus entered Jerusalem. Ask for a student volunteer to read Mark 11:1–11 and ask all of the students to read the shouts of the crowd together (vv. 9b–10).

Recruit a volunteer to repeat the story in his or her own words from start to finish. Then ask the rest of the students if the first student missed anything. Why is the crowd asking for Jesus to save them? Save them from what? Do you think the average person in the crowd truly understood what they were doing? Explain how the crowd missed the significance of Jesus' message of eternal salvation and how we must understand that God's salvation is not temporary, but eternal which requires our eternal worship.

What do you think it would be like for you to worship God publicly and privately every day? What is stopping you from doing that? Is it the crowd?

Share with the students what it means for you to worship God every day and then ask if the students have any stories to show how they worship God.

## TEACHER'S NOTE:

If the Jews saw Jesus as the Messiah, then they were expecting Him to save Israel from the Roman government. They were not expecting Jesus to save the world of its sin. Therefore, their chant of "Hosanna" or "save us now" was more of a political statement than a theological one.

## Life Application

Let each student make a list of five ways they can worship God in private and public. Ask the students to write these down and place them in a self-addressed envelope. Mail these to the students one week later to remind them of the ways in which they chose to worship God.

## Making It Personal

Just as the crowd misunderstood why Jesus came, so can we. The crowd thought Jesus was a political figure that was going to help save them from the government. They didn't realize that Jesus came to save the world from sin, an eternal destination, not temporary. He did not come for us to be part of the crowd that worships Him momentarily. Jesus deserves to be worshiped in our minds, hearts, and in our entire lives for all of eternity.

## Song Connect

"Here Is Our King" by David Crowder Band on *A Collision*

# A Crowd for a King

*By Bryan Whiteside*

### Memory Verse

Hosanna! Blessed is he who comes in the name of the Lord! Blessed is the coming kingdom of our father David! Hosanna in the Highest!—Mark 11:9b–10 NIV

### Scripture

Mark 15: 1–15

### Lesson in a Sentence

The same crowd that worshiped Jesus five days beforehand has now turned on Him.

## Focus

Show the same clip from *Rudy* (1:44:00 or chapter 15 through the end of the film).

Follow the movie clip by asking the students what it would take for the same stadium of people to kill Rudy? How different would the movie be if the teammates who were carrying Rudy off the field decided to kill him less than a week later?

## Discovery

Assign different students to read the parts of different characters (Narrator/Mark, Pontius Pilate, Jesus, and let everyone else play characters of the crowd). Once again, ask for volunteers to explain the scene in their own words.

How has the scene changed since Sunday? How has the crowd changed? How much does the crowd affect people's decisions? Do you think that the average person in the crowd understood what they were chanting? Would you be wearing the clothes that you are wearing if there was no crowd influencing fashion today? It is sad that the crowd dictates people's lives. We saw it then and we see it today. Sometimes we do things that we wouldn't do if there were no pressure to go with the flow. We trust what everyone says without looking into it for ourselves. Peer pressure can be difficult and it takes a very strong and courageous person to stand against it. Explain a time when you have gone with the crowd rather than following your own convictions. What did you learn from the experience? Was the decision a good one or was it one that you regretted? Looking back, what should you have done to stand against the pressure and how would this have changed the outcome of the experience for you? Do you think it would have helped others who may have been skeptical about going along with the crowd? Could you have been an example of standing up for the right thing? Explain a time when you stood up against peer pressure and how your peers reacted. How did this make you feel? Were you proud of yourself or embarrassed?

## Teacher's Note:

Explain what has taken place between chapters 11 and 15 (clearing of the temple, Last Supper, Garden of Gethsemane, trial, Peter's betrayal) so that the students understand the setting of the scene.

## Life Application

Give the students ten minutes to sit, think, and pray about how they react to crowds. Challenge them to really think about all of the images bombarding them every day. Encourage them to see past those earthly images of success, beauty, and consumerism and look to the heavenly images of Jesus which are Faith, Hope, and Love. Issue an individual challenge for each student to pay attention to what the crowd says and what Jesus says.

This is Holy Week in the church. Remember that Thursday is Maundy Thursday (*the night of the Last Supper and Jesus' arrest*) and Friday is Good Friday (*the day of Jesus' death and burial*). Encourage the students to attend any services taking place in your church or community.

## Memory Verse Activity

Read Mark 6:14–29. This passage discusses how Herod gave in to the peer pressure of his wife and beheaded John the Baptist.

Read Daniel 3. This is the story of Shadrach, Meshach, and Abed-Nego who stood up against peer pressure and were saved by God.

## Song Connect

"Meant to Live" by Switchfoot on *Beautiful Letdown*

# The Cross

*By Angela Williams*

**In this lesson, students will:**

✔ Learn that love is followed by obedience, even when obedience comes with difficulty.

✔ Obedience in action means serving other people.

✔ Be challenged to think about what the Cross symbolizes for them personally today.

**Stuff you'll need:**

- ❑ Table
- ❑ Wooden or painted cross
- ❑ Large piece of brown paper
- ❑ Finger paints
- ❑ Index cards
- ❑ Pens
- ❑ Chair
- ❑ Pillows or blankets
- ❑ Hot chocolate
- ❑ Hot-liquid disposable cups
- ❑ Art scissors—ask any scrap booker what these are and ask to borrow them!
- ❑ Trays
- ❑ Poster-board
- ❑ Tea lights

## Memory Verse

For even the Son of Man came not to be served but to serve others and to give his life as a ransom for many.—Mark 10:45 NLT

## Scripture

Philippians 2:5–11

## Lesson in a Sentence

The Cross is a symbol of obedience in brokenness and ultimately points to God's power and the redemption of humankind.

## The Big Picture

The symbols of a feeding trough at Christmas time and the cross during Easter are actually God's greatest displays of power and love toward us. Symbols that generally would be deemed as unclean and shameful are now pictures of God's sovereignty and servanthood toward humankind. God chooses the ordinary to display the extraordinary and the simple to showcase the depth of God's love for people.

What we find with Christ is obedience in brokenness. One of His disciples betrays Him; His closest friends sleep while He agonizes (Mark 14); the crowd that once praised Him cries, "Crucify Him" (Mark 15:13–14). However, He still chooses obedience in the midst of suffering. For Jesus knows that love and obedience go hand in hand. Through Christ's obedience, we get the opportunity to live in the hope and comfort that God is alive and active. Furthermore, the Cross becomes not just an image of obedience, but a promise of redemption. It is the power of God at work (1 Cor. 1:18 NLT). We can live in the truth that God is redeeming everything.

# Focus

### Set-Up
Decorate hot-liquid cups with the Memory Verse. You can buy disposable cups with plastic lids. Type the Memory Verse and print enough copies to have one for each cup. Cut them with different art scissors so the verses have artsy edges. Glue or tape the verse on the cup. Prepare hot chocolate and fill the cups with it. Have trays of hot chocolate ready for your leaders to hand out to the students when they arrive. Encourage the adults to read the verse aloud as they hand each youth a cup of hot chocolate. Put together three stations.

### Station 1
Set up either a wooden cross or draw/paint a picture of a cross on a table. Put a large piece of brown paper on the table in front of the cross. Place finger paint next to the paper. Encourage youth to paint words on the paper stating what the cross symbolizes in their walk with God.

### Station 2
Place index cards and pens on a chair. Put pillows or blankets (bunched up to create multiple sections) on the floor around the chair. Instruct youth to take a card and write areas of their life where obedience is difficult. Encourage them to pray for obedience.

### Station 3
Put some quotes about service and love on a piece of poster-board. Put some tea lights (small candles) on the table in front of the poster-board. Encourage students to think about the quotes and choose someone they would like to serve this next week out of love. Let them light a candle in representation of this person.

Describe each station to the students. Play music for fifteen minutes and let them pick a station. They may choose to go to all or just one of the stations. Discuss the symbolism of each of the stations with your students such as the feeding trough at Christmas and the cross at Easter. What do these symbols generally stand for? Do you see the importance of these symbols relating to Jesus and your lives today?

## TEACHER'S NOTE:
Easter is often a Sunday when students who do not typically come to church will be in attendance. Be certain that you connect with each of these youth helping them to feel welcome and part of the group. While they may know something about the Resurrection, don't assume that they do. After talking about what these symbols generally stand for, ask your students to offer a brief explanation of why the symbol of the Cross means

so much to Christianity? Ask for a recap of the actual events and what these mean to us today?

Show them the brown piece of paper they all painted on. Discuss what was written about the Cross.

Now you have an opportunity to mention 1 Corinthians 1:18, "The message of the cross is foolish to those who are headed for destruction! But we who are being saved know it is the very power of God." For Christians, the Cross represents the power of God because Jesus did not just die on a cross. The story is much bigger than that. Jesus rose from the dead three days afterward!

This would be a great time to show the video in the "Extra! Extra!" section below. If you decide not to use it, ask the students where they see crosses on a daily basis such as on necklaces, part of door frames, windows, and telephone poles.

What does the cross symbolize for them when they see it in the most ordinary places?

Do the crosses remind you of Jesus or do they have a different meaning to you? Do you display a cross somewhere in your life? If so, where?

# Discovery

When you were praying about obedience earlier, did you feel you received any answers from God on how to be more obedient in your service to Him?

Choose a student to read Philippians 2:5–11 aloud.

Divide your students into small groups to look at a certain verse together. Depending on your group sizes, give each group one verse or two. Ask the groups to pick apart the verses they were given. Ask them to talk about how their verse depicts Jesus and relates to Christians today?

Ask the groups to share their answers with each other.

- What does your verse say about the kind of person Jesus was or what He did?
- How does the verse show Jesus as a servant?
- How does your group's verse relate to us as Christians?

Read verse 8 again.

- Why was being crucified an act of obedience for Jesus?
- Why is it difficult to serve and be obedient?
- Is it hard to think of others when one is hurting or has been betrayed? Can you relate?

## TEACHER'S NOTE:
While leading the discussion, you can mention things about each verse if the students are not able to make connections between their verse, who Jesus was, and how this relates to us as Christians today at Easter.

Verse 5: As Christians we should try to portray the selflessness and love for humanity that Christ showed in healing people, spending time with them, and accepting them for who they were.

Verse 6: Jesus was God and yet He chose to take on the role of servant rather than the role of King while on earth.

Verse 7: Jesus chose to live a sinless human existence in order for us to have an abundant life, communion with God, and eternal life in heaven.

Verse 8: Jesus' ultimate display of servanthood resulted in His death on a cross, which at that time was a demeaning, shameful way to die.

Verse 9: Jesus knew that in God's kingdom the last shall be first and the first shall be last. Jesus knew His role on earth was to give His life for others. We, too, can answer this call.

Verses 10 and 11: Easter is our time to recognize what Jesus did for us by giving His life on the Cross. However, there will be a time when all people of all nations will come before Jesus and bow in recognition of His love and obedience.


## Life Application

Ask a student to read verse 5 again.

Point out that the verse calls us to have the same attitude as Christ when He chose to die on the Cross.

- How would your schools change if Christian teenagers were serious about this verse?
- How might you affect your friends and family by reflecting the love and obedience of Christ?


## Making It Personal

Give the students examples of serving people around them. Explain that serving means doing something out of love or concern for someone without expecting anything in return. Ask the students if anyone has chosen a person to serve this week. Tell them that in the Midweek lesson they will have an opportunity to talk about how serving this person made them feel personally and how the person reacted. Suggest that they can also serve someone anonymously and describe in the Midweek meeting how that feels.

Love results in obedience and obedience in action as being a Christian means loving and serving others. This was the lesson for us taught by Christ in His death and Resurrection. We should always follow in His footsteps to live an obedient life.


## Song Connect

"Chapter One" Shane and Shane on *Upstairs*

"Mighty Is the Power of the Cross" Chris Tomlin on *Arriving*

## Extra! Extra!

The video entitled, *The Crowd or the Cross* by Igniter Media Group is wonderful. It begs the question, what will you follow? It says things such as, "The crowd says, be happy . . . the Cross says, be humble." You can view it or purchase it at www.ignitermedia.com.

## Quotable Quotes

*Everybody can be great . . . because anybody can serve. You don't have to have a college degree to serve. You don't have to make your subject and verb agree to serve. You only need a heart full of grace, a soul generated by love.*—Martin Luther King, Jr.

*I don't want to live. I want to love, and live incidentally.*—Zelda Fitzgerald

## TEACHER'S NOTE:

Explain each station before worshiping together. It is also helpful to make small signs to place near each station with directions on how to use each one. You can play music as a sign of starting and finishing the station activities.

You can buy a bag of one hundred tea-light candles for under five dollars and use them for several Sundays in activities or for atmosphere.

# The Cross

*By Angela Williams*

> ## Stuff you'll need:
> - ❑ Black construction paper
> - ❑ White chalk
> - ❑ Song and lyrics: "Waiting on the World to Change" by John Mayer

## Memory Verse

For even the Son of Man came not to be served but to serve others and to give his life as a ransom for many.—Mark 10:45 NLT

## Scripture

Romans 6:4–11

## Lesson in a Sentence

The Cross is a symbol of obedience in brokenness and ultimately points to God's power and the redemption of humankind.

# Focus

Place black pieces of construction paper with a bowl of white chalk on a table behind the students.

Ask students to spread out across the room and find their own little space. Encourage them to use the chalk to write actions they are not proud of, or perhaps words symbolizing any guilt they may be harboring.

You can play the song "Waiting on the World to Change" by John Mayer. The lyrics can be found at http://www.moron.nl/lyrics.php?id=83928&artist=John%20Mayer.

Disclaimer: This is a secular song. It is by an artist who may or may not be a Christian. The lyrics beg the questions, "If we don't like what is going on around us, why do we just sit and wait on the world to change? Why don't we do something?"

# Discovery

Invite the students to share stories about the people they were able to serve in the last few days.

- How many of you chose to remain anonymous?
- How many of you chose to serve a friend? Family member? Stranger?
- Did you try to have the same attitude as Christ?
- How did it make you feel to be serving out of love and obedience to God?
- What are some specifics on the ways you served someone else?

Explain that our ability to serve comes from the redemption we find at the Cross. Read Romans 6:4–11 NLT.

The New Living Translation is great because it speaks of "new lives" (v. 4) we get from dying with Christ. It also states, "sin loses its power in our lives" (v. 6).

Talk about the John Mayer song you played, especially about the lyrics.

- Why does sin get in the way of our being used by God and having a new kind of life?
- Explain why you think teenagers wait to change the world instead of trying to do something now?
- Can God use us to serve other people even when we mess up? Why or why not?
- Do you think teenagers can make a difference in people's lives even at a young age?

Talk about how our sin or guilt can paralyze us from doing good things or cultivating change in the world. Sometimes we believe if we mess up in some way, we are not good enough to serve God. Other times we get so caught up in sin or guilt that we forget to serve. God loves us unconditionally and He wants to use us in His kingdom. We just have to allow Him full control of our lives.

Ask the students to smear the white chalk all over the paper with their hand. Make sure the words can no longer be seen. Explain that because of the Resurrection of Christ, we can have a new life. God sees our sins and guilt as white; they have been taken care of and forgotten.

How did it feel to wipe away all the sin and guilt you had written about?

Let the students take their construction paper home and put it in a place so they can see it in order to be reminded of the redemption we have as Christians through Christ's death on the Cross.


## Life Application

Sin does not have to have power in our lives. We will all sin. We will all find ourselves messing up at different points in our journeys with God. However, sin does not have to be a stronghold in anyone's life. God can and will use us even though we have messed up. Through Christ we are renewed every day. Sin should not be the focal point of our lives.

What can and should be the focal point of our lives as Christians? Obedience? Love? Servanthood? Hope? All of the above?

Encourage students to continue serving others out of love and obedience to God. Explain that reaching out to others, even in our brokenness can result in a deeper recognition of our redemption and ultimately contentment with God.

You can conclude the night with your own story of finding new life in God, freedom from sin, or times when serving brought you fulfillment. Close with a prayer.

## Extra! Extra!

You could take your students to a beautiful setting to study this lesson. If you meet at night, you could take them to a nice place under the stars. If you meet while there is still daylight, you could take your students to a garden. Atmosphere could add to the idea of new life and you could mention how nature is constantly being renewed and recycled.

# Believed, Changed, Proclaimed

*By Amy Jacober*

## In this lesson, students will:

- ✔ Learn of Jesus' love and acceptance in spite of our actions.
- ✔ Realize that sin and the consequences of sin are real but not the end of the story.
- ✔ Acknowledge that Jesus can and does change lives.
- ✔ Meditate on the changes Jesus desires in their lives.

## Stuff you'll need:

- ❏ Large dark-colored T-shirts
- ❏ Several boxes or bags of powdered-sugar donuts

## Memory Verse

Let the redeemed of the LORD say so, whom He has redeemed from the hand of the enemy.—Psalm 107:2

## Scripture

John 4:4–26, 39–42

## Lesson in a Sentence

When someone's life is changed, they cannot hide it.

## The Big Picture

Every once in awhile we hear of someone who has come to know the Lord and goes through a radical and public change of lifestyle. The woman in this lesson was well known in her community but not for good or noble reasons. She was most likely looked down on, talked about, and lacked friends. Most of us don't have sins as public as hers were. We are not considered "bad" by this world. God doesn't care what our sin is. He just wants us all to be saved and sanctified. We all have shameful things in our life. The old question of "How would others think of you if your thought life was projected up on a movie screen?" still makes its point. God *does* know our thought life and still loves us. Loving us does not mean that He is willing for us to continue living in sin. God calls us to something better. When we encounter Jesus, we can't help but change. We also can't help but share with others this amazing experience of being loved by Jesus without condition.

# Focus

## Option 1

Stories about people the students know and relate to can be very powerful teaching tools. If there is someone in your church who had a significant life change when they came to know Christ, invite them to share their story. Be certain when you ask that you explain the theme for the night and give a time limit. Encourage your students to ask questions respectfully.

## Option 2

This is a silly way to make a big point. Depending on the size of your group, divide into at least three teams. Use very large, dark-colored T-shirts (black, navy, dark green). Choose one person per team to slip the shirt over whatever they are wearing. Place students with the T-shirts at least fifteen feet from their teams. As each team assembles, hand to them a large box or bag of powdered sugar donuts. The object of the game is to see which team can get the most powdered sugar on their T-shirt! You might want to really play this up and give goggles to those wearing the shirts, reminding your students that the object is *not* to leave donut bruises! Offer a small prize to the team who wins.

The donuts represent sin. Sometimes our sin leaves marks for the world to see. More often, sin does not show on the outside but there are marks left on our lives that the Lord can see. In this lesson, let's see what happens when Jesus runs across one of those people with the blatant sin that shows up on the outside for the world to see.

# Discovery

John 4:4–26, 39–42 reads like a short play. Ask three people to take the parts: Jesus, Samaritan woman, and narrator. While the rest of the group is out playing, ask these three to read through the passage a few times.

When the group is reassembled, have these three students offer a dramatic reading of the passage.

When finished, ask your students what they heard. Who were the characters? What did they notice? What stood out to them?

You may need to read this a second time as your students follow along in their Bibles.

## TEACHER'S NOTE:

Offer a little background before they start the reading. Explain that Jesus states it was His disciples baptizing others, not Himself. Regardless, there were people trying to set Jesus up to be at odds publicly with His cousin, John the Baptist. This was not the case. The passage is about a Samaritan woman. During this time in history, there was a lot of animosity between the Jews and the Samaritans. In fact, it was typical to take an extra long route through the land of Perea just to avoid Samaria. Jesus spends time again and again honoring those in Samaria. Remember Acts 1:8? Jesus calls His disciples to be witnesses in Jerusalem, Judea, and all of Samaria. He is not concerned with the prejudices that have been in place. In fact, He ignores them and calls for those who follow Him and plan to carry out kingdom work, to be intentional about including people that others wouldn't consider.

## Life Application

Write the phrase "Believed, Changed, and Proclaimed" on a dry-erase board or butcher paper placed where everyone can see it.

Break into smaller groups of four or five. Ask each group to discuss how this phrase relates to the story they just heard.

After a few moments, ask each group to consider the following questions:

- Why do you think the Samaritan woman was so quick to tell others?
- What things happen in your life that make you want to run and tell others?
- Have you ever had big news that you didn't want to share? Why?
- Do you think God could still use someone who sins that way today?
- How do you think she was changed long term after meeting with Jesus?
- What would have happened if the woman had not gone to the city to tell others?

Be sensitive to the fact that you may have non-Christians in your group. If appropriate for your group, transition to the following questions:

- How do you share with others what Jesus is doing in your lives right now?
- Are you silent or do you talk about your faith? Why or why not?

## Making It Personal

While each time together typically ends with prayer, let today's be a *lectio divina*. If you have never done this before, it is a way to focus and pray Scripture. *Lectio divina* is Latin for divine reading which explains its purpose.

## Memory Verse Activity

The Memory Verse for this week is Psalm 107:2. This verse can be a summary of the passage you've read. Ask your students to get comfortable, possibly close their eyes, and resist distractions for the final few moments of class. For the *lectio divina,* read through Psalm 107:2 several times, slowly and deliberately. Pause between each reading allowing time for your students to meditate. Ask them to listen for a word or words that seem to "bubble up." In other words, as you read, which words seem to have more significance. Consider what God is saying to you through this passage for this time on this day. There is no right or wrong answer. The words will have different meaning for everyone. Just know that the Lord will speak when given the opportunity. The beauty of *lectio divina* is that it teaches us how to create space and not rush through a prayer. God is longing to connect with you. While making that connection happen is not your responsibility, being able to create space for its arrival is.

# Believed, Changed, Proclaimed

*By Amy Jacober*

## Memory Verse

Let the redeemed of the LORD say so, whom He has redeemed from the hand of the enemy.—Psalm 107:2

## Scripture

Mark 1:40–45

## Lesson in a Sentence

When someone's life is changed, they cannot hide it.

# Focus

Create a series of "I'd rather" options. Begin with meaningless ones, moving toward the more meaningful.

- Would you rather eat ketchup or mustard?
- Would you rather be smart or popular?
- Would you rather be short or tall?
- Would you rather be happy or wealthy?
- Would you rather be kind or powerful?
- Would you rather be lonely or homeless?
- Would you rather have a fatal disease no one can see or a nonfatal disease that leaves you disfigured?

You get the picture. Ask your students to create additional options.

Spend some time asking and answering as a group. You may even want to take turns allowing each person to create at least one option. Be certain to end with the final one on the above list.

# Discovery

Today you are looking at someone with a disease that was considered fatal and certainly had a disfiguring external presence.

Read Mark 1:40–45 in small groups.

- Why was it so significant that Jesus was willing to touch, talk to, and heal this man?
- Why do you think Jesus asked the man to not tell anyone but to go straight to the priest?
- How was this similar/different from the Samaritan woman's story you previously studied?

## TEACHER'S NOTE:

Leprosy was a term used for several different skin disorders. In the Israelite tradition, it was a disease that left not only the person who had it unclean, but anyone who came in contact with him or her. Being ceremonially unclean meant that the person was cast out, isolated from their family, community, and unable to worship with their people. You can read more about this and how to be restored in Leviticus 13:45–46 and 14:2–32.

## Life Application

Explain that this man was not just a sick man. He was a social outcast. He was someone who was considered unworthy to hang out with everyone else.

- Who are the social outcasts in our world today?
- Do you think we have gotten any better about not looking down on other people?
- What would God call us to do to reach out to social outcasts in the world?

Push your students to think a bit more personally. Be certain to remind them to not use this as a time to gossip or trash someone they know by naming them as an outcast. This is a time to teach sensitivity about recognizing people who are left out, while not making the problem worse by patronizing or pointing them out.

The leperous man was healed and could not contain the good news! He ran around town telling others of the wonderful thing Jesus had done.

Give your students a few moments to think about the good God has done for them, even in the last week. It doesn't have to be as big as being healed from leprosy—just a place where they can recognize God at work in their lives. Ask each person to share how God has blessed them recently.

## Quotable Quote

*Transformation in the world happens when people are healed and start investing in other people.*—Michael W. Smith

## Song Connect

"Shine" by Salvador on *Dismiss the Mystery*

## Service Options

There are many places you can serve those who are overlooked in society. A great organization that is always happy to receive more volunteers is Special Olympics. There are a variety of ways to serve by being intense weekly team captains, cheerleaders, or encouragers for just one day. Consider checking into your local chapter to see how your students may get connected. This is a great activity to do together!

# Don't Be Afraid of Us, We Are YOUR Kids!

*By Amy Jacober*

Surely none of us would ever be afraid of the students in our ministries. And yet, this is a common sentiment of many students across the country. They can smell fear. They know when we are nervous. Some will respond sympathetically, others just enjoy the sport of watching an adult squirm. Equally common with the sentiment that they wish adults would not be afraid of them is the bewilderment that we are. They eat in our homes, sleep in our beds, wear clothes we have bought them, and have grades sent to our mailboxes or computers. It's not like we've never met!

Yet, there you are; a part of the few and brave who as an adult choose of your own free will to talk about: video games, boyfriends and girlfriends, wrestling, Nascar, the top 10 on Billboard, the latest reality show on MTV, algebra and trigonometry, fashion trends, prom, playoffs, detention, crumping, reggaeton, the drum line, and a whole host of other subjects you never thought would be with you again once you pulled that tassel and walked across the stage when you left high school.

You may have been cool when you were their age, but you don't need to be cool anymore. Once you understand and accept this, a lot of that fear will go away. You don't know their favorite songs and you can't (or shouldn't) be wearing their same fashions. If you try to incorporate the phrase "off the hizzle" into your talk, giggles will erupt and nothing you say will be heard or have any credibility. Relax. Be who you are!! The less you try to fit in with them and just listen and learn from them, the better off you will be. You may even like some of their music, shows, or activities. By not trying to blend in, you can actually spend your time and energy getting to know them and learning about their world. The kids need a mentor, someone who can help mold them in positive ways. They don't need someone who is competing with them. They have enough people to compare themselves with as they seek their own identity. If you dress trendier, have all the latest CDs, can beat each of them at "Halo," and know more slang than they do, you come across as a peer, not a mentor.

One cautionary note: Do not take the aforementioned as license to ignore what is important in their world. Take it as an opportunity for you to learn from your students by giving them a chance to be the experts. Listen, experience, play, but do it in your own unique grown-up way. Some of the best times with students come when they share their favorites songs or try to teach you something that you know will make you look like a fool. Amazingly enough, your willingness to look foolish is the very thing that can build respect and a bond.

Here are a few tips on things you can do or avoid doing to better meet and connect with your students, one on one and in groups. This is not an exhaustive list and some may not work for your particular group. Add your own ideas and delete the ones that simply will not work for you.

1. As a leader, you must spend time with the Lord long before you spend time with teens. You cannot give what you do not have. Many leaders are dedicated, even long past the point of their own spiritual and emotional health. Know your own boundaries and stick to these. This can take many forms including boundaries on when your students may call or visit. Be certain that you spend time each week with the Lord through prayer and reading Scripture, NOT in preparation for a lesson.

2. You are the adult. You are no longer in high school and you are definitely NOT competing with any of these students in any way. This means, in fashion, sports, video games—you name it! Feel free to talk with them, shop with them, play with them but do not be in competition. There is nothing more awkward than watching a youth leader who is insecure in his or herself and needs to posture in front of students. Even more awkward . . . if you are super competitive, step away from flag football, basketball, volleyball and any other activity that brings out the worst in you. As odd as this might sound, it really can damage your credibility and witness.

3. Silence is not a bad thing. When in a group setting or one on one, don't jump too quickly after a question to fill the silence. If you really struggle with those awkward moments, count to sixty in your head allowing enough space for your students to consider the question, think, and offer a response. If this does not work, you may need to rephrase the question or ask if they understood what you asked.

4. Be accepting of their ever-changing moods. It is not a matter of teenagers "getting over it" or "adjusting their attitude." It is a biological issue that teenagers, all teenagers, in every generation will have moody days. This is a part of growing up. They will get over this, when they are in their 20's! Keeping this in mind can go a long way in not taking things personally and remembering their mood is not about you.

5. Some teenagers are just as afraid of you as you are of them. They worry what you think of them. They worry if you think they are frivolous or silly. They struggle to find the right words to express what they are thinking or feeling. They want to connect but don't always know how.

6. Blue hair, pounds of black eyeliner, a pierced eyebrow, or saggy pants are not the marks of a troublemaker. You may not understand what they wear or have done to their bodies, but these are external. This does not negate the fact that who we are on the outside has a relation to who we are on the inside. Find out why they have blue hair. Listen to what they intended. They may have just thought it looked fun or liked the shock value. Modesty and clothing with offensive language can be an indicator of an underlying message, but even those can sometimes be questionable. What they see as funny, you may see as offensive. If you have built a relationship of respect, you will be able to speak into their lives and let them know why you find their T-shirt offensive without dismissing them as a whole person.

7. Being grounded, failing a class, or worse does not define a teenager. It is not unusual for a teenager to go through a difficult season while growing up. Even if

their season seems to be extended, do not let this define them. Some of the best youth leaders today were the most problematic, disrespectful, troublemakers when they were teens. Somewhere along the way, someone saw what God always knew—that teen was His child.

This is just a beginning. The list could be much longer. Now it's your turn. What wisdom have you learned along the way? Be encouraged! Being a little nervous at times is normal. The more comfortable you are in your own skin, the more comfortable you will be with your students. You are blessed to have the opportunity to serve teenagers. Enjoy the adventure!

# Jacob: A Manipulative Man Changed by God's Grace

*By R. Scott Okamoto*

---

**In this lesson, students will:**
- ✔ Examine the nature of their relationships to God.
- ✔ Recall and analyze struggles they have in life.
- ✔ Recognize change as evidence of God's grace.

**Stuff you'll need:**
- ❏ Sturdy tables for arm wrestling
- ❏ Simple prizes for everyone who participates (candy, stickers, etc.)
- ❏ A watch or stopwatch

---

## Memory Verse

Blessed is the man who endures temptation; for when he has been approved, he will receive the crown of life which the Lord has promised to those who love Him.
—James 1:12

## Scripture

Genesis 32:22–30

## Lesson in a Sentence

Spiritual transformation is a struggle and God rewards those who persevere.

## The Big Picture

Most Sunday school attendees will have read the story in Genesis of Jacob wrestling with the angel. Many will be taught that Jacob was so spiritually mature he was able to wrestle with God Himself and win. I remember a poor Sunday school teacher explaining it as some dream, probably to avoid telling young students they can rumble with God. Another pastor talked of the dream or illusion as a metaphor. Yet others have valiantly taught the story in literal terms, highlighting the spiritual maturity Jacob held over the rest of us by even attempting to wrestle with God. Do a Google search of "Jacob wrestles the angel" (as I did), and you'll see a wide range of interpretations of the story as people try to fill in the gaps in the narrative. Some say Jacob wrestled the Man because he knew He was an angel. Others say he does not realize he's wrestling with God until the hip trick. So, the best way I can think of to present this passage to students is to do so honestly and simply. Many honest theologians will admit that the more they read this passage, the less sense it makes. Our faith in God sometimes presents more questions than answers.

In this story, we see Jacob changed physically as his hip is wrenched; and in the next passage we see him reconciling with his brother, Esau. Since Jacob had manipulated and duped Esau out of his birthright, he had to make careful plans to make amends with his violent brother without getting killed. However, God wants Jacob to trust Him; so what seems like a good plan gets scrapped the minute Jacob overcomes the angel and receives God's blessing. God's grace comes in the form of physical injury along with the change of Jacob's identity to *Israel*, meaning one who has "struggled with God and with men and [has] overcome." To figure out this passage, we have to explore what it means to struggle with God and with men and how we might do so correctly. After all, we want God's blessing, too.

# Focus

Have an arm-wrestling open tournament. Pick two people to get started. Then ask other students to come up and challenge the winner of each contest. As the official for the tournament, you will simply time each contest and write down how long each pair wrestled. Try to get at least a few students to participate and feel the strain of the physical conflict. After a few rounds, ask the arm wrestlers to describe their experience. What emotions did they feel? What made them want to keep pushing, even when they felt their strength waning? For those who watched, what did they notice about the nature of the contests? What did the combatants look like?

# Discovery

To get students to look at Scripture for themselves, ask them to read Genesis 32:22–30 in groups of three. What do they notice about verses 24–26? (It simply says Jacob and the Man wrestled from night till daybreak.)

Ask the arm wrestlers to comment on the idea of wrestling all night as opposed to the amount of time they actually spent arm wrestling in the previous exercise. Ask what conditions would force them to wrestle all night with anything. Ask the students what sorts of things have kept them awake all night before: a problem, a conflict with someone, an issue in life; what caused them to struggle an entire night?

## Life Application

In groups of three or four, ask students to recall and share difficult times that took perseverance to overcome. Ask them to identify how they were hurt or injured—emotionally, physically, or both. Then ask them to speculate how God used that event in their lives. Might there have been a blessing as a result of this experience? Once the groups have had time for discussion, ask them to share with the larger group.

## Making It Personal

Can we really wrestle with God? Certainly we can resist His will, but that is what we call sin. Jacob's story seems to be an anomaly. Fight with God? Physically even? What chance do we have against the Creator of heaven and earth? Heck, what chance do we have against the Rock or a bouncer at the local nightclub? As it turns out, we have a good chance, so long as we rise to the challenges God presents to us. God challenges Jacob, even going so far as to injure him, but allows Jacob to hold on and not yield. Despite the range of interpretation for this passage, no one would dare claim that Jacob was simply stronger than God. Jacob is in no position to taunt God, yelling, "Who's your daddy now!" Absolutely not—Jacob holds tightly to God as a child to his parent after the wrestling has subsided. He becomes Israel, receives a blessing, and goes on to make amends with his brother.

## Song Connect

"Time Takes Its Toll" by Bebo Norman on *Between the Dreaming and the Coming True*

## Quotable Quote

*Without struggle, there is no progress.*—Frederick Douglas

# Jacob: A Manipulative Man Changed by God's Grace

*By R. Scott Okamoto*

## Memory Verse

Blessed is the man who endures temptation; for when he has been approved, he will receive the crown of life which the Lord has promised to those who love Him.
—James 1:12

## Scripture

Genesis 32:22–30

## Lesson in a Sentence

Sometimes we fight with those we need and love the most.

# Focus

The purpose of this lesson is to show how we sometimes struggle against those closest to us.

Ask students to recall movies they've seen where parents and children argue or fight. Have them recall as much of the scenarios as they can. When several movies have been mentioned, ask the students to explain the subject of the arguments. If possible, bring a clip or two of your own to illustrate a good example of parents and children arguing.

If you are opposed to using movies or just wish to focus on personal experiences, invite the students to discuss their conflicts with their parents.

# Discovery

Read Genesis 32:22–30.

Ask your students to close their eyes and listen attentively as you read this Scripture several times. Ask them to listen for words or phrases that stand out to them after each reading.

When you have finished reading, give your students two minutes in silence for them to consider why particular words or phrases stood out.

You may be tempted to talk through the entire two minutes in order to keep your students focused. Allow your students and yourself the complete silence of two minutes.

Ask students to describe the struggle between Jacob and the Man. Do they see anger—hostility? What words stand out in the sparse description of the struggle? Is it surprising that Jacob is so polite when he says, "Please tell me Your name?"

## Life Application

When the Man touched Jacob's hip and displaced it, Jacob knew he was wrestling with God. And yet, he did not stop the struggle. He held on tightly and asked for a blessing. When we argue with our parents or caregivers, we recognize them as authority figures. However, we would not dare let the arguments lead to separation from them because we know we love and need them. Ask students to comment on the relationship Jacob has with God. Ask them to discuss ways we can learn from this relationship.

# Forgiveness and Faithfulness

*By David Upchurch*

In this lesson, students will:
- ✔ Learn the effects of forgiveness for themselves and others.
- ✔ Learn to let go of revengeful thoughts.

Stuff you'll need:
- ❑ A VCR or video player
- ❑ One or two recorded football games
- ❑ Pens and paper

## Memory Verse

Bear with each other and forgive whatever grievances you may have against one another. Forgive as the Lord forgave you.—Colossians 3:13 NIV

## Scripture

Genesis 50:15–21

## Lesson in a Sentence

People who experience true forgiveness experience God in a deeper way and declare His glory and His plans for the world He loves.

## The Big Picture

In a fallen world few virtues are as powerful as forgiveness and grace. As one reads through Joseph's life story, what unfolds is a lesson in forgiveness and faithfulness. He was hurt by members of his own family, his boss's wife, and even a friend who forgot about him. Imprisoned in a foreign country, Joseph had every reason to become bitter and seek revenge. Yet, throughout his life, Joseph remained convinced that God had a plan for his life. With that in mind, he moved past the hurt through forgiveness and allowed God to use him to save entire countries from starvation and famine.

# Focus

Together with your students, watch a couple of recorded college or NFL football games to illustrate the penalties of certain reactions to hurts in life. When we experience pain and disappointment from those close to us, we need to be careful how we handle the situation. A revengeful response to an offender can sometimes get us into trouble. When you are watching the football games together, look for the yellow penalty flags that come flying out from the referees during a fight on the field; and then carefully watch to see who gets penalized. If a player strikes out against another player in anger or revenge, he is most often the one who pays the price for his reaction. An instant replay will usually show the whole story but at that moment, the officials often catch and penalize *the reaction* of a player. As a believer it is important to always remember that revenge is God's business, not ours.

Joseph is a great example of the way to handle hurt. We can learn much from his life and his response to those around him as he kept his eye on what was eternally important.

# Discovery

Joseph's story begins in Genesis 37. Read about his dreams in verses 5 and 9.

Often God's plan begins to become a vision of future reality when we are teenagers. This was the case for Joseph. Remember he is about seventeen when he has dreams of his family bowing down to him. (Talk about a dream!) But before that dream could come true, Joseph's journey in life would lead him into a series of unforeseeable, unfair situations which were necessary to prepare Joseph for the fulfillment of God's plan for his life.

When we catch up to Joseph in chapter 50, his dad's life is ending (vv. 15–21). Through Joseph's story we get a glimpse of the effect forgiveness has on one who truly forgives. Joseph's brothers are worried that after the funeral of their father, Joseph will drastically change and so will the "peace" they have known with one who has the power to get even. Think about it: Since Joseph's revelation of his identity, the brothers must have constantly been looking over their shoulders. They are worried and anxious about their relationship with Joseph now that their father is gone. Verse 20 reveals that revenge is the last thing on Joseph's mind but the brothers have no way of understanding the meaning of complete forgiveness. God used Joseph to save lives during the famine thereby giving him a purpose rather than allowing him to dwell on the wrongs done to him by his own family.

Being wronged brings pain and pain generally brings self-centeredness. Slowly, the hurt begins to consume your thoughts as you look for ways to "protect" your heart throughout the days and weeks, months and years that follow. Joseph would never have been effective if he had not forgiven his brothers. Forgiving them allowed him to see God's presence and plans. Moving past his circumstances and the effects of his brothers' evil led to a new life for Joseph and thousands of people. Forgiveness brings life. Just think about the Cross!

The *Merriam-Webster Dictionary* defines forgiveness "to give up resentment of or claim to requital for" a wrong done to you. If Joseph had held on to resentment, he would have been living in the past. Despite the terrible things that were done to him, through God's power, he was able to move on. We can't tell how long it took for Joseph to get over the real pain of his life being turned upside down but we know that he did. Read his words in Genesis 45:5–8: "It was not you . . . but God. . . ." That is the perspective of someone who knows God is the only One in control of his life.

Joseph saw God in the midst of evil and pain and desired to see God's plan, his dream, fulfilled. As a result of hearing the confession of his brothers (Gen. 44:16), he sees a change in their lives as well. Their hearts are broken. The brothers had watched as their father grieved over his loss of Joseph. And they knew how much it would hurt for any other brother to be lost. God works in the lives of all who are involved when forgiveness is allowed to flourish. When they realize Joseph is alive, they are stunned; but gradually they grasp his forgiveness and it means their family has a future. Also, thousands were saved because God, through Joseph, interpreted Pharaoh's dream and he began to store up food for his people to carry them through the predicted famine. Who knows, there could be someone watching how you handle a hurtful situation; and the way you respond could lead that person to God.

Forgiving others allows us to become more like Jesus. When we are hurt or wronged, we tend to focus on our pain and getting revenge on the person who caused our suffering. By focusing on ourselves and our hurt, we may miss the opportunity that God is giving us to practice forgiveness. Joseph looked beyond the present and saw that good had come out of an evil plot because of God's plan. Joseph never wavered in his resolve to be faithful to God. This faithfulness was clear in Joseph's encounter with Potiphar's wife (Gen. 39). After he was thrown in jail, Scripture tells us that God's presence was with him and in fact he was put "in charge" of the prisoners. God gives Joseph the power to interpret dreams of the prisoners and one day he is called to interpret the dream of Pharaoh. Joseph interprets the dream and tells Pharaoh what God has in store for the land of Egypt. Joseph is then placed in a position of authority in fulfillment of the plan of God.

Too often we spend time and thought on revenge for our hurts. God is pretty clear that He is the One who will handle revenge without our help. It is His desire to heal our hearts. Notice throughout the story Joseph never plots to get even. He doesn't sit around crying or feeling sorry for himself in Egypt or in jail. Joseph could have dwelled on all of the wrongs: the lies, the murder plot, being sold into slavery, jealousy, false accusations, and the forgetfulness of a friend. But he doesn't, and when he recognizes his brothers, his heart is not hardened but soft and he weeps.

Doctors tell us that bitterness and resentment are also harmful to our health. Note the statistics and quotes that follow in the Midweek lesson. When we keep track of how many times someone has hurt us, we harm our physical and spiritual health. That kind of thinking derails our physical, emotional, and spiritual life. Learn to forgive and move on as quickly as possible.

There are so many lessons to learn from Joseph's life and example. The one that rises to the top is that of forgiveness. Joseph recognized God and the plan He had for his life. He forgave his brothers in the hope of seeing God's plan come to pass. He remained faithful to his God in unfair circumstances. His heart was soft and he didn't seek revenge. As a result, thousands of people were saved and God was glorified throughout his lifetime.

## Application

Forgiving accomplishes more for eternity while getting even makes the situation or relationship worse. Forgiveness is *the* unique quality of the gospel and Jesus preached salvation that is the forgiveness of sin (Matt. 18:35; Luke 3:3; 5:24; 17:4).

Don't miss this. If you've forgiven the offender, then you are able to care for and support him. Genesis 50:21 states that Joseph took care of his brothers and their families. That's forgiveness!

## Connections

Leviticus 19:18
Deuteronomy 32:35
Matthew 5:23–24

# Forgiveness and Faithfulness

*By David Upchurch*

## Memory Verse

Bear with each other and forgive whatever grievances you may have against one another. Forgive as the Lord forgave you.—Colossians 3:13 NIV

## Scripture

Matthew 18:21–22

## Lesson in a Sentence

Forgiveness changes lives and is not forgotten.

# Focus

What is forgiveness? What is an apology? Allow students to define these terms as best they can. Years ago in the Far East, a radio station began an apology show for people to apologize on the air instead of in person. For a certain amount of money, a DJ would read an apology on behalf of another, in effect saying "I'm sorry" for whatever. Would you forgive someone who apologized this way? Does this qualify as an apology? What are the necessary components of an apology? Someone once apologized to my wife and me by saying, "I'm sorry if you felt hurt." Is that an apology? Do I have to forgive him?

# Discovery

Read Matthew 18:21–22.

"What!?!" Peter must have shouted this in his mind and, knowing Peter, he might have shouted it out loud.

"You've got to be kidding, Jesus, seventy times seven?!?! That equals 490 and I can't keep track that long or count that high."

That's the point; don't keep track. In 1 Corinthians 13:5 ". . . love keeps no record of wrongs" (NIV). In our human way of thinking, seven seems like a lot of times to forgive someone! Yet, Jesus had something bigger in mind.

Early in 2007, America witnessed several funeral services for the 38th president of the United States, Gerald R. Ford. One thing every one of the speakers at those funerals mentioned was his pardon of former President Nixon. Forgiveness is so powerful that it gets the attention of a nation and helps to shape it. In fact, it may be the one thing people remember more than anything else.

In the Scripture in Matthew, Jesus is focusing the responsibility on the one who needs to forgive because forgiveness changes lives. It changes your life by freeing you from negative thoughts and feelings. The ability to forgive is also good for your health. Consider these scientific findings:

Fred Luskin, a psychologist from Stanford University, says, "Holding on to hurts and nursing grudges wears you down physically and emotionally. Forgiving someone can be a powerful antidote." Charlotte van Oyen Witvliet concurs. She's a professor of Psychology at Hope College in Holland, Michigan, who conducted a study with 71 volunteers that showed people who don't forgive experience "steep spikes in blood pressure, heart rate and muscle tension."

Forgiveness, Witvliet found, helps people to remain calm. "Forgiveness isn't about condoning what happened," Luskin said. "It is about breaking free from the person who wronged us."—*Reader's Digest, March 2002, p. 173*

A study conducted by the University of Michigan and partially funded by the National Institute of Mental Health, found young adults aged 18–44 were less likely to forgive others than middle-aged adults (45–64) and older adults (65 and up). Younger adults were also less likely to believe they had been forgiven by God. People who forgive reported decreased psychological distress, including fewer feelings of restlessness, hopelessness, and nervousness. Young adults who reported high levels of self-forgiveness were more likely to be satisfied with their lives. Older adults who reported high levels of forgiveness for others were more likely to report increased life satisfaction.—http://dailynews.yahoo.com, Journal of Adult Development 2001, December 31, 2001

Forgiveness changes the lives of others because it actively demonstrates love. I once heard it said, "People might remember what you say or do but they will never forget how you made them feel." People around you need to know they are loved. That is what God said to you in the Cross. We were once enemies of God (Rom. 5:10), but not now because God forgives. To be able to forgive also involves grace, so, in a small sense we become more like Jesus when we forgive someone. That just happens to be God's plan for us—to be more like Jesus (Rom. 8:29).

Forgiveness changes history. It changes eternity for those who trust Jesus. It changes tomorrow for those who forgive because their relationships get a new start.

## Application

Who do you need to forgive? Are you waiting for that person to do or say something? Make a list and begin to pray today for persons you feel have wronged you, and in your prayer tell God you want to be able to forgive the way He forgives.

# How Quickly We Forget—
## Spiritual Compromise

*By Amy Jacober*

In this lesson, students will:
- ✔ Articulate that God requires that we worship only Him.
- ✔ Recognize that the world pushes idols at us all the time.
- ✔ Understand that we have a choice of whom or what we serve.

Stuff you'll need:
- ❏ List of movie quotes from http://www.imdb.com/title/tt0020929/quotes
- ❏ Index cards
- ❏ Markers
- ❏ Crayons
- ❏ Dry-erase board and markers

## Memory Verse

I am the LORD your God, who brought you out of the land of Egypt, out of the house of bondage. You shall have no other gods before Me.—Exodus 20:2–3

## Scripture

Exodus 32

## Lesson in a Sentence

God has made it clear that He is not interested in partial commitment.

## The Big Picture

While there are many topics not mentioned in Scripture (Internet, AIDS, hip hop), there are principles that transcend time. One of those principles definitely worth remembering is straight from Exodus 20:2–3: *"I am the LORD your God, who brought you out of the land of Egypt, out of the house of bondage. You shall have no other gods before Me."* God is not about to share space with anyone or anything else. Scripture talks again and again of God as longsuffering, relentlessly pursuing, and loving. Make no mistake; God is not a pushover. As loving and patient as He is, He is also jealous and requires our complete lives. We live in a world that is at best tolerant of Christianity but does encourage faith that impacts every corner of our lives. Our students may love Jesus but they also love celebrities, clothes, money, sports, and a whole host of other things. God calls us to more. He demands that we get our priorities straight, placing God above all.

# Focus

## Option 1

Enlist one of your students to help you with this project ahead of time. It's not a grand secret that teenagers have a particular knack for memorizing movie lines. Compile a list of movies you know your students love. Once you have that, check out the Internet movie database at http://www.imdb.com/title/tt0020929/quotes. Look for lines from the movies you know your students watch.

At your meeting, create a movie feud. Split your group into at least two teams. Invite one member from each team to come to the front of the room where you will read the movie line. The object is for this person to guess from which movie the line came. Rotate through all members of the teams at least one time. Award ten points if the designated person can get the answers on their own. Award five points if they have to consult with their team. The winning team is the one with the greatest number of points.

Why do we remember these facts so well? Some things just stick in our minds because they consume our time and attention. Without answering aloud, can you think of a few things that have your attention more than God?

## Option 2

This is an exercise in concentration. Give each student at least two index cards. Have plenty of markers or crayons available. Ask each student to draw the same picture on each card: a sun, flower, or car. The drawing can be complicated or simple. You do not need to be a major artist to do this. Be certain to give an even number of cards to each student if you give more than one set. Once all of the cards have pictures, collect them, shuffle, and spread them out facedown on a table. For example, if you have ten students, you will have twenty cards. Lay them out five across and four down. Expand as you need to if you have more cards. If you have a larger group, create two or more games running at the same time. Taking turns, each student flips over two cards. If the cards match, the student gets the pair. If they do not match, the cards are flipped back facedown and the turn moves to another person. Continue until all of the pairs have been found.

What did you have to do to get a match? (Sometimes it was just luck. Other times you had to pay attention and remember what cards had been shown before.)

# Discovery

Life also requires us to pay attention to what we have heard, seen, or done before. Some things take more effort and attention than others.

In groups of three, instruct your students to read Exodus 32. Tell them to be looking for "scenes" in the story. When movies or TV shows are being created, they go through a storyboard stage. It is sort of like a cartoon but keep in mind that this is to be an action shot with characters and dialogue. You can either have each group create their own storyboard or you can work this as a group. A large dry-erase board is an excellent place to storyboard, or a large piece of butcher paper will do just as well.

## TEACHER'S NOTE:

Even if your students know much of the story of the Israelites and their Exodus, spend a few minutes reviewing what has happened up to this point. You may want to read Exodus 1—31 in preparation. The Israelites were living and serving in Egypt; Moses was born in Egypt; Moses was raised in Pharaoh's household; Moses rejoined his people as an adult; he led the Israelites out of Egypt; they wandered the desert; he brought the Ten Commandments to the Israelites from God; a little more wandering, and finally a time when God is speaking with Moses face to face on Mt. Sinai. This brings us to the moment of this passage. Moses is up on the mountain and the Israelites are getting restless. Be certain to help your students focus on the Israelites as a whole and not Moses alone. The commandments and way of life were for all of the people, not just their leader!

## Life Application

You've got the story down. The Israelites forgot about the instructions God had given them through Moses shortly after he went away. How does this compare to the way teenagers act when they are away from church or their youth group?

What makes it so difficult to remember what God has asked of us? Is it difficult to remember or is it difficult to live our lives the way God has asked?

Calves were not only the symbol of blessing and prosperity but the calf, as opposed to a cow, was a symbol of youth and growth. What symbols of youth and prosperity do we have today? How much time and money do you think is spent on these things?

Who is influencing you? In the passage we read, Aaron was easily swayed by the people and led them to idolatry. He could have stood up, reminded them of what Moses and consequently, God, had said. But when questioned by Moses later, Aaron passes the buck saying, "you know how those people are." Sound familiar? What are teenagers like? Do you think teens influence the music, clothing, and gaming market or does the market influence teens? Or both?

Ask your students how many shows they can name from MTV, Comedy Central, VH1, CCM, Fox, CW, or any television or radio stations that you know cater to adolescents. The fact that there are entire stations that cater to adolescents is amazing! Unsure if this is true? Check out www.teenresearch.com. This is one of the largest research firms focusing solely on teenagers today. Still a skeptic? Look at their client list. It reads like a who's who of those looking to learn from, influence, and make money from adolescents.

## TEACHER'S NOTE:

Cattle were of great importance to the Israelites both agriculturally and economically. They were sources of milk and meat, as well as income. When all was well, they represented wealth and prosperity. They were the ultimate symbols of blessing. Can you imagine your favorite celeb wearing a diamond and gold cow? Bling! Bling!

## Making It Personal

God has made it clear that He wants all of our life—not just Sundays or youth group times. He wants our school life, our dating, family, Internet, shopping, and any other area of our life. He cares what we wear on our body and what we put in it. He cares how we treat others and how we think of others. He cares that we are honest, not whether we get caught or not. Our words and actions are important.

The world pushes us to other things and places—anything to take the place of God.

What do you struggle with that is taking the form of an idol in your life? Take a few moments in prayer to ask God to remove that desire from you.

Close in prayer, thanking God, not only that He loves us, but that He loves us enough to let us know exactly what He desires and requires of us.

# How Quickly We Forget—
## Spiritual Compromise

*By Amy Jacober*

## Memory Verse

I am the LORD your God, who brought you out of the land of Egypt, out of the house of bondage. You shall have no other gods before Me.—Exodus 20:2–3

## Scripture

Revelation 3:14–22

## Lesson in a Sentence

God has made it clear that He is not interested in partial commitment.

# Focus

## Option 1

Give each student a sheet of paper and pen.

Here's the deal. For the next few moments, consider what you would do if someone handed you $1,000,000. How and where would you spend it? As best as you can, break it down and spend it to the last dollar.

Share all of your lists. If your group is large, ask them to share their lists in groups of five or six. What was repeated? Cars? Houses? Clothes? Islands? Vacations?

Everything we have comes from God. How does your list reflect where you place God in all you do? This is not to say that you cannot have a car on your list; but if you set aside $70,000 for a car and $1,000 for ministry, what does that say? This is make-believe, but how does your real life match up in what you offer to God? You may not have $1,000,000 set aside but you do have time and resources right now.

## Option 2

Welcome your students and let them know that you have two kinds of drinks for them! Be sure to have enough cups for every student. Assure them that you did not put anything weird in any of the cups and they are perfectly safe. In half of the cups, have coffee that has cooled to room temperature and in the other half, place soda or milk that has warmed to room temperature. Ask them to take a sip and tell you what they think. Inevitably, there will always be one or two students who actually like the lukewarm liquid but the majority will not be happy with their drinks!

A variation on this is to bring in fries and a sundae or shake that were bought a few hours earlier. The fries will be limp and cold, the sundae or shake will be melted and separated. Get the point? God doesn't want lukewarm worship. It must be hot or cold—not in-between.

# Discovery

John is largely credited with writing the book of Revelation. There are many things in this book that are difficult to study or understand. However, there are a few things that are very clear.

John has a few words for the church in Laodicea.

Read Revelation 3:14–22 out loud as an entire group. After it has been read at least once, spend a few moments with explanations. Laodicea was a city known for its wealth. It was located on a road between Ephesus and just west of Colossae. In other words, it was in the middle of several well-known cities and other Christian communities. Laodicea was known for banking, medicine, and fabrics, firmly establishing it as a city of means. The one thing they lacked was water!

Read this passage again in smaller groups listening for mention of banking, medicine, and fabrics and their lack of a strong water supply.

Ask each group to offer a summary of the main message of this passage.

## Life Application

The church at Laodicea was claiming to be as wealthy spiritually as they were materially. This is clearly not how God was seeing them.

Ask your students to read Revelation 3:15–16. How do they interpret this?

This passage is misunderstood and misquoted by many! It is not about being "hot" on fire for God. Rather, it says because they are neither hot nor cold . . . they are not being what they are supposed to be—so much so that God is ready to vomit them from His mouth. This is a strong image, not one of being mildly disappointed.

The church at Laodicea looked good on the outside, yet on the inside they were not who God created them to be.

Spend some time talking with the students about who they think God has created them to be. Are they just taking up space or are they part of a precious family, loved and created with a purpose?

How do you understand and handle discipline? Do you think parents and teachers should still have a right to discipline? Why or why not?

Here's the crazy part—in the end, the Laodiceans are rebuked. They are called to shape up and get their lives in order inside and out. This is the same call God places before us. He promises to be there for us and He lovingly disciplines us when we are wrong.

God set the rules for following Him before the Laodiceans. They knew this and forgot, looking more to their own resources than to God. Close in prayer considering this same principle today.

## Song Connect
"Hold Fast" by Mercy Me on *Coming Up to Breathe*

## Connections
Colossians 2:1; 4:13

## Memory Verse
Moses carried the Ten Commandments down the mountain on stone tablets. While this would be a bit cumbersome today, there is still value in the symbolism. Stones are heavy and long-lasting. If you can, get some smooth stones for each person in your group (bring a few extras just in case!). Using permanent markers, write out the passage of Exodus 20:2–3 on the stone. Give each student a stone to take home.

# Status, Popularity, and How Much Jesus Cares

APRIL 27 2008

*By Amy Jacober*

In this lesson, students will:
- ✔ Understand that Jesus is willing to befriend anyone.
- ✔ Learn that even in biblical times there were classes of people with status and wealth.
- ✔ Recognize that God requires the same devotion from the wealthy and powerful as He does from the poor and lowly.
- ✔ Discuss our culture's disproportionate obsession with celebrities and put it back in perspective.

Stuff you'll need:
- ❏ *Amazing Grace* DVD
- ❏ DVD player
- ❏ Candy bars in king-size, regular, and mini-sizes

## Memory Verse
But many who are first will be last, and the last first.—Mark 10:31

## Scripture
Luke 19:1–10; Matthew 9:9–13

## Lesson in a Sentence
God calls all of us to be obedient with our whole lives, regardless of age, ethnicity, wealth, or status.

## The Big Picture
We live in a world where wealth, prestige, and popularity rule. Every day, we see examples of people with any or all of these qualities who are in trouble with the law, making bad personal decisions, or losing their lives because of negligence. Rehab is no longer a stigma; it is becoming the norm. If there were ever a time that we should buy into the cliché "money doesn't buy happiness," it is now. If the truth were known, many of our students will strive to reach these earthly goals without giving thought to the price they will pay to achieve these status symbols. They forget that God doesn't care how much money you have or how prestigious you are. He calls all people, regardless of their status in life to follow Him with every part of their lives. There are not enough Oscars, Grammys, fancy homes, corporations, or Rolls-Royces to impress God into letting someone slide.

# Focus

## Option 1

Rent the movie *Amazing Grace*. This is the story of William Wilberforce and his quest to end slavery. In the film, he has one of the most powerful positions in government in one of the most powerful countries. He has a choice to make with his life: to take a stand at the risk of being misunderstood, or to work for more than twenty years in what he sees as service to God and humanity.

There are many clips from this film that would be appropriate. Watch the movie and choose scenarios you believe would best speak to your students. In the movie, Pitt and Wilberforce discuss the fact that they are young but they don't want that to stop them from doing great things. Another scene discusses living their lives as God has called them to do. In one scene, Wilberforce wrestles with the idea of being a powerful member of Parliament, but at the same time, desiring to serve God.

What might God be calling us to do today?

## Option 2

Spend a few moments asking your students to share how their week is going. If they are quiet, rephrase and ask for any high or low from the week. Before they get going too much, cut it off. Tell them you wanted to pass out a snack quickly. Offer the same candy bar in three different sizes, give two king size, three regular size and the rest as the mini size. Once these are passed out, ask the two who received the king size to share what has been happening this week and really engage them in conversation. Allow those with the regular size to talk some. If those with the minis try to talk, cut them off quickly redirecting the conversation. You may even let them know that if they really want to share, they can give their candy to those with the king size in exchange for being able to talk about one thing.

This will take just a few moments and your students should catch on quickly. While this is clearly a minor example of what happens in the world all the time, it illustrates the difference between those with resources and power and those who are less fortunate. Ask your students to give illustrations they have seen in real life.

# Discovery

Luke 19 introduces us to a tax collector named Zacchaeus, who was one of the wealthiest people in town, yet not a part of the ruling class. In some ways he was an average worker but he also possessed the extreme backing to get what he wanted.

Before the class, enlist a few of your students or your leadership team to create a skit presenting Luke 19:1–10. Exaggerate to make the point that Zacchaeus was wealthy, powerful, and disliked! If you have a really creative group, they can adapt the story to a modern setting using banking, cell phone companies, Internet, or any other item commonly used and needed by those in society. Be certain to have the group practice a few times so they are able to seriously portray the message intended.

At the end, read the passage from Luke.

## Teacher's Note:

The job or office of a tax collector was created by the Roman Empire. In order to get this job, the person had to bid for it. It was not only secure employment but came with a great deal of profit. It was acceptable to the Romans for the tax collector to collect the required amount of taxes plus whatever additional money that he wanted. Most of these positions were held by Romans but a few were given to Israelites. Since the position was a Roman creation, an Israelite taking this job was seen as an act of betrayal because the tax collector was profiting by cheating his own people. A modern day example might be a slum lord who buys a building never intending to offer clean safe housing, while still demanding high rent.

## Life Application

Brainstorm with the students about powerful people recognized in today's society. Make a list of these people in categories. While none of these categories are exclusive, some people have contributed or served the community (school-board members, governors, senators, the surgeon general). Others are powerful because of their wealth (Donald Trump, Oprah Winfrey, Bill Gates). And finally some are powerful just because they are well known (Paris Hilton, movie stars, athletes). Place this list where it is visible to everyone.

Break into small groups, with one appointed leader in each group to keep the conversation on track. Ask the students to discuss what they believe God expects of each of the people on the list. Are there different rules for those who have wealth or status? How much more difficult or easy would it be to honor God if you were privileged in one of these ways? Why does the world, including Christians, look up to these people so much?

Read Matthew 9:9–13. Jesus called Matthew as one of His disciples, to be one of the elite. Matthew was not a righteous, kindhearted, generous man. He was a man disdained by the majority of society. He was a cheat and a betrayer. Matthew used his own people for monetary gain. Jesus called Matthew, and Matthew followed. He literally walked away from the life he had been living. No easy task and one which caused others to question Jesus and Matthew.

How would it look if one of the people on your list made this sort of radical change? Would you believe it? How would that make Jesus look?

## Making It Personal

While we do not all have the same privileges, we all have some privilege. We live in a country that offers free education. Food and clothing, employment, and medical care are available to almost everyone.

Consider your life today. What would need to change in order for you to follow Jesus with your whole life?

Invite your students to spend a few minutes considering what they must do in order to use the privilege they have to honor God. If they choose Option 1 in the Focus section, remind them of the film clip. William Wilberforce was a member of the government. He could have chosen to work for his own gain and no one would have fought him on it. He also could have dropped out of government when he began to realize that they were approving of human slavery. He did not choose either of these. He chose to take advantage of his status and power, motivated by his faith, to bring change into the world. Every great man or woman begins as a young boy or girl. There is no reason someone in your group cannot grow up to be a world leader impacting the world in a way that honors God.

While Jesus cares about all of us, He does not care if we are rich, poor, famous, unknown, or powerful. Money and status do not impress the Creator of the universe. Close in prayer, asking your students to pray for one of the persons on the list they created of powerful people today.

# Status, Popularity, and How Much Jesus Cares

*By Amy Jacober*

### Memory Verse

But many who are first will be last, and the last first.—Mark 10:31

### Scripture

Mark 10:17–31

### Lesson in a Sentence

God calls all of us to be obedient with our whole lives, regardless of age, ethnicity, wealth, or status.

## Focus

This project will take a little preparation. Ask the parents or guardians of several of your students to bring some of their kids' favorite or most valuable possessions to you. You may need to convince the parents that you will take good care of the items, especially the very expensive ones. On the day of your class, display all of these items. (Have a leader closely watching the items so there is no opportunity for one to be taken inadvertently.)

When each student identifies his possession, ask the student how important this item is to him. What would he be willing to trade for it? What about simply giving it up? How important is it to have money to be able to buy what you want in life? Do you believe money can help you get all you need for life?

## Discovery

The Bible has a lot to say about money. For today, check out what the Scripture in Mark 10 has to say about one guy in particular. This isn't just any guy. He is young and he is rich. He has everything he needs to be powerful and get anything he wants in life.

Read Mark 10:17–31 as a group. Ask your students to gather in smaller groups of three to four persons and read the passage again. Give each a list of the following questions to discuss. Remind them that they don't need to cover all of these and that they may come up with others on their own. The point is to read the passage and determine what God is saying.

- What is the young man asking Jesus?
- How does Jesus respond?
- Do you think it is right for Jesus to ask for everything? Why not just a portion of his wealth?
- What does Peter say they did to follow Jesus?
- What do you think Jesus means by saying that it is more difficult for the rich to enter the kingdom of heaven? What if the rich person helps a lot of people and uses his or her money for good?
- How do you feel about Jesus saying the first will be last and the last first?
- Are there other questions you want to add?

## TEACHER'S NOTE:

The young man in this passage is asked about his following the commandments. While your students have likely heard the commandments, many do not know where to find them. Flip to Exodus 20:1–26 and read through the Ten Commandments. Realize also that in Israelite tradition, the Ten Commandments are not the least of what it takes to follow God. Rather they are a summary of the entire law covered in Exodus, Leviticus, Numbers, and Deuteronomy.

## Life Application

Hand out paper, an envelope, and pens or pencils to your students. Play a song quietly as you instruct them to write a letter to God. Ask your students to put on paper what they are doing to try to earn God's favor. What do they feel God is calling them to surrender to Him? Remind them that God's grace is free but many of us still try to earn our way to heaven. God cannot bless that which we hang onto tightly. Have the students seal the letters in the envelopes.

While the students are writing, set up a shredder. Maintaining a prayerful attitude, invite your students, as they are ready and only if they are ready, to come and shred their letter. This is a way to symbolically give up what they have been trying to earn and to choose to surrender what God is requiring of them. Close by asking the Lord to remind them of the commitments they are choosing at this time.

## Song Connect

"Big Enough" by Ayiesha Woods on *Introducing Ayiesha Woods*

## Quotable Quote

*Whoever is careless with the truth in small matters cannot be trusted with the important matters.*—Albert Einstein

# Doubts and Struggles About Evil Prospering— Why Does Evil Go Unpunished?

*By Sharon Koh*

In this lesson, students will:
- ✔ Learn to make good moral decisions when faced with peer pressure.
- ✔ Recognize that poor decisions can lead to serious consequences.
- ✔ Learn that following the crowd isn't always the best course of action.

Stuff you'll need:
- ❏ Case studies of morally difficult situations for consideration
- ❏ Pens and paper

## Memory Verse

Dear Friends, do not be surprised at the painful trial you are suffering, as though something strange were happening to you. But rejoice that you participate in the sufferings of Christ, so that you may be overjoyed when his glory is revealed.
—1 Peter 4:12–13 NIV

## Scripture

Habakkuk 1

## Lesson in a Sentence

All choices in life have consequences—either on earth or in eternity.

## The Big Picture

Many Christian students see all the things that they are taught NOT to do take place regularly in their daily environment. Sunday school teachers and youth leaders uphold moral standards such as honesty, integrity, and godly character. But, cheating, lying, and illegal experimenting take place all around the students with few or no consequences. "It's only illegal if you get caught!" is an oft-repeated saying.

It is difficult to hold a Christian perspective on morals that seem to only have eternal consequences. It is even more difficult to hold to these moral decisions when peers are mocking one for being self-righteous and cowardly.

This lesson comes from a similar frustration that the prophet Habakkuk voiced to God saying, "The wicked hem in the righteous, so that justice is perverted" (Hab. 1:4 NIV).

# Focus

Copy the following case studies for students to consider in small groups. Ask them, "What would you do in this situation? Why?" During reflection time, be sure to emphasize the second question (why?) and allow students to find a basis for their moral decisions. It is far too easy for students to give the right answers without thinking through the reasoning behind them. This hinders their character development far more than it helps.

## Case Studies

1. Billy is a hardworking honor student on the basketball team. Most school days, Billy stays at school for practice, returns home to do chores, and then does his homework. Many nights, Billy does not get to start his homework until 9:00 P.M. Recently, some of Billy's teammates figured out a way around this problem— www.turnitin.com. They could change the time stamp and the report of plagiarism on the receipts they printed for their homework! This, coupled with Cliffs Notes, would certainly reduce the amount of time Billy has to spend on his English essays. If you were Billy, what would you do?

2. Jenny hangs out with the same group of friends at lunch every day. She enjoys her friends very much because of their sense of humor. There is never a dull moment at lunch! However, lately, her friends have taken to making fun of the "losers" at her school. They mimic the same few "losers" loudly and exaggeratedly every lunch period—always within earshot and view of those who are being mocked. This makes Jenny uncomfortable because she can see the hurt that her friends are inflicting, even though it is in the name of fun. If you were Jenny, what would you do?

# Discovery

Read Habakkuk 1.

1. What is Habakkuk complaining to the Lord about?
2. Why is the Lord tolerating the injustice and unrighteousness that Habakkuk sees?
3. Summarize God's response. What does He command Habakkuk to wait for?

# Life Application

Have students reflect on their day-to-day, week-to-week lives. Ask them to consider the times when they are frustrated because others seem to be getting away with the very things they have been instructed not to do. Have them describe to each other specific circumstances when they have felt the same way Habakkuk feels in Habakkuk 1 (raging against injustice, watching evil prosper, feeling punished for trying to make good moral decisions).

## Making It Personal

After students share their struggles with one another, lead them in a time of prayer and mutual encouragement. Let each student feel supported and understood in a safe place. Commend them for good decisions they have made.

### Teacher's Note:

The difficulty with this lesson lies in its application. It is easy for students to come up with the right answers—don't lie, don't cheat, don't bully. It is a lot more difficult when the temptation is specific and the immediate promise is that they won't get caught. Peer pressure certainly adds to the struggle. However, if you can help your students find deeper reasons (integrity before God, honoring God's wishes, eternal rewards in Christ) for their decisions, it will be easier for them to stand alone when the next morally difficult situation presents itself.

## Connections

First Corinthians 4:1–5 contains some excellent teaching about judging and waiting for Christ to be the Judge. It explains well the need to be patient in the above-discussed type of situations.

# Doubts and Struggles About Evil Prospering— Why Does Evil Go Unpunished?

*By Sharon Koh*

## Memory Verse

LORD, I have heard of your fame; I stand in awe of your deeds, O LORD. Renew them in our day, in our time make them known; in wrath remember mercy.
—Habakkuk 3:2 NIV

## Scripture

Habakkuk 3

## Lesson in a Sentence

It is okay to be honest about doubts and struggles—God is big enough to handle them.

# Focus

Ever have a hard time believing that some of the news stories you hear are real? Do you doubt them? Sadly, many of these are true stories and we really do live in a world that is lacking in thought.

This is a silly and fun way to segue into talking about doubts. Tell your students you are going to read ten short news stories to them and they get to vote on which is real or fake. Choose your stories from www.dumbcriminals.com. At the end, let them know that they were all true! If you want to mix it up, create a few fakes of your own. I promise, they will not seem farfetched compared to what people really do.

- What caused you to doubt these stories?
- What causes us to question or doubt anything in life?

# Discovery

Read the text in Habakkuk 3 (or, if time permits, read the entire book of Habakkuk).

Ask students to pay attention to the conversation that Habakkuk is having with the Lord. At what point do Habakkuk's mood and attitude seem to change from frustration to awe and respect?

Why did this heart change take place?

## Life Application

Ask students to talk about times when they have been frustrated or angry with God.

Were they afraid to express these feelings? Why?

It is in these times of our honesty and openness to God that He is invited to meet us where we are. What a blessed thought! Ask your students to share a time when they doubted God but saw after the fact that He really was present and at work the entire time. Hearing from one another on a topic like this can go a long way to encourage a student who is currently struggling.

Give your students a few moments of time to themselves to talk with God. Encourage them to be really honest in thanking God for the blessings He has placed in their lives. At the same time, they should ask for God's guidance and help with struggles or situations they may be facing in their daily walk.

# Instructions for Older Women

*By R. Scott Okamoto*

In this lesson, students will:
- ✔ Appreciate the role of matriarchs in their family.
- ✔ Be able to identify some key temptations and pitfalls for women and all people.
- ✔ Learn how to encourage the matriarchs in their family.

Stuff you'll need:
- ❑ Newspapers from the current month
- ❑ Store catalogs
- ❑ Paper and pens

## Memory Verse

"Honor your father and mother"—which is the first commandment with a promise—
"that it may go well with you and that you may enjoy long life on the earth."
—Ephesians 6:2–3 NIV

## Scriptures

Ephesians 6:2–3; Titus 2:3–5

## Lesson in a Sentence

Just as men need to be temperate, worthy of respect, self-controlled, and sound in faith, in love, and in endurance (vv. 1–2), women have much to contribute to society and to the state of family.

## The Big Picture

The focus should not be on what is prohibited, but rather the significant role Paul gives women in society and the family. The book of Titus was written to help Titus work with the people of Crete. Crete is often remembered as the pagan island society rich in Greek mythology along with its unique worship of the bull. Remember the story of the Minotaur in the labyrinth at Knossos? As with many of the combative Greek cultures just north of Crete, dishonesty, gluttony, and laziness were characteristics Paul addressed throughout the letter.

So, while many Christians might focus on the seemingly restrictive and cautionary tone of the passage, it is important for us to understand that while our own culture can be said to have characteristics similar to the Cretans, this passage is more of an exhortation than a condemnation. Paul is telling the older women that they play a vital part in the church community. No matter the social trends or forces, all women need to rise above them and pursue God.

# Focus

Ask students to make two lists on a piece of paper. The first list (column 1) is to be things they appreciate about their mothers, grandmothers, or favorite matriarchs in their lives. In a second list (column 2), students should identify things that distract them from living a godly life.

# Discovery

If the two columns are not already adjacent to each other, put them together. Have students imagine how hard it would be to pursue all their hopes, dreams, and desires, all the while keeping God as the focus of their lives. Now tell them to imagine doing all that and trying to help children do all that as well.

1. Ask students what their goals are for their lives. These can be spiritual, as well as, personal.
2. Ask students to identify the temptations and distractions that hinder them in their pursuits of these goals. (You many give examples such as video games, friends, television, etc.)
3. Have students calculate the number of hours they spend doing things they enjoy. Include hobbies, video games, sports, any activities they love to do. (For younger students you can make a ballpark list and come up with a rounded estimate.)
4. Have students calculate the estimated cost of the things they would love to buy. (For younger students you can make a ballpark list and come up with a rounded estimate.)

## Life Application

Ask them to think of their mothers. Most teens have not thought much about the personal lives of their mothers. What things do they know their mothers want? (These can be personal and material such as new clothes, a new car, a better job, etc.) Use the newspaper ads and catalogs to find things students would want their mothers to have.

Ask students to identify what things their mothers want for them, their children.

Finally, ask students to consider all the things their mothers do, and how many material items their mothers forgo in order to provide for their families. Also, how many personal hopes and dreams do mothers put on hold or even let go of in order to fulfill their roles as mother?

## Making It Personal

It's pretty much a given that children often take their parents for granted. In traditional families where the father goes to work, the mother is often underappreciated for the tremendous responsibility she has in order to keep a household running. If the mother works, she often has to do double duty and make a living in addition to these responsibilities. Paul understands the importance of the mother figure as a model for her children and as a crucial part in the body of Christ. Remind the students that their mothers and/or matriarchal caregivers have tremendous responsibility.

## Service Options

There are a lot of overworked, stressed out, tired moms in the world. Consider working with your pastor and/or children's minister to see if there are some moms who might want a break or need a little help around the house. Arrange, with your students, a time to serve those moms who work so hard. It can be anything from mowing the lawn to a few hours of cleaning or babysitting.

A second option is to create a "ladies only" evening. If you have female students who can pull this off and would go for it, have a girls' night with moms. The girls host the affair and it can be anything from a movie with snacks provided by the girls, to manicures and snacks. Make it as low-key or fancy as fits your group.

# Instructions for Older Women

*By R. Scott Okamoto*

## Memory Verse

"Honor your father and mother"—which is the first commandment with a promise—
"that it may go well with you and that you may enjoy long life on the earth."
—Ephesians 6:2–3

## Scripture

Titus 2:3–5

## Lesson in a Sentence

Students learn how much our mothers care and how much they do for us in accordance
with the Scripture.

# Focus

Ask students to write down the top five things their mothers are constantly telling
them. These can be things their mothers ask, yell, scream, nag, etc. Depending on the
dynamics of the group and the ages, have students share their answers by calling on
them or having them volunteer their answers. Some may be humorous, and some may
be universal. Make a note of the responses by the group such as rolled eyes, nods,
laughter, oohs, and aahs.

# Discovery

Write down some of the most common responses and pick a few of the ones you think
follow the spirit of the passage in Titus. Point out that even though the rants of our
mothers might get monotonous and annoying, they are ultimately made out of love
for us. Some will be corrective. Others will be cautionary. Still others might be encouragement. Be sure to show how these all follow the spirit of Paul's words in Titus.
Chapter 2 begins with a challenge to teach what is in accord with sound doctrine. In
this case, sound doctrine is a part of following the Word of God (v. 5). It may be true
that our mothers are encouraged to be self-controlled and busy in the home, in addition
to loving their husbands and children, but these things are all a part of living within
the context of God's Word.

## Life Application

As we learned in the previous lesson, our mothers make sacrifices for us. The women of Crete were being asked to give up their traditional ways of thinking and living. Slanderous talk, drunken behavior, and irreverence were their vices. Reminding students of this should make them feel pretty good about their own mothers. Regardless of what stands in the way of following God's Word, mothers have the tremendous responsibility to often forgo their own desires and dreams in order to make their families function. The first goal in verse 4 is to love their husbands and children. If our mothers are following God's Word, they will be making sacrifices and often busting our behinds to make us better people.


## TEACHER'S NOTE:

It is worth mentioning that differing views will likely be encountered when we discuss the topic of parenting and the roles of men and women. It will be important to be sensitive to the varying views of the students who might find some of the perspectives of this lesson to be problematic.

# Crisis Mode

By David Upchurch

---

In this lesson, students will:
- ✔ Learn to call on God in times of crises for help and survival.
- ✔ Learn that crises have been a part of life since the beginning.

Stuff you'll need:
- ❏ Bibles with maps
- ❏ Paper and pens
- ❏ Movies or DVDs: *Snow Dogs* and *March of the Penguins*
- ❏ DVD or VCR player

---

## Memory Verse

Do not be anxious about anything, but in everything, by prayer and petition, with thanksgiving, present your requests to God.—Philippians 4:6 NIV

## Scripture

Isaiah 37:14–20

## Lesson in a Sentence

The important steps after a crisis are acknowledging that God is in control, and then spending time in concentrated prayer.

## The Big Picture

Life is about crisis whether it is big or small. *When* one turns to God affects the whole circumstance and often determines the positive or negative results after a crisis. The key to Hezekiah's handling of the crisis with Sennacherib was that he took the circumstance to God *first*. Advisors and friends are valuable but talk often means inactivity if God's perspective and plan are not first considered and made a priority.

# Focus

How many *world* crises can you think of right now? How many *national* crises? How about *state or local? Personal?* What makes a crisis, a crisis?

Some may call a crisis an *opportunity.* Why?

# Discovery

Read Isaiah 37:14–20

If your Bible has maps inside, take a look at them. Find a map of Old Testament Israel and/or Old Testament nations. You'll notice that Israel is sandwiched between the super powers, Egypt to the southwest and Assyria to the northeast. Because of its location, Israel became the battleground for these two warring nations.

Since the nation of Israel was generally smaller and weaker, one tactic the more powerful kings would use was to offer protection to Israel. Then they could station troops in Israel's borders in preparation against an attack. Israel would also pay some sort of *tribute* (i.e. money or resources) to a nation in hopes of being spared destruction. However, if one of Judah's kings chose to stand up to one of these super powers, out came the chariots and fighting men and everyone got ready to rumble.

Hezekiah was one of those kings who chose to stand up to the bully on the block. In chapter 36 he stands up to the challenge given by Sennacherib delivered by his commander. Hezekiah sensing an imminent crisis, tore his clothes and put on sackcloth, a sign of mourning. Then, he sent for the prophet Isaiah. Isaiah's word comes back telling the king not to worry. *Whew,* Hezekiah must have thought it's over. Yet Sennacherib was insulted by the lack of a response and he sends another message to rattle Hezekiah and the nation. In it he mocks God and Hezekiah's faith (vv. 10–12).

Now, Hezekiah might have wondered if the city of Jerusalem could stand the attack against such military power. He could have also questioned Isaiah's message. After the second threatening message from Sennacherib, he seems to sense that the siege might be aimed at other foundations, those of a spiritual nature. So, he goes to the temple where he pours out his feelings, declaring his faith in God's power and plan. Always remember that God is not scared of your feelings or your doubts. He already knows your situation and is there with you whatever the circumstance. Prayer should always be personal and expressive, not a memorized poem or repetitious rambling (Matt. 6:5–7).

Wise counsel helps one get another perspective and Hezekiah had close friends like Isaiah to talk to and ask advice, but ultimately a crisis that tests your faith requires you and God to get together. Friends should encourage you and give you a *semi-objective* view but when it comes to the personal nature of faith, you must go to God. In fact ask your friends to pray, too. Prayers in times like these will grow the roots of faith deeply in the soil of your heart and all of those involved. What can happen is that we call a friend or two, tell our story, and complain a little. And that's it. But the crisis isn't over. Other times the crisis can be so overwhelming that we panic or run but we should stop and pray first. Pray for a wise solution and be obedient to the course of action that seems most biblical and/or moves you closer to Jesus. Consider the potential outcome of a circumstance in regard to your action, if it will cause you or someone to question God's nature or plan, you need to reconsider and be sensitive before making a decision. Plan in your heart and with your life to live in a way that shouts, "God comes first!" That will surely shrink some of the circumstances because none of them are bigger than God.

Hezekiah does just that when he approaches God and acknowledges Him (vv. 16–17 NIV). Notice how he addresses God, ". . . LORD God, . . . Almighty or Lord of hosts (or armies which would be very appropriate), . . . enthroned between the cherubim, . . . God of Israel, . . . God of kingdoms, . . . maker of heaven and earth, . . . the living God." Notice he doesn't pray for strength or for the situation to go away but instead his prayer and request are based on God's name and reputation and then God's action. As Hezekiah grounded his prayer in God and God's promise, he was praying a prayer God loves to answer, since God is faithful and true. When we learn to pray like this for God's glory and plan, our selfish prayers to change other people and circumstances cease. We will grow closer to God as our faith in His plan grows. We will see more answers and we'll desire more and more to become people of prayer.

## Life Application
Can you tell the difference between an inconvenience and a crisis?

Don't wait until you are so desperate that the last One you turn to is God.

Don't miss what is happening for an eternal purpose because of a narrow focus on present circumstances and inconveniences.

Check out 2 Kings 18:5 where Hezekiah is mentioned.

There are a couple of movies you can share with the students that illustrate crisis and survival. *March of the Penguins* is a story of penguins and their extreme display of community and survival, as fathers go 125 days without food while they brave one of the most violent winters on earth, to care for their future chick. This is a great illustration to show how crises are a part of life and the will to survive.

*Snow Dogs* is another great movie where the character, Ted Brooks, played by actor Cuba Gooding, Jr., tries to take up sledding after he has inherited a team of Huskies. As he is learning the ropes, the dogs take off hard and throw him off the sled and down the mountain. He gets up to see his shadow dwarfed by that of a bear and he takes off running. Once safe, the precipice on which he is standing falls and begins a slide downhill past trees and obstacles. Once stopped, he finds himself on thin ice that is cracking from his weight. Finally, as he begins to fall off the ice into the river, he dials 9-1-1 on his cell phone only to realize he is out of his "area." This movie humorously illustrates survival of one crisis after another.

## Extra! Extra!
What really makes people satisfied with their lives? Amazingly, the secret may lie in a person's ability to handle life's blows without blame or bitterness. A study of Harvard graduates found this perspective to be true. The study, reported in the *American Journal of Psychiatry*, noted that one potent predictor of well-being was the ability to handle emotional crisis maturely.

## Spiritual Practice
Pray with your hands open. Pray about specific crises, and as you do, picture them, lay them before God, and then leave them there. Allow God to replace the crises with His peace, love, and hope. (For more on this try one of Richard Foster's books on prayer or spiritual disciplines.)

# Try a Night of Prayer

*By David Upchurch*

## Scripture

1 Thessalonians 5:17

## Memory Verse

Do not be anxious about anything, but in everything, by prayer and petition, with thanksgiving, present your requests to God.—Philippians 4:6 NIV

## Lesson in a Sentence

Changing a routine and discovering creative ways to pray encourages a more positive and uplifting prayer time.

## The Big Picture

Often we get used to doing the same old thing over and over so eventually there seems to be no life to it. We wind up just going through the motions. Prayer is too important for it to become dull. Try some new experiences and watch these corporate times together become powerful events.

# Discovery

### Try a Night or Concert of Prayer

With some groups, it might help to enlist some students to pray beforehand so they don't get overwhelmed and put on the spot. Depending on the length of time for your Midweek program, you could break up the night in four segments like the acrostic A-C-T-S. Spend fifteen minutes in Adoration of God for who He is, fifteen minutes in Confession (this could be general instead of specific sins, due to the setting, or written down instead of spoken aloud, or even a confession of our need for God), another fifteen minutes in Thanksgiving for blessings received, and then fifteen minutes in Supplication for friends and family.

*Popcorn prayer* is a great way to pray together. Variations are ways to change things up. Pray through the alphabet of God's names as a group. Start with "A" and let students praise God for being the *Almighty, Abba,* the *Amen* and so on; then try "B" the *Beginning, Best.* The whole alphabet is full of praise. Check out the Model Prayer that Jesus taught the disciples and break it into phrases: *Our Father . . .* let students focus on that for a few minutes then, *Hallowed Be Your Name . . .* Try Psalm 23 or some of your favorites.

A *labyrinth* is a great experience in prayer if the students are prepared and debriefed.

Walk one if you haven't had the chance. It can really make an impact. One walks the path in prayerful expectation toward the center. The goal of all prayer is God, so remind the students this is more than just another experience. Around the edges and/or in the middle, you can have a Bible or other symbols and Bible verses that help spark prayers, or let the space be for them to meet with Jesus. The walking back out can be unique, too, and an experience of community as they pray for each other. Do some research beforehand. Then you may tape out or create your own path, borrow a portable labyrinth, or go to a church that might have one marked out on their campus.

Try *prayer stations* scattered throughout the room to create a great atmosphere for a night of prayer. Give each area an issue or prayer request to focus on by writing it on a poster. Open with prayer and then let students freely go where they feel led. When students go to a specific station, it triggers them to pray for that specific issue . . . school, family, friends, church, etc. Other stations could include psalms or Scripture from the Bible to spark a prayer of praise, thanksgiving, or intercession.

On some nights you could *forego the actual singing* of worship songs and just put the words on a screen or type them out. As the students think through each song, they can respond by writing out a prayer or simply spend time praying. Another variation would be to try simply reading one of today's choruses or some type of responsive reading.

There always seems to be a need in a group of students, so there could be some who would simply let others pray for them. Ask for volunteers by phrasing it in such a way for them to remain seated and let others in your group *lay hands on them* and pray. You could pray for upcoming tests, big decisions, family matters, personal struggles, etc.

Experiment with *postures of prayer*. Throughout the Bible, God's people prayed kneeling down, lying face down, hands raised or outstretched, head bowed or looking up. Getting students to experiment this way helps them pray more often as they discover it doesn't have to be routine.

A *night or period of silence* may be tough for some smaller groups, but try it. Place signs or words around your space indicating a time of silence for prayer. The text should guide them to pray specifically. You could debrief with some conversation before you leave because many times the Midweek meeting centers on community and friends.

*Focus on world missions* through prayer for a night. The global community is at the students' doorstep or at least their mouse pad. Many missions organizations put together prayer calendars and list needs weekly. Choose a country or two and spend time praying strategically for that group of people to be reached. Find out more about the country and its missionaries as you pray for them.

You might be amazed at how well your students do this. They are constantly looking to try something new, so any little twist can be a catalyst to a lifestyle of prayer. Many times adults will think students can't pray for an hour. When we've tried some of these ideas in the past, we've all been amazed at how fast time flies. Praying continually has to start somewhere. Encourage the students to start praying at other times and get the students to think about creative triggers such as: Every time the school bell rings they say a prayer, every time they walk through a door, get in a car, look at themselves in the mirror, open their backpack. Students can come up with their own system for reminding themselves to pray.

# Unlikely Faith

*By Amy Jacober*

**In this lesson, students will:**
- ✔ Identify Rahab's act of faith.
- ✔ Recognize confession of faith in the midst of risk-taking.
- ✔ Be encouraged to consider where God is asking them to take risks.
- ✔ Evaluate their willingness to recognize God in all circumstances of life.

**Stuff you'll need:**
- ❏ Two flags
- ❏ Downloaded story from www.jesusfreaks.net

## Memory Verse

For by grace you have been saved through faith, and that not of yourselves; it is the gift of God, not of works, lest anyone should boast.—Ephesians 2:8–9

## Scripture

Joshua 2:1–21; Hebrews 11:31

## Lesson in a Sentence

Faith often comes at the most unlikely of times to those who are willing.

## The Big Picture

Rahab was not exactly up for the "godly woman of the year" award. In fact, if she were in your youth group you'd be making an appointment at a clinic to check for diseases and praying she and those she had been with were healthy. Prostitution was just as abhorred in biblical times as it is today. This was not a youth leader kind of woman. Yet this woman, who was considered a lowlife, had faith that changed not only her life, but the lives of those around her. She took a huge risk in trusting the spies knowing that if they did not come through, the king could find out and turn on her. She chose to stand up for what she had been hearing, accepting as truth that God was Lord of all. She made this declaration clear in verse 11. She was willing to believe and when presented with the opportunity, acted on what she knew to be true. This was without "fixing" her life to become someone worthy. She was still a prostitute presented with the reality of God at work in the world.

# Focus

## Option 1

### Capture the Flag

Split your group into two teams. Decide your time limit in the beginning. If at the end of the time neither team has captured a flag, count the number of people in their respective jails and declare the team with the largest number the winner.

Designate half of a large area to each team with a clear center boundary line. If your church doesn't have a large area, consider going to a park close by. Each person may wander within their own area freely but in order to capture the opposing team's flag, they must cross to the other side. Once they are on the opposing team's side, they are fair game to be captured.

Teams begin face to face on their own side. Blow a whistle and send each to hide their flag on their own side. Students must be able to see the flag so it is to be hidden conspicuously.

After a few minutes, blow the whistle again to signal the start of the game. The object is to make it through the opposing team's side, capture the flag, and make it back to your own side without being touched. You may have no more than two people posted within fifty feet of the flag as guards. If someone comes close to stealing the flag, the guards may move closer.

If a person is touched by a member of the opposite team while they are in enemy territory, they are "captured" and taken to jail. Each team chooses a jail for a holding place. While in jail, there may be one guard keeping watch. Prisoners can be set free when one of their own teammates is able to make it to the jail and tag them without being tagged. A rescuer can free only one person at a time. He or she must run back across the borderline and return to the jail in order to free a second person. If the rescuer is tagged by the guard before he or she tags the person waiting to be freed, he or she must also go to jail.

If the game begins to move slowly, yell "jail break" allowing the prisoners of both sides to go free.

Once a flag is found and captured, it must be carried across the boundary line. If the one who stole the flag is tagged before he or she makes it across the line, the team reclaims their flag and hides it again.

## Option 2

Many of us have amazing people right in our own communities. These are people who moved from a secure job to start their own business or who adopted a needy child or offered a job to someone out of jail. The possibilities are endless. Risk is everywhere. If you know of someone in your church or community who has done something amazing, ask them to come and share their story.

Since this is the week of Memorial Day, if you know any veterans who would like to relate some of their experiences, this would be both appropriate and interesting.

# Discovery

Read Joshua 2:1–21 aloud to the group. Read it through once to hear the story. Next, ask your students to get comfortable and close their eyes. Tell them that you are going to read this story through two more times. As the students listen, ask them to choose what character they would be in this story. Joshua? Rahab? The spies? The king? Messenger of the king?

If your group is larger, break into groups of four and invite them to read it once again from their own Bible. Consider the following questions as a guide for studying this passage.

- With which character did you most identify? Why?
- What do you think you would have done if spies had come to your door?
- Do you think Rahab had faith or was she trying to save herself?
- Should the spies have trusted her?

Read Hebrews 11:31. Rahab's faith is quite clear.


## TEACHER'S NOTE:

Rahab is told to tie a scarlet cord in her window. Scarlet is similar in usage to the color purple, designating royalty. This is also reminiscent of those Israelites in Egypt marking their doorposts for the angel of death to pass over.

Jericho was a significant city in the history of Israel. It is the first one Israel conquered under the leadership of Joshua. It was on a major thoroughfare from Jerusalem to the west to Amman to the east and considered a wealthy community in general.


## Life Application

Every day there are people doing amazing things in this world. They take risks to make a difference knowing that there is the possibility of their attempt backfiring.

Talk about some of the biggest risks you or someone you know have taken. Encourage each student to share at least one story.

Read a selection from www.jesusfreaks.net. You will find excerpts from their books and links to Voice of the Martyrs, a group committed to educate and eliminate persecution of Christians in the world. Ask your students to respond to what they hear— belief, disbelief, moved to want to do something, or still searching? Were the students aware that there are people today risking everything to follow God's calling? How might we learn from those in the past who risked everything? Share with them this Web site and the books they can check out after this time together.


## Making It Personal

Rahab was an unlikely heroine expressing an unlikely faith. One of the great things about God is His willingness to use those of us who are imperfect to change the world. Age, gender, background, status, and wealth do not matter. There are hundreds and thousands of opportunities every day to serve God and make a difference. Some are large, some are small; but they are there.

Allow a few moments in silence for each student to hear from God what He may be calling them to do. This may need to take the form of a guided prayer depending on the level of comfort your students have with silent times before God. Is there something so big that it could not be accomplished unless God was in it?

# Unlikely Faith

*By Amy Jacober*

## Memory Verse

For by grace you have been saved through faith, and that not of yourselves; it is the gift of God, not of works, lest anyone should boast.—Ephesians 2:8–9

## Scripture

Matthew 14:22–35

## Lesson in a Sentence

Faith often comes at the most unlikely of times to those who are willing.

# Focus

This is a rather wet take on musical chairs!

Offer movie passes to whoever wins this game. Rather than using chairs, ask your group to stand in a circle. Enlist two of your leaders to make a "bridge" that each person must walk under. The two who are making a bridge hold a small water balloon above everyone's heads. As the music stops, pop the balloon. The person who gets wet is out! Be prepared for this to turn into an all out water balloon fight!

Realize that some will drop out once they think they may get wet. For those who stay, they are taking the risk to gain the prize. Make a big deal about the movie tickets you are giving away. If you are able, throw in snack bar coupons or something else unexpected to further drive the point of the reward at the end of a risk.

# Discovery

As students gather in class and get settled, have a strong reader begin. This is quite effective from the back of the room, but it must be read by someone with a commanding presence. Read through Matthew 14:22–35 in its entirety.

Outside, several of you took a risk by playing the game. Not a big deal really, but a risk nonetheless.

Ask your students to open their Bibles and read Matthew 14:22–35 in small groups. Ask them to determine the person who was taking a risk and the outcome.

A lot of people focus on Peter sinking and needing Jesus' help to keep from drowning. Realistically, Peter was the only one to get out of the boat. It was Peter's action that led the whole group to declare, "Truly You are the Son of God!"

## Life Application

Sometimes the risks we take lead to something spectacular. Sometimes risks fail in the way we expected but bring a result we never could have planned.

Brainstorm in groups about what God might be calling you or your group to do. Is it a 24-hour prayer chain? Intentional witnessing to friends? A monthly visit to a retirement center? Letters of encouragement to missionaries in the field? Adopting a child in need from **Compassion International** or **World Vision?** There are so many things God may be calling you to do. Peter kept His eyes on Jesus and did the impossible; he walked on water, if only for just a few moments.

Remind your students of Rahab. In today's lesson, Peter, one of the disciples was the focus. While a little rough around the edges, he was considered a godly man. Rahab was a harlot. She was not a woman considered to be worthy of being recognized in the community, let alone to be in service to God. It is not a matter of getting your whole life together in order to be loved and used by God. In the moments of service, God is able to enter in and change us from what we once were to a new creation. The old indeed passes away. Sometimes more slowly than others but still, change comes.

Once again, spend a few moments in silent prayer asking God to reveal what He is asking of the students personally. They may need to ask forgiveness for something in their life. They may need to ask for courage to do what God is calling them to do. It could be both. Encourage the students to focus as much as possible and really listen for God.

## Song Connect

"I Believe" by Building 429 on *Rise*

## Quotable Quote

*To one who has faith, no explanation is necessary. To one without faith, no explanation is possible.*—Thomas Aquinas

# Teenagers with Special Needs

*By Amy Jacober*

Have you been looking for something new and different for your students to do which will draw them closer to Christ and to one another? Are your youth tired of the same old thing? Are they ready to be stretched and challenged to think beyond themselves—even if only for an hour or two per week? This is an opportunity to reach out to a hidden and unreached people group right in your own neighborhood.

Who are these unreached, isolated people? They are teenagers with special needs. Statistics say that over 15% of teenagers in America have an identifiable disability. How many of these students do you know? How many of them participate in your youth group? What would it take to include them and to show them and their families God's love?

Following are a few guidelines to enhance inclusion of people with special needs in youth ministries followed by real life quotes from youth pastors and youth who have stepped out in faith to follow Jesus' example of caring.

## Why Welcome Someone with a Disability?

First Corinthians 12:22 teaches that contrary to being "weaker" members of Christ's body, persons with disabilities are "indispensable" to its proper functioning. Our worship, fellowship, and outreach are incomplete without the abilities and gifts they contribute. However, instead of being valued for their unique gifts and abilities, people with disabilities often find that they are ignored, isolated, pitied, or patronized—even by well-intentioned believers. Fortunately, many are learning that those with disabilities are more like their able-bodied peers than unlike them. All people have similar physical and spiritual needs, desires, and concerns.

As we seek to reach out in our communities, it is important that we include people with disabilities in our lives and that we encourage ministry with them, not just to or for them. We must endeavor to remove barriers of attitude, communication, and architecture that exclude people with disabilities from full participation in the body of Christ.

From the moment a person enters your gathering, they need to be welcomed as someone created in God's image with gifts and talents to share. Their unique needs also must be acknowledged, so they can enjoy full access to the love of Christ.

I praise you because I am fearfully and wonderfully made; your works are wonderful, I know that full well.—Psalm 139:14 NIV

## How to Welcome Someone with a Developmental or Mental Disability

Most teens with mental challenges can learn to live, work, and socialize with a small amount of caring supervision. Some people miss social cues, do not learn easily from experience, and are physically and socially immature. For these friends, your youth group could be a haven of acceptance and affirmation, free from the rejection and stress they experience in other places. To improve your personal interaction:

- ✔ Talk to the person directly, not through a companion or family member.
- ✔ Treat teenagers with developmental disabilities as teenagers, not as children.
- ✔ Be patient and flexible. Converse in a normal tone and warm manner. Give instructions slowly, in short sentences, one step at a time.
- ✔ Someone with a developmental disability may react to social situations in a nontypical way. Respect their request to be left alone, not to be touched, or to participate without speaking.
- ✔ Allow the person to try tasks or answer questions on his or her own, to make mistakes, take a longer time, and to persevere. Be aware of your potential impatience to take over doing things for the person that he or she could do independently.
- ✔ Build confidence and skill by helping to develop interests and the opportunity to share them.*"Let your conversation be always full of grace . . ."*

*". . . only what is helpful for building others up according to their needs . . ."*
—Colossians 4:6; Ephesians 4:29 NIV

## How to Welcome Someone with a Physical Disability

Millions of Americans use wheelchairs, canes, walkers, braces, or crutches. Attitudes can limit people as much as architectural barriers. Ignorance can give rise to condescending or rude behavior toward those with physical disabilities, particularly someone who uses a wheelchair. Here are some tips for improving personal interactions with those who have a physical disability:

- ✔ When speaking with someone who uses a wheelchair, place yourself at eye level by sitting or kneeling. This reduces strain on their neck and yours.
- ✔ Do not lean on the wheelchair as this invades the person's space.
- ✔ Allow the person, as much as is possible, to choose where they would like to be seated. Keep wheelchairs, walkers, and crutches within reach of the person who uses them.

## Helpful Tips for Everyone

Everyone should be welcomed with courtesy and thoughtfulness. When meeting someone with a disability, remember they are first and foremost a person—who happens to have a disability. Let your words emphasize their worth and abilities. Here are some general suggestions for interacting with someone who has a disability:

- ✔ Don't ignore people with disabilities. Acknowledge them as you would anyone else and make an effort to include them. Everyone appreciates a warm smile and friendly conversation!
- ✔ Don't give excessive praise or attention to a person with a disability; it can be patronizing.

- ✔ Speak directly to someone who has a disability, not to his or her companion, attendant, or interpreter.
- ✔ Act naturally. Some people tend to change their tone of voice and nonverbal language with someone who has a disability. This may come across as demeaning.
- ✔ Let people do and speak for themselves as much as possible. Choice and independence are important to us all.
- ✔ Extend a hand of welcome. In most instances, touch is appropriate and important and an offer to shake hands is accepted. If someone is unable to shake hands in the usual way, offer to shake their left hand. If someone is unable to lift their arm, gently clasp their hand. If someone is averse to such contact, try to be accepting and greet him or her with warm words.

Do not forget to entertain strangers, for by so doing some people have entertained angels without knowing it.—Hebrews 13:2 NIV

## Are You Looking for Growth in Your Youth?

Here are growth points experienced by typical youth in youth ministries where students with special needs are welcomed:

a. They gain a deeper understanding of the unconditional love of Christ.
b. They look at and experience acceptance in a whole new way.
c. They develop a new level of patience.
d. They gain an appreciation of others' challenges.
e. They learn to look past outward appearances.
f. They gain a broader view of life and may be able to glance beyond their self-centeredness.
g. They grow in their work ethic or determination as they watch the determination exhibited by their friends with special needs.
h. They learn the value of a slower pace.
i. They learn that what seems to be a small accomplishment may be a HUGE cause for celebration.
j. They learn to be less threatened by identifying and naming their own weaknesses; it's okay not to be perfect.
k. They see new vocational possibilities.
l. They count their blessings.
m. They reach a new comfort level when interacting with persons who are different from themselves.
n. They make new friends.
o. They experience the JOY of serving others!

## What Youth Groups Have Experienced When Teens with Special Needs Have Been Included

*For me, it was an opportunity to spend time with our youth while helping them learn to serve. An extra added bonus was that they were able to see God's love for all people.*
—Youth Director at Calvary United Methodist Church

*There is something about the kids with special needs that you cannot find anywhere else. They are truly God's secret keepers. They have such an amazing outlook on life that puts me in awe. Their innocence and humility make me feel as though I am the one with the disability, that there is something so pure and simple about life that I can't understand or just can't seem to grasp and live. These kids truly model Christ's love to each other and anyone willing to be a friend. After working with them, I realize how much more there is to a person than their physical or mental abilities or limitations. It is a person's soul that shines bright with Christ that matters, and these new friends make me want to shine brighter.*
—Julie, Junior at Fairfax High School (Julie comes from a non-Christian family and gave her life to Christ while serving as a buddy.)

*My buddy, Christopher, is 19 and is affected by mental retardation due to severe epilepsy and brain tumors as a child. His multiple brain surgeries caused him to have mood-swings and little-to-no self-control. On the third day, during the talk about how everyone is made in God's image, Chris stood up and yelled, "God made a mistake with me! God didn't make me right!"—pointing to his scars on his head. While at the time I felt embarrassed and frustrated, trying to convince him to sit down and listen, the conversation that came later will forever be seared in my mind. I assured Christopher that everyone has a special purpose in life and that God cherishes us all, regardless of ability or disability. I was as affected by my argument as Christopher was. He calmed down and stopped doubting his worth and I realized that God doesn't care how "able" a person is, but how a person lives their life with the abilities they have. This conversation with Christopher was one of the most rewarding conversations I have ever had. During that twenty minute discussion, I realized that it wasn't just that I was following Chris around, making sure he didn't get into trouble, but that we were reciprocally learning from each other. The reactions that Christopher had to the group talks and camp experiences gave me a completely different outlook on my own life. I am forever transformed and have been given new eyes and a new heart because of kids with special needs.*—Will, Senior at Fairfax High School

# Seeking God and Being Misunderstood by Others

*By Amy Jacober*

**In this lesson, students will:**
- ✔ Learn that not everyone will understand those who seek to follow and honor God in all that they do.
- ✔ Discuss the pros and cons of seeking God.
- ✔ Identify times when they have trusted God and when they have held back from God.
- ✔ Be encouraged by God's promises and provision.

**Stuff you'll need:**
- ❏ Playlist of songs
- ❏ Potentially 2 MP3 players
- ❏ Butcher paper or poster board

## Memory Verse
What then shall we say to these things? If God is for us, who can be against us?
—Romans 8:31

## Scripture
1 Samuel 1–2

## Lesson in a Sentence
Some people are just not going to "get" how you live or the choices you make when you decide to follow God.

## The Big Picture
If following Jesus were a human idea, then obedience would always be accompanied by success and acceptance. Reality is that following Jesus is not our idea but God's. Scripture makes it clear that His ways are not ours. Often we are most misunderstood when we are focused on Jesus, following Him closely. It can be confusing when you choose to honor God in your dating life and you are the only one of your friends not invited to the prom. It can be equally confusing when you have prayed for your parents for years only to be made fun of at home for being a "Bible thumper." There may even be more difficult times to come. Others may choose to lie or distort your good intentions as you struggle to decide whether to respond in kind or to turn the other cheek. When it feels like almost everyone is against us, God is for us. He hears our

cries. It is in these moments of being misunderstood that we may deeply identify with Jesus and His struggles on this earth.

# Focus

## Option 1
### Humdinger!
This game is similar to the charades of humming done as a race. Split into two teams with each creating a playlist of songs for the other. Have one person from Team A be the moderator for Team B and vice versa. Have each team select a volunteer to begin the game. The moderator whispers the song title to the volunteer and only through humming, the volunteer tries to get his or her team to guess the name of the song. The person on the team who guesses trades with the volunteer and the process is repeated. Keep this going until the entire list is done. Whichever team finishes first, wins.

## Option 2
For a slight twist, ask two of your students to create a playlist with popular songs on their MP3 player. Instead of just telling your students which song to hum, have him or her listen to the song while trying to hum it to their team. Be careful not to turn the volume up too loud so the team hears it through the headphones. If this is the option chosen, keep the number of songs on the two lists the same.

# Discovery

Ask your students to describe their ideal family. Does it include grandparents close by? What about a mom and a dad? Chances are they did not list more than one wife for their father. Before they begin reading the Scripture, set the backdrop for this passage. Elkanah is the husband of both Hannah and Peninnah. This was a time in history where polygamy was a part of the culture. While hard to believe in our world, this was perfectly acceptable. This does not mean that it was perfectly easy. There could be jealousy and alliances that no one could have predicted, not to mention favorites. Try not to get hung up on the two wives part of the story and focus more on Hannah. She longs to be a mother, is mocked, misunderstood, and finally comes to peace with her desire.

Break your students into groups of four or five. Give a sheet of butcher paper or poster board to each group. Ask them to read 1 Samuel 1 through once in its entirety and a second time thinking of it in scenes. On the poster board, create either a timeline or a storyboard of what has happened in the passage. What are the major scenes? Which elements are important?

Be certain that you spend time with your students and your leaders by joining each group for just a few moments to keep them on track and answer any questions which may arise.

Once finished, ask each group to share, noting what parts each group held in common as important, and where they differed. Hang the posters on the wall. Be certain to point out 1 Samuel 1:12–16, if this did not come out clearly in the group poster presentations.

## TEACHER'S NOTE:

The Israelites were not a God-honoring society as a whole at the time when Samuel was born. In fact, "everyone did as he saw fit" (Judg. 17:6 NIV). This was not a holy people seeking to honor the Lord. Elkanah and Hannah did not fit into their world. They were seeking God and being obedient to His commandments even when the world around them was not. Sound familiar? Leaders and students trying to honor God in the world as it is today are in the minority.

## Life Application

Hannah was seriously misunderstood. When she is at a personal low, crying out to God, things only seem to get worse. To make it even more painful, it was Eli, the priest, accusing her of being drunk. He did not ask why she cried or what was happening in her life. Still, Hannah stood her ground and Eli accepted her explanation. In fact, he encouraged her to go in peace, petitioning God on her behalf.

Read again 1 Samuel 1:20. After years of sorrow, Hannah's prayers are answered as she had hoped for and she became pregnant. In response, Hannah offers praise to God! She raises Samuel until he is weaned and then honors her promise. Hannah takes Samuel to Eli to serve the Lord. Ask each group to read 1 Samuel 2:1–11.

What has God done in your lives that deserves praise? How has God blessed your group? Your community? A specific family? Your own life?

Create a prayer of thanks to God for something He has done in your life personally or for the group. You will know your students best. The creative process of writing this out together can be an additional blessing to some. For others, group work can be a struggle. Encourage them to work together as a community reminding them that no one wants to throw a party for one. Times of praise are like a celebration, to be shared and not hidden. Offer options asking your students to create a written prayer, a rap, song lyrics, or some other form of prayer that suits them.

## TEACHER'S NOTE:

Reframing the idea of writing a prayer as a song is a great way to encourage students to be engaged. A mistake many leaders make is trying to be creative to keep the attention of the students, yet not paying attention to who the students really are. If your students love hip hop, don't push them to write a country song. If your students lean toward country, don't push them to write a rap. Do what works best for your group.

## Making It Personal

What sort of things do people beg God for today the way Hannah did? How do most people respond once their request has been answered?

Spend a few moments thinking back over what you have asked the Lord for in your life. God never promises to simply give whatever we ask. He is not a cosmic Santa who will deliver PDA's and the latest PlayStation. He does not magically make the guy or girl you have a crush on instantly like you. In fact, sometimes God's response of "No" is protection and blessing in disguise.

Allow at least ten minutes for your students to be alone with God. You may want to play music softly in the background to help set the tone and to drown out small distractions. Ask them to seek God and consider the following: What is your heart's desire? Have you asked God for this? Are you ready for the response? What if it is not the response you expected?

Close in prayer asking God to prepare each of us for the responses He gives. Thank Him for His faithfulness and ask for His help in persistence and patience. (Remember, Hannah prayed for the same thing for years!)

# Seeking God and Being Misunderstood by Others

*By Amy Jacober*

## Memory Verse

What then shall we say to these things? If God is for us, who can be against us?
—Romans 8:31

## Scripture

Nehemiah 2; Jeremiah 20

## Lesson in a Sentence

Some people are just not going to "get" how you live or the choices you make when you decide to follow God.

# Focus

We learn to realize that following God in this day and time will sometimes place us in situations of struggle and confusion. As we see in the books of Nehemiah and Jeremiah, following the call of Jesus isn't always a bed of roses, but we learn through reading the Scripture that it is always worth the effort. There are many instances where our faith is tested, and there may be others who are watching us to see exactly what this "faith" we possess is all about. Our actions or reactions in situations may turn out to be a catalyst for change in the life of someone who is struggling to find their way in this world. If we allow Him, God will use our lives in amazing ways, sometimes for circumstances we are not even aware of.

# Discovery

Ask your students what they expect from their parents when they follow the rules at home. What about what they expect from their teachers when they follow directions in class or on assignments? What do they expect from neighbors or police when they follow the rules in their communities? Most answers will be some of a *quid pro quo*. If I follow your rules, you will give me something. If I follow your rules, you will give me an allowance (and sadly, many parents will give it no matter what!) If I follow the instructions in class, you will give me good grades (It doesn't matter if they did well or not, as long as they followed the rules.) You get the pattern!?

Once you've had a good conversation about this, ask what they expect from God when they follow His ways?

Break into two groups. Explain that you are going to look at two guys who were just trying to do what God had called them to do—probably not expecting the outcome they got!

## Group 1

Read through Nehemiah 2. Ask this group to create a mini drama to explain what is going on in this Scripture. Help them to focus by telling that regardless of what details they include, the point is that Nehemiah knew God was calling him to restore a community. Others, including those in power, mocked him as he tried to help the Israelites. Feel free to share the story as written or have them make it modern, simply getting the point across.

## Group 2

Read through Jeremiah 19:14–15, Jeremiah 20, Jeremiah 37, and Jeremiah 38. These passages make a great newscast. The main point is that Jeremiah keeps doing what God says and life gets harder. He gets beat up, put in stocks, sent to prison, thrown down a well, and loses friends. This is not exactly how most of us think things will happen if we follow Jesus. Another untypical response is found from Jeremiah in chapter 20. He responds and it is not with sugar-coated praises. He is frustrated and angry. Yet, he does not give up. There is a freedom that comes when students learn that others have been treated poorly for following Jesus, and they can struggle but that does not give them permission to stop being obedient.

## Life Application

Many arguments and bad decisions occur when expectations are not met. We expect to be blessed when we follow Jesus. God has not abandoned us though some will feel the effect of living in a sinful broken world more than others.

How might you respond if you had experienced what Nehemiah or Jeremiah experienced? How do you respond when your experiences are not met today?

This is a great time to talk about life expectations. How do we continue to live joyfully when life gets hard? What happens when you don't make the team or fail at a test that you actually studied for? Even more, how do you find joy when parents divorce or you get expelled for drinking at school? Some struggles will come in trying to honor God. Some will come as consequences for poor choices. Regardless, struggles will come. It is in these struggles that we may most identify with the pain Jesus felt on the Cross.

## Memory Verse Activity

Turn to the Memory Verse. You may even want to have this printed on a sheet of paper or a card for them to take home. Take five minutes in silence asking your students to read and reread this verse. What does it mean to them? Do they believe it? If yes, do they live it? If no, what is keeping them from believing it? Or living it?

Give them a few moments to write on that same piece of paper a place in their life where they either need to thank God for being for them when no one else seemed to be or to ask God for His support when it seems they have been forgotten.

## Song Connect

"Does Anybody Hear Her?" by Casting Crowns on *Lifesong*

## Extra! Extra!

While there are many examples of people who were not looked upon favorably when they sought to honor God, two notables are Mother Teresa and Martin Luther King, Jr. While your students most likely know their names and have a very simple understanding of what they did, they probably are not aware of the years of struggle and opposition each of these people faced. They sought God with the desires of their hearts and were mocked, ignored, harassed, and struggled throughout their lives.

Study the backgrounds of these two individuals and ask the students to consider how Romans 8:31 related to their life struggles.

# Faith in Obedience

*By Sharon Koh*

In this lesson, students will:
- ✔ Consider how difficult it was for Abraham to be obedient to God's command.
- ✔ Recognize situations in their own lives that require that sort of radical obedience.
- ✔ Consider what motivates this kind of obedience (faith).
- ✔ Have an opportunity to commit and *do* what Jesus has asked them to put into practice—both generally and specifically.

Stuff you'll need:
- ❑ Paper bags (lunch bag size), each containing one *set* of
- ❑ Strips of paper with the following instructions (each on its own sheet):
  —Do ten jumping jacks.
  —Put your head in your hands and hold it there.
  —Stick out your tongue.
  —Draw a sunset on the board.
  —Sing "Happy Birthday" to someone in the room (pick someone who is not celebrating his or her birthday).
  —Spread out your arms and pretend to be flying around the room like an eagle. (Feel free to improvise and come up with other creative instructions.)

## Memory Verse

You foolish man, do you want evidence that faith without deeds is useless? Was not our ancestor Abraham considered righteous for what he did when he offered his son Isaac on the altar? You see that his faith and his actions were working together, and his faith was made complete by what he did.—James 2:20–22 NIV

## Scripture

Genesis 22:1–18; James 2:14–24

## Lesson in a Sentence

Obedience is much more than what we say or think; obedience is what we do and how we live.

## The Big Picture

Most of us would say that we want to be obedient to God. We desire to follow His commands . . . but at what cost? The kind of obedience that the Lord requires of us is an obedience that could come at all costs—like it did for Abraham. Oftentimes, this kind of obedience is a demonstration of our faith.

# Focus

This exercise is an exercise in obedience.

Have students split into groups of six or seven (or however many instructions you placed in it). Hand each group a paper bag containing folded instructions. Without looking into the bag, ask each student to reach in and choose a strip of paper.

Then, at the same, tell the students to spread out and obey the instructions on their sheet of paper.

This should create a comical scene, and students should have fun watching each other embarrass themselves.

Later, ask them if it was hard to follow instructions knowing that it would make them look silly in front of the others. Our obedience to God's commands is not always easily understood by those around us.

# Discovery

Read Genesis 22:1–18 together and answer the following questions:

1. What were God's instructions to Abraham?
2. What did Abraham do in response to these instructions?
3. How much did Isaac mean to Abraham? (See Genesis 15:1–5; how would God be able to fulfill His promise of descendants if Abraham sacrifices his only son?)
4. Why did Abraham leave his servants behind? Did he know what they would think if they saw what he was about to do?
5. How do you think Isaac felt when he voiced his question (after the third day)? What was Isaac trying to say?
6. God is pleased with Abraham. Why?

Now, read James 2:21–24.

1. Abraham is remembered in the New Testament as "righteous." Why was he considered righteous?
2. Read verse 22 again. This verse connects righteousness and faith together. What is the relationship between the two described here?
3. How does faith relate to obedience?

## Life Application

The command that God gave Abraham was a difficult one to follow because it meant demonstrating *faith* that God was going to fulfill His promise (of a lot of descendants) some other way. If Isaac, Abraham's only son, is dead, and Sarah is too old to have more children, then Abraham would have to trust that God had some other plan in mind.

When have you had to demonstrate faith in obedience? That is, when have you had to be obedient in actions *and* have faith that God would provide for you some other way?

## Making It Personal

Allow students to consider the above question and then to discuss in small groups. Ask them to be as specific as possible.

## TEACHER'S NOTE:

The idea of "faith in obedience" is an abstract one and not all students will understand it immediately. Help them first to see that Abraham's faith was demonstrated *through* his action (of being willing to sacrifice Isaac). If necessary, you may have to illustrate with an example from your own life first.

## Song Connect

"I Will Lift My Eyes" by Bebo Norman on *Between the Dreaming and the Coming True*

# Don't Settle

*By Sharon Koh*

## Memory Verse

But someone will say, "You have faith; I have deeds." Show me your faith without deeds, and I will show you my faith by what I do.—James 2:18 NIV

## Scripture

Genesis 11:27—12:5

## Lesson in a Sentence

When God calls you to go somewhere with Him, go all the way there—it just might be the Promised Land.

# Focus

**Simon Says**

This game is a classic. Nevertheless, it illustrates our lesson well. Students only obey when the command starts with "Simon says."

To make the activity more complex, combine "Simon Says" with "Telephone" and have students pass the command down a line before the last person has to follow the instructions.

# Discovery

Read Genesis 11:27—12:5. Ask the students to pay attention to the difference between Terah's and Abraham's obedience to God's command.

1. Where did God tell Terah to move to from Ur of the Chaldeans? Where did he settle instead? Where did he die?
2. Where did God tell Abraham to move? Where did he settle?

When God initially had this family uproot themselves to relocate, he had the Promised Land of Canaan in mind. The father, Terah, attempted the journey, but he settled on the way to his destination. He never made it to Canaan. Instead, he died in Haran. Abraham, Terah's son, made it all the way to Canaan, and this is where the Lord had always intended for them to settle.

## Life Application

Have you ever felt called to do something for Jesus and gotten discouraged along the way? Perhaps there was a project that became too daunting to complete? Perhaps there was a goal that took too long to achieve?

Terah was called to move to Canaan, but he never got to see the land "flowing with milk and honey" because he settled and died in Haran. Would you like to be Terah who settled and died on the way to the Promised Land, or would you like to be Abraham who made it?

## Making It Personal

Ask students to think of something they would like to achieve in their lives. Ask them if it is something they think would be pleasing in God's sight. Then, ask them if they are actively pursuing this goal, or if they have lost heart during the length of the journey. Take time to share with one another in community, and then pray to encourage all to keep their eyes on the prize.

# David/Solomon: From Parent to Child

JUNE 15 2008
FATHER'S DAY

By R. Scott Okamoto

In this lesson, students will:
- ✔ See their fathers and father figures in a new light as they examine their life lessons in relation to David and Solomon.
- ✔ Examine the lessons we learn from looking at the lives of our fathers.
- ✔ Learn to pursue wisdom and discernment as we learn from both the spoken and unspoken lessons our fathers teach us.

Stuff you'll need:
- ❏ Ask students to bring in old pictures of their fathers when they were young. Bring in pictures and portraits of wise men from previous generations. The older the better—Abraham Lincoln, Martin Luther King, Jr., paintings or drawings of ancient philosophers, or wise kings. Include more recent pictures of men that students may know, such as the head pastor or even of their fathers if you can get them. Just be sure you can say a few words about each picture.

## Memory Verse

A Father of the fatherless, a defender of widows, is God in His holy habitation.
—Psalm 68:5

## Scripture

1 Kings 2—3

## Lesson in a Sentence

Successful, Godly leadership shares many similarities with successful, Godly fatherhood.

## The Big Picture

Although we can assume very few of us are planning on becoming kings of God's people, we can certainly gain insight into leadership and, to a lesser extent, discipleship by looking at this advice given by David to Solomon. Whether we plan on becoming actual leaders of a community or in a church, or simply want insight into the riches and rigors of parenting, David's firm, authoritative advice sheds light on issues of logic, justice, and maintaining Godly order.

Perhaps more importantly for us, we see a son, Solomon, taking his father's wise counsel and building on it with God's help before putting it to use. While many of us have, at times, assumed our parents are from different planets or lack any semblance of a clue when it comes to life, the astute observer will take note of all that his or her parents have lived through and use all that knowledge and experience as a foundation for his or her own life. Whether through wise advice or drawing upon life experiences, our parents, in this case our fathers, can be invaluable sources of wisdom and insight.

# Focus

Display or show one by one the pictures and drawings. Have students share the pictures they have brought, and ask them to share something about the persons in the pictures. Remind them that at one time, their fathers were kids just like them. Point out that their father's generation is considered the Greatest Generation by most people. Looking at what they went through can help us respect them and learn from them. List the historical events, wars, and accomplishments of this generation. The goal is to tie the students' fathers to their generation.

# Discovery

In the Scripture passage, we see Solomon acting wisely. This wisdom can be attributed to his father's guidance. We see Solomon relying on his father's advice and building on it by asking God for wisdom and discernment.

Discuss how David dies, telling Solomon to "be strong, and show yourself a man," in 2:3. Solomon then has several people executed. Next we have Solomon's prayer in chapter 3, asking for wisdom and discernment. What conclusions can we make about Solomon's character, particularly in light of his handling of the two harlots at the end of chapter 3?

Ask students to share something their father has taught them. Press them for life lessons and philosophies as opposed to specific lessons such as, "Don't talk with your mouth full!"

## Life Application
- Ask students if they know the year their fathers were born. If they don't know, ask them to guess.
- Ask them if they know anything that was happening in the world at that time.
- Discuss the life lessons we can gain from learning what the Boomer generation went through. Living through wars, political scandals, economic ups and downs, and social trends can give us insight into how we approach life and faith.
- Ask each student to speculate as to how all the experiences of their father's life might give them perspective and insight into their own lives now.
- Discuss how students might find ways to build upon their fathers' and caregivers' instructions and teachings.

## Making It Personal

I remember the first time I realized my father had once been a real live human being. He had found his high school yearbook along with some photos in an old box. He showed me his yearbook from what seemed like a million years ago, but what froze me was a picture that slipped out. In it, my dad was sixteen, my age at the time, sitting at the beach between two pretty girls. He was looking over his shoulder at the camera with a tough, cool expression. He had a white T-shirt on with a pack of cigarettes rolled up in his sleeve. One of the girls was touching his arm as she smiled at the camera. Now, my dad as he sat next to me was and still is, a nerdy dentist. He was a deacon at our church and about the most conservative person I knew. I could not believe the cool looking dude in the picture was the same guy as my dad! He, of course, pointed out that he wasn't a Christian at the time and never really smoked. But what I remember most was that I was filled with questions about his life. What had he dreamed of? What did he experience? What was life like six thousand years ago? It quickly became clear to me that he had experienced many of the same things I was experiencing as a teenager. Peer pressure, girls, school, sports, life-decisions looming—he had been through them. Later, he would live as an army captain in the Vietnam era, though he was never sent, and he would witness the assassination of President Kennedy, the first man on the moon before having me with my mom. Since then I have taken every opportunity to learn about those who have come before me. I don't always agree with my father about politics, theology, or even who will win the World Series. But, I appreciate his perspective he has gained from his experiences and pray for God's wisdom to enable me to take that perspective as I go through life as a father, a professor, and a Christian man.

Getting young men and women to appreciate their parents' lives can be a significant step in their development as wise, discerning Christians. When we realize that we don't start our adult lives from scratch, but rather have the opportunity to build on the foundations laid by our parents and caregivers, we can then ask God, like Solomon did, to add to that as we become men and women.

# David/Solomon: From Parent to Child

*By R. Scott Okamoto*

## Memory Verse

A father of the fatherless, a defender of widows, is God in His holy habitation.
—Psalm 68:5

## Scripture

1 Kings 3:3–14

## Lesson in a Sentence

Analyzing Solomon's prayer when he became king teaches us the value of our father's legacy and the value of praying for wisdom and discernment.

# Focus

Put students in groups of three or four. Have them share situations they either were involved in or they witnessed in which a tough decision had to be made. If they feel comfortable doing so, have them share how that decision turned out. Was it a good decision or should another course have been taken?

# Discovery

Read aloud 1 Kings 3:3–14.

Point out how the passage begins with a reference to David's legacy.

Point out what pleased God about Solomon's prayer, or have students identify what, specifically, pleased God.

## Life Application

Lead a session of prayer in which you pray to thank God for our earthly fathers, leaders, and caregivers and the legacy they have left for us, and pray for wisdom and discernment in all areas of life—as children, as students, and as followers of Christ.

## Teacher's Note:

Please be sensitive to those in the group who do not have fathers. Be sure to point out that the role of father can be fulfilled by teachers, relatives, and caregivers. The last thing we want to do is make a student feel badly for not having a father. Also, it is possible and even likely that students have or are currently undergoing a rough period with their parents. There is also the possibility of all manner of abuse, neglect, and just plain bad parenting. The goal is to make the distinction that we should praise good fathers, and more importantly, we should see David and Solomon as prime examples of how the relationship should work.

# Being a Dorcas!

*By Ivan Wild*

In this lesson, students will:
- ✔ Learn the story of Tabitha/Dorcas.
- ✔ Recognize ways they can help others.
- ✔ Understand that helping others is part of doing the good work they were created to do.

Stuff you'll need:
- ❏ 3x5 Cards
- ❏ Pencils or pens

## Memory Verse

For we are God's *workmanship,* created in Christ Jesus to do good works, which God prepared in advance for us to do.—Ephesians 2:10 NIV

For we are God's *masterpiece.* He has created us anew in Christ Jesus, so that we can do the good things he planned for us long ago.—Ephesians 2:10 NLT

## Scripture

Acts 9:36–43

## Lesson in a Sentence

God will use ordinary people to do great things that will last forever if we are faithful in doing *good works.*

## The Big Picture

If someone said, "You remind me of Dorcas," would you be offended? Being called Dorcas back in the day of the early church would come as an honor. Dorcas was a lady in the church of Joppa who was known for her kindness and giving to the poor. She made clothes for widows, and always went around helping others.

Dorcas was living out what God intended her to be—a *masterpiece* of good works. She was not rich, famous, or a leader. She had no power, position, or authority in the church but she was known as a disciple (one who followed Jesus) that was used by God to bless many people. She no doubt touched many lives in practical ways that demonstrated the love of God. In fact, many of the widows who received the clothes she made, came to mourn her death and begged Peter (an apostle with ability to do miracles by the power of God) to come and do something. As a result, she was brought back to life and many people became Christians because of her life.

Dorcas is an example for us to imitate. We might feel small or insignificant and wonder how we can ever be used by God or live up to the expectations of being a Christian. Simply by helping others in need we are being a masterpiece of good works. God is not asking for outrageous or extreme good works, but to do what we can right where we are. When we do, big things will happen, lives will be changed, and God will be glorified.

## TEACHER'S NOTE:

*Dorcas* is the Greek translation of the Aramaic name *Tabitha*. Both names mean *gazelle*, which is a graceful and quiet animal.

# Focus

Choose the option that works best for the students. Modify as needed.

## Option 1

### Scavenger Hunt Game

Divide the students into teams. The first several items should be things found in and around your facility or outside, if possible. Make sure that some of the last items on the list can be found on the student, such as pencils, a white shoe, or Ipod. Since the very last item requested is the key item, ask for any change or dollar bills last. Ask each team to place items in the middle of the floor to see who has the most. The team with the most total items wins. Once items are on the floor begin to explain how $1.00 a day can feed a child in a Third World country, or how $50.00 can replace the old toys in the church nursery. Then challenge the groups to either take back their money or leave it for a mission-type project. Then together, choose a project the students would like to support.

## Option 2

### "Deal or No Deal"

Give 3x5 cards to each student and have them write down one or two things they can do that will demonstrate helping others. Some suggestions are mowing someone's yard, cleaning up an area of the church, volunteering at a local charity, or collecting canned goods for the needy. Tape the cards facedown on the wall or board and number the back of each card. Have each student select a numbered card for the job that they will commit to do. They are allowed to exchange one card for another. The object is for each student to do something that helps someone else. In order for the game to mimic the television show, "Deal or No Deal," make some cards with actual prizes such as a gift card, candy bar, or a CD. To receive the gifts, the projects have a harder degree of difficulty. Examples: Candy bar = bring a canned food for food pantry. CD = cleaning the church nursery. Have an extra bonus card to make the challenge and give away the prize. The winners are those who help others and give to the needy without rewards.

# Discovery

Read the story in Acts 9 and ask the students why the widows were mourning when Dorcas died? Why would they bring the clothes she had made them? Allow time for the students to answer. Help the students to understand that because of Dorcas' kindness and generosity toward them, the widows wanted to honor her by bringing the clothes. Ask the students what they would like to be remembered for.

## Digging Deeper

Dorcas was known for helping people but what was God doing through the life of this woman? Did God have a purpose for her by allowing her to get sick and die? What was Peter's part in God's plan for Dorcas?

Peter responded to the call for help from others and he had faith in God for a miracle. What if Peter had never gone to Joppa, the city where Dorcas lived? Perhaps we would only know of a person who did good works but because of this story, we see the awesome power of God to bring back to life a person who died. As a result of God performing a miracle, many people believed in the Lord. Dorcas was used by God in a practical and a supernatural way. Does God still work in practical ways and supernatural ways? Give students time to answer.

## Making It Personal

Tell students to take a minute to reflect on how they were created in God to do good works. Ask them to pray about the good works they can do where God might be glorified. Remind them of the games they played and the projects they committed to doing. Pray as a group or allow time for personal prayer. During the time of reflection, play some music your students might enjoy including Switch Foot, Pillar, Third Day, or any familiar praise and worship songs.

## Connections

There are several verses that proclaim how God helps us. In turn we are to help others. Examples include: "help in times of trouble" (Ps. 46:1 NLT), "I will strengthen you and help you" (Is. 41:10 NLT), "the Holy Spirit helps us in our weakness" (Rom. 8:26 NLT).

## Extra! Extra!

Extreme help. I watched a news report about a couple who adopted seventeen severely handicapped children, both physically and mentally. They took babies that no one wanted, loved them, and raised them as their own. For twenty years, this couple has been providing a quality of life for these children that is better than any institution could give, and they did at their own expense and sacrifice. If they can give so much of themselves, then certainly I can give a little to help others.

## Quotable Quotes

*When a person is down in the world, an ounce of help is better than a pound of preaching.*
—Edward Bulwer-Lytton, 1803–1873

*Some people give time, some money, some their skills and connections, some literally give their life's blood. But everyone has something to give.*—Barbara Bush

# Being a Dorcas!

*By Ivan Wild*

## Memory Verse

For we are God's *workmanship,* created in Christ Jesus to do good works, which God prepared in advance for us to do.—Ephesians 2:10 NIV

For we are God's *masterpiece.* He has created us anew in Christ Jesus, so that we can do the good things he planned for us long ago.—Ephesians 2:10 NLT

## Lesson in a Sentence

We are God's *masterpiece* (NLT)/*workmanship* (NIV), not a famous painting but created by God to do good and helpful things for others the way Dorcas did.

# Focus

You will need a box of unused Popsicle sticks, Elmer's glue, and pens for this activity. Give each student some Popsicle sticks and ask them to write the words of the Memory Verse on the sticks. Together, build a *masterpiece* as you reflect on the lesson. This is a throw back to preschool but teens will start talking and laughing as they work together to build an object.

# Discovery

Reread Acts 9:36–43 and answer the following questions.

- Do you think the clothes Dorcas made were the good works that God prepared in advance for her to do?
- Were Dorcas' good works for special events or more of a lifestyle of helping others?
- What are some of the differences and similarities between event-oriented good works, or a lifestyle of good works? Which type of good works is Ephesians 2:10 referring to?

(Possible answers for event-oriented good works: works to gain recognition, feels obligated to serve, or does something only once or twice a year. Lifestyle-oriented good works: one who looks for opportunities to help others, meets the need of a person with no obligation to do so, or does something for no recognition.)

## Life Application

Think of people you know who remind you of Dorcas. What are some of the things they have done? Allow time for students to share short stories. Is it possible to show others in school that you are God's masterpiece? In what way? How difficult would it be or what might happen if you did good works at school?

Each and every one of us is created in the image of God. When we become a Christian, we become a new person in Christ Jesus. This is what "God's workmanship or masterpiece" means. Workmanship describes having a purpose because something was carefully designed, and a masterpiece describes the glory of the Artist. God wants to use us to show off His glory in things we do and by the way we live. He has given each of us the ability to do good things. The more we do good works, the more we become who we are meant to be. It is not a matter of being the most talented or the best looking, but simply being who God created us to be. The key is to recognize that we are masterpieces and God has good works for us to do. Pray for God to show you opportunities to demonstrate His workmanship.

## Connections

Good works should not be confused with salvation. It is impossible for us to work our way into being God's workmanship or masterpiece. God has given us salvation so that we may do good works for others. Understanding Ephesians 2:10 and the story of Dorcas helps us to develop good works and reveal our true nature of being God's workmanship and masterpiece.

## Quotable Quote

*A kind and compassionate act is often its own reward.*—William John Bennett

# The Power to Choose

*By Jim Krill*

### In this lesson, students will:
- ✔ Learn who the prophets were and what they tried to communicate.
- ✔ Understand how God wants us to act as people with power, wealth, or influence.
- ✔ Realize how God reacts to those who abuse power, wealth, or influence.
- ✔ Learn how God rescues the oppressed.
- ✔ Be able to recognize different groups of power in the world today and whether or not they are abusing the power they have.

### Stuff you'll need:
- ❑ The movie, *The Iron Giant,* rated PG
  This is a great resource containing many profound lessons.

## Memory Verse
Sing to the LORD! Give praise to the LORD! He rescues the life of the needy from the hands of the wicked.—Jeremiah 20:13 NIV

## Scripture
Nahum 3:1–19

## Lesson in a Sentence
Having power does not give one the right to be cruel or violent.

## The Big Picture
Those who abuse power on earth and use it to do harm to others will have to answer to God who will judge them and ultimately avenge the oppressed and afflicted victims of abusive power.

# Focus

## Option 1: Jr. High (Possibly High School)
Use the movie, *The Iron Giant,* to demonstrate how we have choices in using the power we possess. In particular is the scene where Hogarth intervenes to keep the Iron Giant from blasting everyone away with his gun. Hogarth tries to tell him he doesn't have to use his gun. Just because he has the power doesn't mean he has to use it.

In the movie, go to chapter 23 entitled, "I'm Not a Gun"—play from 1:01:23 to

1:07:33—about six minutes. You are cutting it off before it is resolved, but this is okay. You should plan to show the resolution in the Midweek lesson.

This is a great tool to demonstrate that we make choices to use power for good or evil. In the Midweek lesson, the resolution shows the sacrificial love of Christ who gave up His life to save us, and who ultimately triumphs because death does not have dominion on Christ, or us.

## Option 2: High School or College or Small Groups

Involve your students in discussion on the misuse of power by people in their lives.

Ask them to think of a time when someone misused their power to get something they wanted. Or maybe a time when they witnessed someone using their power to hurt others. Ask the students to discuss their feelings and reactions to these situations. Examples could include:

- Coaches
- Parents
- Teachers
- Bosses (for those with jobs)
- The Police
- The Government
- A Friend

# Discovery

Read Nahum 3:1–19 NIV.

These may be difficult verses to understand. We may need to look at a little bit of history to figure out what is going on here. This passage is brutal, descriptive, poetic, harsh, and convicting. Nahum names Nineveh's evil and its impending destruction. Indulge the students in a discussion about the meaning of a prophet.

Nahum describes Nineveh as "the city of blood" and "full of lies, full of plunder, never without victims!" Assyria was a powerful empire that had massive amounts of wealth and "plunder." They accomplished this through brutality, lots of bloodshed, lies, and always at the expense of victims. What people, groups, governments, or nations can you think of that exist today or in the past that remind you of Assyria? How are they similar? How are they different?

Verse 4 tells us what went wrong in Nineveh. "All because of the wanton lust of a harlot . . ." (Wanton means "without restraint or inhibition" or "unrestrained, heedless of reasonable limits, or characterized by greed and extravagance.) Nahum describes Nineveh's evil as lust of a harlot. It lured men in with its pleasures, only to steal their freedom and ultimately, turn God against them (v. 5). What types of things, ideas, places, or people are you aware of today that try to lure others in with their pleasures? Nahum says that they became "enslaved" . . . Can people become slaves to pleasure or power? Name some people, groups, companies, or governments that have been lured in by wealth, power, and pleasure.

(For college-aged groups: Read verse 16 again. What nations today do these verses remind you of? What does this look like in today's world?)

Read verse 19. Although Nineveh, and therefore, Assyria, were powerful and wealthy—they were hated. Verse 19 says, "everyone who hears the news about you claps his hands at your fall, for who has not felt your endless cruelty?"

## Teacher's Note:

Here is a little background on Nineveh and prophets. A prophet is not a psychic who claims to know the future. Prophets are messengers from God who come to be mirrors to civilizations who have lost their way. A prophet is usually "a voice of one calling from the desert"—a lone voice who goes counter to those around him, usually resulting in persecution or death because of his message. In his book *God's Politics*, Jim Wallis describes prophets and prophecy as follows:

> "Prophecy is not future telling, but articulating moral truth. The prophets diagnose the present and point the way to a just solution."

So prophets provided judgment of the current situation, as well as a way out. That is where the prophecy comes in—they provided a picture of what the future could/would look like—given the current circumstances.

The book of Nahum is a prophecy about the fall of Nineveh, the great capital of the Assyrian Empire. Nahum was speaking to the Assyrians, announcing that God had had enough of their evil, corrupt, greedy ways and was about to eliminate them from the map. (This has literally happened to all the great powers throughout time. They enjoy their short bouts of seemingly absolute power, but ultimately are overcome by their own corruption and lust for power and wealth.)

For a more in-depth background on Nahum, read the intro to the book in *The Renovaré Spiritual Formation Bible* (NRSV).

## Life Application

It is safe to assume that most of us are not rulers of countries, presidents, or dictators. We are not kings or emperors. But each of us has power. God gave us power when He created us. How we use that power determines our devotion and worship of God. Do we use our power for good? Or do we abuse our power by disobeying the laws of God and living for ourselves?

## Making It Personal

Make sure that students know that God has given us the privilege of power through our mere existence and free will.

## Option 1

Students should recognize that they always have a choice in the use of their power, whatever form it may take, for good or for bad. Remind them of the prophecy of

*Youth Ministry Sourcebook*

Nahum and the destruction of Nineveh and the Assyrian Empire as a result of God's judgment. Invite them to be the prophets of this age. They should keep an eye out for those abusing power and those who are being abused. Encourage them to speak out against abuses of power that they may encounter.

## Option 2

Ask the students how they feel about people who use power to abuse others? If you are wealthy or powerful and have influence over others, how can you better use that power and influence to do good?

## Quotable Quote

*I think the Bible is a book about power in ways we don't understand very much. It's a book about power and how safe it is to share power. So God makes a universe which among other things involves the sharing of power. Even allowing things to have the power of existence is a kind of sharing of power. A rock, by existing, is given the gift of a certain kind of power to be there, and to weigh something, and to last. And all of creation involves the gift of the power of existence; some have the power of mobility, and others have the power of reproduction, other creatures have the power of communication, and other creatures have the power of self-awareness, and we find ourselves as human beings being given so many layers of power. God is a safe person to carry power, but the question is: how safe are we to carry power?*—Brian D. McLaren, *Power, In Ways We Don't Understand*

# Power Redefined: The Power of Christ

*By Jim Krill*

## Memory Verses

How God anointed Jesus of Nazareth with the Holy Spirit and power, and how he went around doing good and healing all who were under the power of the devil, because God was with him.—Acts 10:38 NIV

The thief comes only to steal and kill and destroy; I have come that they may have life, and have it to the full.—John 10:10 NIV

## Scripture

Philippians 2:1–11

## Lesson in a Sentence

The power of sacrificial love shown by Jesus on the Cross is an example of how God did not abuse His power, but used it for the good of all mankind, and expects us—as followers of Christ—to use any power we have for good.

# Focus

**The Iron Giant, Cont.**

If you used this film for the first lesson, you can show the resolution of the story and relate it to how Jesus uses His power, not to kill or destroy, but to save life and to heal.

Continue showing the film from wherever you left off.

Discuss how the Iron Giant was like Jesus.

# Discovery

Read Philippians 2:1–11. After reading, ask students to relate any stories they know from the Bible where Jesus uses His power. Ask them how, and for what reason, He used His power.

## Life Application

God, in all His infinite power and glory, comes to earth to do good. He uses His power to heal—not to kill or destroy.

How can we be more like Jesus and use the abilities, talents, wealth, influence, and power that we have to do good? To help others?

# For Freedom

*By Amy Jacober*

In this lesson, students will:
- ✔ Understand that Jesus wants more for us and from us than a checklist of behaviors.
- ✔ Be encouraged to learn that Jesus provides an escape.
- ✔ Consider what sin is holding us down.
- ✔ Be given space to claim freedom in Christ.

Stuff you'll need:
- ❏ Dry-erase board
- ❏ Markers
- ❏ Weights of some sort (see Option 2)
- ❏ Strips of paper
- ❏ Tape
- ❏ The song "The Freedom We Know" by Hillsong
- ❏ Words of the song preprinted

## Memory Verse

Stand fast therefore in the liberty by which Christ has made us free, and do not be entangled again with a yoke of bondage.—Galatians 5:1

It is for freedom that Christ has set us free. Stand firm, then, and do not let yourselves be burdened again by a yoke of slavery.—Galatians 5:1 NIV

## Scripture

Galatians 5:1–15

## Lesson in a Sentence

Freedom in Christ means we no longer have to earn His favor.

## The Big Picture

Too often the measure of a Christian today reads like a checklist of do's and don'ts forgetting completely that Christianity is about a relationship. There is a fine balance between living in a legalistic manner and living as though our actions don't matter at all. Jesus calls us to choose actions as a response to our relationship with Him, not in order to earn His favor. Some students may feel they will never be good enough. Others feel that a loving God will not hold them accountable for anything. The truth lies somewhere in between. You will know your group better than anyone else. Gear this lesson in the direction that is needed most for your students.

# Focus

## Option 1

This is a lesson on **Knots.** Create circles of six to ten people. In the circle, have each person reach across the circle grabbing the hand of someone across from him. Be certain to grab only one hand of the same person. Once the students are connected, they must work as a group to break free from their knot. They are to move and shift until the knot is untangled and the group is in a circle once again.

The lesson is that way too often we give up and choose to stay tangled up when realistically, and with a little effort, we can be set free.

## Option 2

On a dry-erase board, ask your students to make a list of things that help to define a Christian. These are things such as: doesn't drink, doesn't cheat at school, doesn't lie to parents or others, doesn't have sex before marriage, doesn't steal, and so on. Let your students come up with as many as they are able.

Choose one of your students to become a living example. You will want to set this up with him or her ahead of time to be certain he or she is ready for it and will cooperate. Ask the student to do a small exercise like push ups or jumping jacks. Have a set of heavy items waiting. These can be heavy books that you add to a back pack or bag, actual weights, string around soup cans so they can be draped around your student's shoulders or whatever. The form it takes is not nearly as important as the sheer burden of weight that it will become. For each item listed on the dry-erase board, name it, and place a weight for your student to bear. With the burden of the weight, ask your student to again do the exercise. Once he or she is finished, ask them to stand, holding all of the weight.

While the other students read or talk among themselves, check with the student to make sure he or she is okay. Be certain to point out to your students that he or she is still standing with all of that weight.

# Discovery

In groups of three, read Galatians 5:1–15.

- What do you think this means at first read?
- What does yoke of slavery mean?
- How do we live like people who are still enslaved?

Reread Galatians 5:13–15.

- How do you understand these verses?
- What does the sentence mean to—"not use your freedom to indulge the sinful nature"?
- What do you think God is calling His people to do based on this passage?

## Teacher's Note:

This passage can be difficult in that the meaning can be lost in the focus on circumcision. Paul uses this obvious sign of living under the law. Explain to your students the significance of the circumcision under the law and the new order ushered in by Jesus. People no longer needed to meet each item in a checklist. In fact, Jesus came to set people free from the law.

The tricky part is that while this may seem easier at first, it is in fact a more demanding way to live. Jesus is not asking for people to follow a set of rules; He is asking for their lives. We have been set free from sin and the burden of living by the law and are called to live out the relationship we have with Christ.

## Life Application

Before your students get into group discussions, direct attention to your student weighted down. Explain that while the items mentioned are important for holiness, they are a result of a relationship with Christ, not a way to earn that relationship. Begin to slowly take the weights away from your student. Ask him or her what it has been like to stand burdened while everyone else was reading and talking. What does it feel like now that the weights have been removed? Remind your students that these things really do weigh us down. Often, they have been a part of our lives for so long that we don't even notice them anymore.

Ask each group to decide what would change about the life of a teenager if he stopped trying to live by checklists and chose instead to live in the freedom Jesus offers.

Consider giving the following questions as guides.

- Would life get more or less difficult?
- Is there a price for freedom?
- Why is there a warning about indulging in sin?
- How do we avoid this?
- Which is more difficult, to love your neighbor or yourself?

This passage is a strong statement calling each of us to freedom. This is neither patriotism nor independence. In fact, the freedom Jesus offers is one of interdependence and no longer being shackled by sin.

## Making It Personal

Ask each student to look back over the list of items written on the dry-erase board. Hand each person a strip of paper, a marker, and a copy of the words to the song, "The Freedom We Know" by Hillsong. While you play the song, ask your students to consider the words as they listen.

Instruct your students to write one item on their strip of paper that is weighing them down from which they need to be set free. Invite them to bring their strip of paper to a designated spot. The first person makes a ring with their strip and the others add their strips, thereby creating a paper chain.

Daily burdens do not seem so bad. Even our *little sins* don't seem to be a big deal. Understanding that Jesus doesn't even want us burdened with these can change one's entire perspective. No single person offered an entire chain though some probably could have.

As your students look at the chain, invite them to spend a few moments in prayer asking the Lord to help them truly live in freedom.

## Song Connect
"The Freedom We Know" by Hillsong on *Mighty to Save*

## Quotable Quote
*We cannot be truly Christian people so long as we flaunt the central teachings of Jesus: brotherly love and the Golden Rule.*—Martin Luther King, Jr.

## Service Option
While this lesson is about freedom in Christ, this time of year reminds us of the freedoms we experience every day. Get in touch with a local branch of the military or some connection in your community. Invite your students to write notes of encouragement and prayers to those serving in the military. Make sure these get sent.

# For Freedom

*By Amy Jacober*

## Memory Verse

Stand fast therefore in the liberty by which Christ has made us free, and do not be entangled again with a yoke of bondage.—Galatians 5:1

It is for freedom that Christ has set us free. Stand firm, then, and do not let yourselves be burdened again by a yoke of slavery.—Galatians 5:1 NIV

## Scripture

John 8:31–41

## Lesson in a Sentence

Christ alone brings freedom.

# Focus

## Option 1

### Two Row Tag

Break your group into two teams. Have each team line up shoulder to shoulder facing each other with at least ten feet between the two rows. Ask for a volunteer from each team. One is "it" while the other gets chased. They run around and between the two lines of people until one is tagged.

### The Twist!

The person being chased can run up behind someone from his own team and gently push that person into the middle, making him become the one being chased. Now "it" is left outside the rows and the other person is inside.

If "it" tags the chasee, then the chased becomes "it" and choose someone from "its" team to become the new person being chased.

There are many ways this game can illustrate freedom and being chased by sin. We often choose to run aimlessly, forgetting that we have the authority to refuse to be trapped any longer.

## Option 2

Check out the Web site www.snopes.com. This Web site offers a warehouse of urban legends that are being spread on the Internet. We are all subject to being trapped or conned if we are not armed with the proper information to keep us safe and free.

Choose a handful of the legends and truths the Web site suggests. Print these and pass them out to your students. Ask them to choose which ones are true and which ones are legends. How do they know?

Remind them that in life, Christ offers what we need for freedom but it is up to us to listen. When we don't listen and respond to God, we choose to be at risk for the scams this world has to offer.

# Discovery

Read John 8:31–41.

After the entire passage has been read, reread verses 31–36.

Jesus promises freedom.

- What does He say brings freedom?
- What is He saying the people are to be freed from?

This concept of being set free from sin seems simple, but it becomes a lifelong journey.

## TEACHER'S NOTE:

Set this passage in context reminding your students that this is a book written to the Gentiles who were struggling with all of the teachings of Jesus. They struggled with the popular Greek teaching that He was divine but not human. Explain to your students that in this passage, Jesus was affirming that His listeners were descendents of Abraham but they were not acting like their father and the children should reflect their father.

## Life Application

In small groups, ask your students to list definitions of freedom.

- Are their definitions applicable to this passage?
- Do we have a big enough idea of the meaning of freedom?
- Name some things that keep teenagers trapped (image, drugs, popularity, grades).
- How real are these pressures? How do they cope?
- Invite your students to discuss what they think it means to be a slave to sin.
- Ask them to describe a life of freedom from sin.
- How does the freedom of one person help others to be free as well?
- How does the truth of Jesus set you free?

Close by offering a few moments for students to consider the things in their lives which are keeping them enslaved. Then ask them to shift their prayer by asking the Lord to set them free. Ask your students if any have received an answer from God about what needs to shift in their lives to truly live as free people.

# Down, but Not Out

*By Amy Jacober*

## In this lesson, students will:
- ✔ Learn of God's extravagant love.
- ✔ Consider failures in their own lives.
- ✔ Recognize that everyone has ups and downs in life.
- ✔ Learn that God can still use us in spite of what we have in our past, and at times, because of what we have in our past.

## Stuff you'll need:
- ❏ Papers for folding
- ❏ Sheet of paper for each student
- ❏ Pens or pencils
- ❏ Butcher paper
- ❏ Markers

## Memory Verse
Brethren, I do not count myself to have apprehended; but one thing I do, forgetting those things which are behind and reaching forward to those things which are ahead, I press toward the goal for the prize of the upward call of God in Christ Jesus.
—Philippians 3:13–14

## Scripture
Judges 13:1—16:31

## Lesson in a Sentence
God is able to redeem any person in any situation.

## The Big Picture
Every day in the media we hear news of terrible things that are occurring in the world. There is no shortage of stories of teenagers committing embarrassing, silly, and even horrible acts almost daily. Some people feel that their past actions are way too much for God to ever forgive. They surmise that if God *is* able to forgive their sins, surely He would not welcome them back into relationship and service with Him as well. This is extravagant! This is too much! This is not like any person we have ever known. From a human experience, we can at times find forgiveness for others, but overall we tend to keep people at a distance. We learn heartbreaking lessons from trusting the wrong people, so we become determined not to be let down or taken advantage of again. God sees it all in a very different way. Today, we look at Samson. By every right, he was

privileged and should have known better. And yet, he messes up—and not with just a little embarrassment. If a person today did the things he did, the church would make certain he never even led prayer. God, however, does forgive and uses Samson for His glory, even after his moral failure.

# Focus

## Option 1
Tell your students that you are challenging them to a strength contest. Really play this up and make it a big deal!

Ask the students if anyone thinks they can fold a piece of paper four times? Six times? Eight times? Ten times? Twelve times? Keep going until someone says they think they can do it. Have the person come up front and place him or her in the center of your group so that everyone can see him. If you have more than one person who accepts the challenge, place them in a row for all to watch.

Let the students try their hardest. Reality is that no one can fold a paper more than eight times but it sure is fun to watch them try! Feel free to try different sizes of paper as well. Large or small, eight is the limit for a real fold.

When they have finished, let your students know that today you are going to look at someone who was very strong but also had limitations.

## Option 2
### Commonalities
Split your students into three teams. Assign at least two leaders as facilitators/judges. Each team creates a list of five pairs. For example: a hockey player and a nurse, soybeans and a cow, a hip hop artist and a skydiver, and so on. For each pair given, the team must decide what the pair have in common. A hockey player and a nurse both see blood often—the more creative the connection, the better.

Once you have the lists, call out the first pair for all three teams to hear. Give one minute for the three teams to brainstorm and then call on them to share their responses. (Be certain as you work through the list that you rotate which group is asked first in order to be fair. If you don't, your students are sure to point this out!) Work your way through all the lists. The judges decide each time which team has created the most creative/interesting connection. Give fourteen points to the winning team each round. The winner is the team with the most points at the end of the game. Offer a small prize for the winning team.

# Discovery

Every person has highs and lows in their life. The study of Samson's life is similar to an unending roller coaster ride.

Before you begin, tape a large sheet of butcher paper on a focal wall so that it runs lengthwise. You will come back to this after the entire passage has been read.

Ask if anyone likes a good romance story. What about action stories? Stories that include gore or betrayal? Announce that you've got a story for them that includes all of these and more.

Remember when you were in grade school and the teacher would read a chapter from a book after recess? Settle in, get where you can hear, and listen up for the story of Samson!

Give your students a sheet of paper and pen or pencil. Tell them to draw a line down the center of the paper. On one side, write the word *highs* and on the other side write the word *lows*.

Choose someone who is a very animated and strong reader to read the story. This is a long section of Scripture but it reads like a story. Have the student read Judges 13:1—16:31. Ask your students to record on their paper each time they think Samson was at a high point in life and each time they think he was at a low point.

Together, you are going to create a timeline of Samson's life. Draw a line across the center of the paper. Ask your students to look back over their high and low lists. Begin at Samson's birth and work all the way through to his death. Write any high in Samson's life above the line and any low below the line. Notice anything? It literally runs up and down, up and down. You may even want to try to show the extremes of the good and bad in his life. Draw the really good things way above the line and the really bad things very far below the line.

Samson is known as one of the strongest men in the Bible. He was chosen, set apart, messed up big time, and yet was still used by God in amazing ways—even to the point of his own death.

## Life Application

Gather students in groups of three to four. Be certain you have a leader in each group. If you need to, increase the size of the group to ensure a leader is present.

Guide the group in a discussion.

- What things did you notice that stood out in Samson's life? Why?
- Was there anything in particular that you could relate to?
- What things do you think people do that are unforgivable?
- Are there different standards for what God forgives and for what people forgive?

If you knew someone had a reputation as being a cheater, arrogant, strong, privileged, and being with a prostitute, is this the kind of person you would choose to lead the youth group devotion? What about being on the worship team? Give the sermon on a Sunday? To lead a Bible study? To build a church? To serve on a mission team? To cook for a mission team? To do construction for a mission team? To serve as a night guard for those on the mission team?

Where do we draw the line in what people are allowed to do in service to God based on their lives? Where does God draw the line?

## Teacher's Note:

Be careful not to leave the impression that what a person does is of no importance to God. God calls us to nothing short of holiness. What is counter to a human's perspective is that God calls all people to holiness and sees them as righteous, even when they have been disobedient and lacking in morals in the past. It is never too late to follow Jesus and allow Him to change your life.

## Making It Personal

Ask each student to think about times when they have messed up.

If they are willing, have them share a time they messed up and how forgiveness or redemption came after a while. It may be that a leader needs to prime the pump and share the first story.

We have all messed up. It would be dishonest to say that we have all messed up the same amount by the world's standards. God views everything in such a different way! Remember the parable of the prodigal son—the son who goes out and spends all of his money and has to come crawling back to his father? The son who was good and stayed home, serving the family and doing everything he was supposed to, is the one who is angry and bitter. Maybe your *messing up* isn't in lying to your parents, or stealing something from the mall. It may be that the way you have messed up is in your attitude and in your heart, similar to the older brother in the story.

Samson had many blessings, many times of obedience, and many times of sheer stupidity in making choices. In the midst of all of that, however, God still used him. God didn't have to; He chose to.

Spend a few moments considering something in your life that needs to change. You may not be visiting a prostitute like Samson (and I really hope none of your students are!) but you may be looking at porn on the Internet, or gossiping about people at school, or sneaking money from your mom's purse. What do you do that would make you seem to be unfit to serve God?

Pray and ask for God's favor in spite of your sin. Pray and ask that God will help you step away from what you have been doing and that you will make choices that honor Him, your family, friends, and all those who pour into your life.

## Connections

There are so many places in Scripture where you can see this same story played out again and again. Examples are Noah getting drunk, Miriam questioning her brother, Peter losing his temper, and many more. One of the clearest and most familiar for your students will be the prodigal son. This parable is often used and there is a reason for that. Consider looking at this one more time to reiterate the point (Luke 15:11–32).

## Song Connect

"Beauty from Pain" by Superchik on *Beauty from Pain 1.1*

## Quotable Quote

*When a man undergoes treatment from a doctor, he does not need to know the way in which the drug works on his body in order to be cured. There is a sense in which Christianity is like that. At the heart of Christianity there is a mystery, but it is not the mystery of intellectual appreciation; it is the mystery of redemption.*—William Barclay

# Down, but Not Out

*By Amy Jacober*

## Memory Verse

Brethren, I do not count myself to have apprehended; but one thing I do, forgetting those things which are behind and reaching forward to those things which are ahead, I press toward the goal for the prize of the upward call of God in Christ Jesus.
—Philippians 3:13–14

## Scripture

Acts 7:58; 8:1–3; 9:1–2, 3–19

## Lesson in a Sentence

God is able to redeem any person in any situation.

# Focus

### Team Dodge Ball

Divide students into two teams. Have some area for play with defined boundaries and a centerline to divide the area. Use either chalk or tape to create a clear middle boundary. Each team takes one side of the area of play. Give each team three foam balls or other soft ball. When you blow the whistle, let them fly! If a person is hit with the ball, he or she must move to the other side. The team with the most players when you call time wins. Remind your students to be careful, aiming for below the waist when throwing and not to throw too hard.

This is an easy silly game with a big impact! For a special summer treat, bring out some frozen ice cream or popsicles!

Granted this is a game, but it is a good segue to a discussion of battle—a battle about Saul, better known as Paul. Paul killed Christians, either himself or by making sure it happened. Not exactly what you typically look for in a minister!

# Discovery

So what do you know about Paul? He wrote lots of letters, was one of the best-known persons in the Bible, defined much of the Christian church today, was a missionary, and an apostle.

But what was he before he became super evangelist?

In groups of three, read Acts 7:58; 8:1–3; 9:1–2. Spend some time talking about what Saul had done. He didn't just lie or give attitude to others. Threats, death, persecution, and imprisoning believers were more his game. He would put most criminals to shame.

After talking about what Saul did, read Acts 9:1–19.

- What specifically happened to Saul on the road to Damascus?
- What was he told to do?
- What role did Ananias play in Saul's life?

## Life Application

Bring in several newspapers and tabloids for your students. Ask them to go through these looking for headlines and stories of people most churches would not see as fit for ministry. Have a sheet of butcher paper taped to the wall with several rolls of tape close by. Ask them to create a giant collage of the headlines and stories they chose.

Once the paper is filled, read off some of these headlines to your students. Why are these the ones they chose? What makes them think the people in these stories might not be considered fit for ministry?

Many Christians have a habit of focusing so much attention on the outside of a person that they miss the inside. Many of us judge others, not really knowing them.

Saul was clearly not the kind of guy any of us would want in our youth groups. He was a bully, not to mention a murderer. And yet, this is the same man, who after having met Jesus, devoted his entire life to the very thing he had hated.

Guide your students in a discussion considering the following:

While most of us don't expect much better from people who are famous, many of these stories from the news are about regular people in cities and towns just like yours. (If you get a local paper, it really will be people from a town that is just like yours because it is yours! For this reason you may want to stick to state or national papers.)

- What people do we judge as unfit for ministry?
- What about being in our youth group?
- God calls those who are sinners to Himself. How can we be imitators of Him and not decide who is and who is not fit for a relationship with God?
- What changes would happen in our lives if we actually lived this way?

Close with prayer, asking God to allow you to see others the way He does. Allow a few minutes of silent prayer, asking each student to pray for someone they had considered being too far from God. Pray for that person to meet Jesus in a strong way just as Saul did on the road to Damascus.

# What Are You Known For?

*By Janelle Comfort*

In this lesson, students will:
- ✔ Realize the different things they allow to define them.
- ✔ Realize that God defines them as His children.
- ✔ Desire to be a representation to others of the love that Christ has shown to them.

Stuff you'll need:
- ❏ Tape
- ❏ Note cards (per student) with names of well-known people or characters on each one (For fun, write your name or your senior pastor's name on a card, too!)
- ❏ Paper
- ❏ Pens/pencils
- ❏ Markers

## Memory Verse

What marvelous love the Father has extended to us! Just look at it—we're called children of God! That's who we really are. . . .—1 John 3:1 MSG

## Scripture

1 Samuel 16:1–7

## Lesson in a Sentence

The world tells us that we are defined by what we do and what we look like, but Christ tells us we are defined by who He says we are.

## The Big Picture

Everyone is trying to figure out who they are and who they are supposed to be in relation to others. As Christians, Scripture makes this clear for us. We are all children of God who are uniquely created to love our Creator and His creation. However, we cannot fully love God or other people if we do not first understand how much He loves us as His children. We have to weed through the lies and stereotypes of this world and begin to see the truth of who God says we are. Our identity must lie in the reality that we are a child of God. If that is where we place our identity, then others will begin to see it as well, and *that* is powerful!

# Focus

## Who's Who Activity

This is an activity where students have to ask questions of everyone else in the room in order to figure out their *secret identity*. A leader must tape a note card with the name of a well-known person or character on each student's back (name facing outward for readability). The student will not know whose name is on their back, but they will be able to read everyone else's. Allow the students an allotted amount of time, ten to fifteen minutes depending on the size of your group, in which they can ask anyone in the room questions about who their *secret identity* is. Students must figure out who they are by only asking yes or no questions of the other students. Once the students figure out who they are, they must continue playing and helping others discover who they are. The game ends once all students have discovered their identity.

# Discovery

Explain to your group: We are going to look at the story from the Old Testament in which Samuel had to find and anoint God's chosen new king over Israel.

Ask a volunteer to read 1 Samuel 16:1–13. If you are working with junior high, it might be easier to break the passage up between two readers—verses 1–7 and 8–13.

- What are qualities you think a person should have had in order to be king?
- Was Samuel looking for those qualities or for what God desired?
- Why do you think God chose David?

Ask another student to read 1 Samuel 13:14.

According to this passage, why was David chosen to be king? (David is referred to in this verse as the "man after God's heart.") Do you think God wants us to be men and women after His heart? What does that mean?

Read 1 Samuel 16:7 again. This verse applies to us today just as it did in David's situation. Too many times we let our outward appearance and talents define who we are. Instead, God says that those things are not what really matter and that we should not let certain stereotypes or other people's opinions shape the person we are. Unfortunately, too often we do just that. We tend to care too much about the world's expectations of us, rather than God's expectations of us.

Think of a time when you were living or acting a certain way simply because that is who you thought you were supposed to be. Share this story with the students, making clear some of the things that used to define you. (Be sure you are open and honest with students. They remember real life stories and these often have a greater impact than any three-point talk you may give!) Make sure this story ends with your discovery that your past ideas of what defined you only made life harder. Once you realized how God saw you, you were able to discover the real you.

## Teacher's Note:

David was chosen to be king because of his heart for the Lord. To everyone else, the negatives outweighed the positives for David. The only positive thing they saw in him was that he was handsome. Everything else was against him—he was a boy who was the youngest of eight brothers, had a low paying job, and was forgotten by his father. Not what some would expect from a king. It is good for students to understand the contrast of the world's expectations of a king, and God's expectations of a king. They must understand that God desires for us, as His children, to be "after His heart."

## Life Application

Prior to the lesson, on a sheet of white paper, draw a large stick figure in the middle of the page and write at the top "I am . . ." Make photocopies of these sheets so there are enough for each student and adult. Give each student a sheet along with a pen or pencil and a thick marker. With either a pen or pencil, tell the students they are going to have to finish the sentence "I am . . ." with as many phrases or words as they can come up with. They can write all over their paper. Students might need some help with this. Examples would be: "I am . . . Jon, a baseball player, a writer, a brother, a boyfriend, a jock, a guitar player. If you are working with younger students, it might be a good idea to do your own paper first and show it as an example prior to beginning. Next, have everyone write down some of the things that others expect them to be—a good student, a great singer, the peacemaker at home. If time allows, you can have some students share a few of the things they wrote down and why.

While looking at these pictures, it is important for us to realize that we can let all of these phrases and expectations become a mold that we feel we have to fit. All of a sudden it matters more that I am a good baseball player, rather than the way I actually treat my teammates.

Hold up your own picture. Now who does God say we are? Are these the only things that define us? Let's look at Scripture and see.

Ask a volunteer to read the Memory Verse, 1 John 3:1.

Then, ask each student to grab a marker and write in big bold letters across their page (over everything else) *Child of God.*

This is what matters (pointing to the words you just wrote over your figure). God made us to be His children first before anything else and *that* is what matters.

## Making It Personal

Break into same gender small groups of no more than ten students with either an adult or a student leader to facilitate discussion. Refer back to the game we played at the beginning of the night.

In what ways do you think the game we played tonight might relate to our own search to figure out who we are?

The game was a reminder to us that we are all trying to discover who we really are. Naturally, we don't tend to figure out who we really are on our own—we want help from others! In the game, you still had to play until everyone figured out who they were. In the same way, God desires us to help each other see who He has created us to be. That is what we are going to do here. We are going to talk about the things that make it hard for us to be ourselves and then we are going to pray for each other. The first step to helping each other be who God has created us to be is for us to be honest with each other, and to ask God for help.

Ask the students to say at least one thing, a stereotype or an expectation, that makes it hard for them to be themselves and why. (If you are working with younger students, you may have to ask them a broader question such as: What is the hardest thing about life right now and how does that make you feel?)

After everyone has shared, remind students that what they have shared is important to God. Then, together, ask God to help us all be the men and women that He wants us to be. Close in prayer by asking students to pray for the person on their left.

## Optional Memory Verse Activity

Give each student a cutout heart to take home. Ask them to write the Memory Verse on one side and the words *I am a child of God* on the other. Encourage them to put it in a place where they will see it often. They could tape it to their mirror, their door, or they could even use it as a bookmark. Explain that these hearts are to be a reminder to us when life gets hard, that God, the Creator of the universe, not only knows us, but He calls us His children.

## Connections

There are verses throughout Scripture that remind us we are children of God. They are references to our sonship through the Spirit (Rom. 8:15–17), and God creating us (Ps. 139:13–16), among others.

# What Are You Known For?

*By Janelle Comfort*

## Stuff you'll need:

Option 1
- ✔ 8 to 10 Paper cutout hearts for each student
- ✔ Pen/pencil for each student

Option 2
- ❏ A whiteboard or easel with large paper
- ❏ Markers

## Memory Verse

What marvelous love the Father has extended to us! Just look at it—we're called children of God! That's who we really are.—1 John 3:1 MSG

## Scripture

Gaius and Demetrius: 3 John 1:5–12

## Lesson in a Sentence

Our identity lies in Christ and who He says we are, and because of His great love for us, we must love others.

# Focus

## Option 1

Give each student an equal number of paper hearts and a pen or pencil. The object of this game is to see who can give away the most hearts. Students need to initial all of their hearts so that everyone will know who gave it away. Each time they give away a heart that was given to them; they need to initial that one as well. The initials will act as a certification that the heart was given away by that person. You can only give hearts away to one person at a time and cannot give it back to the same person you got it from right after they have given you a heart. You must give another heart away to someone else before you can give one to the person who just gave the heart to you. Give the group a certain time limit (ten minutes usually) in which they must give away the hearts. After the time is up, calculate the top three *givers* and award them a prize.

## Option 2

### Word Association

This activity is to get students thinking about who and what they think of when they hear the word *love*. Write the word *LOVE* in big letters on either a whiteboard or an easel. First, ask students to come up and write whatever words come to their mind when they hear the word love. Once you have various ideas written on the board, ask the students to again come up. This time they will need to write the names of certain people they think of when they hear the word love. Discuss the different aspects of love that the students brought to mind.

# Discovery

Choose a volunteer to read 3 John 1:5–8.

According to the writer of the letter, what was Demetrius known for?

Have the volunteer reread the verses so students can listen to Scripture and then answer the question.

Demetrius was known by his love and hospitality. He would open his door for strangers and let them stay in his home. When we look at the Gospel of John, we find more about love. As our volunteer reads these next verses, I want you to think about what the disciples of Christ are to be known for.

Have another student read John 13:34–36.

So, according to this, what are we as Christians to be known for?

Ask students to give examples of how we can be known by our love.

Scripture gives us examples of how we can be known by our love when Paul explains certain characteristics of love. Have a student read 1 Corinthians 13:4–7. When we are patient—we show love. When we are kind—we show love. When we aren't selfish—we show love. When we trust, protect, and hope—we show love. There are so many different ways that we can show love to those around us. Let me share with you a story . . .

(Think of a time in your life when your actions of love were noticed. Tell students your story and explain to them the importance of showing Christ's love to those around them and the impact it can have on another person's life.)

## TEACHER'S NOTE:

John writes this letter to his friend and fellow church leader, Gaius, to encourage and thank him for all he has done. We discover that Gaius is known for his faithfulness and his love. As Christians, God does not want us to be known by a list of things that we have accomplished, or by the way we look. We are to be known by the way we show love. Our greatest commandment is to love God and to love others; therefore the love that He has placed inside us should be the only thing that defines us. We are loved by God and that love must cause us to overflow with love for others.

## Life Application

If you used Option 1, remind students of the heart game they played earlier . . .

Ask them what they liked best about it, and what they feel was the purpose of the game.

Explain that each time you give love to someone; you are doing the single most important thing that Christ has asked you to do. Most people think the object of life is to *get* the most love, so they just stand around waiting for someone to give love to them. For the Christian, though, the object of life is to *give* love away to others, just like we did with the hearts.

If you used Option 2, remind students of the words they wrote earlier. (For a great visual, get out the easel, or point to the white board so students have a reference.) Ask them by which definitions of love they would prefer to be known. Is it the ideas and thoughts that were written down earlier and what the world says love is, or is it what John and Paul describe throughout Scripture? As Christians, we are called to love as Christ has loved us and that is a totally different kind of love.

In closing, ask each student to take a blank heart and write the name of a person they feel could use a little extra *love* for the rest of the week. Challenge them to find a way to show love to that person without expecting anything in return. Remind them of 1 Corinthians 13 and the various ways that we can show love.

Finish the night by inviting students to pray silently for the name they wrote, and then you finish with a prayer asking God to unite their hearts as one, so together they will be known by His love.

## Quotable Quote
*Every time you smile at someone, it is an action of love, a gift to that person, a beautiful thing.*—Mother Teresa

## Connections
Be on guard. Stand firm in the faith. Be courageous. Be strong. And do everything with love.—1 Corinthians 16:13–14 NLT

# Group Project

*By Amy Jacober*

In this lesson, students will:
- ✔ Consider the communal nature of Christianity.
- ✔ Learn to work together and apply this to their lives.
- ✔ Discuss the struggles of trying to honor the Lord against the odds.
- ✔ Be reminded of the need for teamwork with other believers in all of life.

Stuff you'll need:
- ❏ Wading pool
- ❏ Large and small buckets
- ❏ Fence or wall
- ❏ Printed *scripts* of Nehemiah 1:1—3:32
- ❏ Butcher paper with drawn map of Jerusalem
- ❏ Tape
- ❏ Downloads or prints of Jerusalem's gates from the Internet
- ❏ Preprinted questions for discussion
- ❏ Paper *rocks*

## Memory Verse

Bear one another's burdens and so fulfill the law of Christ.—Galatians 6:2

## Scripture

Nehemiah 1:1—3:32

## Lesson in a Sentence

Following and serving God is not a solo project.

## The Big Picture

Nehemiah was not called to a small task. Neither were we when we accepted a life of following Jesus. God has a habit of calling His children to do only things that can be accomplished with His help. The journey can be daunting but it is possible! For some of us today, just getting through school, our neighborhoods, or our families can seem like a rather daunting task. For others, dreams and callings of something much bigger are already underway. Regardless of where you are today, this life was not meant to be lived alone. There are things to be done that require more than one set of hands and eyes. Needing others does not make us weak; it makes us human. The greatest builders in the world had teams; the greatest composers could not play their symphonies alone; and the greatest doctors could not heal without a team of medical care professionals.

Interestingly, you don't need to be *the greatest* at anything if you are willing to work with a team. Extraordinary things can and will be accomplished by very average people who recognize God at work in their lives and come together around that one commonality.

# Focus

## Option 1

Split your group in half. Ask each half to create the most unique pyramid they can. Be certain to remind them of safety along the way. It is always good to have a spotter or two to ensure no one falls to their peril!

Ask each group to present their pyramid with your leaders serving as judges. Remind them that there is no way to build a pyramid by yourself. Every person is to participate in some way. Give Popsicles to the winning team first. Since it is summer, offer Popsicles to the losers last.

## Option 2

You will need a fence at least six feet high for this activity. On one side of the fence, fill a wading pool with water and place as many one-gallon buckets as the number of teams you will choose along the fence. On the other side of the wall, have a ten-gallon bucket or empty water cooler bottle equal in number to the one-gallon buckets. Divide your group into teams of at least two and no more than four. The students' goal is to fill the large container as quickly as possible using the water from the wading pool on the other side of the fence. Give Popsicles to the winning team!

As this is summer and a great time to play outside, you may also want to have some water balloons filled for the end of the game, allowing your leaders to create a little havoc with your students. Be certain no one gets hurt and remind your competitive or zealous leaders that this is just for fun!

Ask your students if this could have been done on their own? Was there any way to complete this task without a team or did you have to work with others to get the bucket of water over the wall and to the larger bucket?

**TEACHER'S NOTE:**
Have a few extra T-shirts on hand just in case any of your students arrive in all white. The intention is not to get soaked, but you never know!

# Discovery

Nehemiah 1:1—3:32

Before you meet, get a large piece of butcher paper and draw out a rough map of Jerusalem, including the wall and gates. This can be found in many Bibles or on the Internet by searching Bible Maps, Jerusalem Gates. Label each of the gates mentioned in Nehemiah. Leave room on one side of your map to list the names of all of the groups who worked to rebuild Jerusalem.

Also, print and make at least ten copies of Nehemiah 1:1—2:20. The Narrator copy, should be Nehemiah 1:1—3:32. You are going to create a melodrama straight from the Scriptures. You will have a narrator reading most of the text with a handful of others reading their specific parts. It is helpful for you to highlight the specific parts on each copy so the person does not miss his or her cue. When you get to Nehemiah 3, ask the narrator to read pausing with each person or group mentioned in the process of working on the wall and gates. List the names of these on the map you have taped to the wall. You will need the following parts.

- Narrator
- Nehemiah
- Hanani, Nehemiah's brother
- King Artaxerxes
- Queen
- Sanballat, Horonite, and Tobiah
- Men traveling with Nehemiah

Once the entire passage has been read through once, hand out the following questions for small groups to consider.

- Who are the people who are back in trouble in Nehemiah 1:3? *(The Israelites, in spite of everything God has done and provided for them, are back in trouble.)*
- What did Nehemiah do when he learned his people were back in trouble in 1:4–5? *(Nehemiah wept, mourned, fasted, and prayed.)*
- What does Nehemiah confess in 1:6–7? *(the sins of the Israelites, including himself in that description.)*
- What does being a cupbearer to the king signify? *(Nehemiah would have been a trusted servant, an important position in the court.)*
- How is Nehemiah described in 2:1–2 and why is this significant? *(He is described as sad. It would not have been acceptable to be sad before the king and could be dangerous.)*
- What does Nehemiah do just before answering the king for what he wants in 2:4? *(He prays.)*
- Why would it be important to get letters to show the leaders in the Trans-Euphrates in 2:7–9? *(Nehemiah knew that it could be risky and wanted to follow all of the proper channels of authority to do what God called him to do.)*
- In 2:10, why were the leaders in this area not thrilled to meet Nehemiah? *(He was there to promote the welfare of the people they were ruling.)*
- What did Nehemiah do once he arrived at Jerusalem in 2:11–17? *(He went out at night to look at the wall and gates, only then revealing his plan.)*
- In Nehemiah 2:19, the leaders of the area tried to confront Nehemiah accusing him of rebelling against the king. What precautions had Nehemiah taken to be certain this was not the case in 2:20? *(He said that God would prosper them and as servants to God, they would rebuild the wall and gates of Jerusalem.)*

## Teacher's Note:

Hearing the word *gate* is not all that impressive in our context today. We have a gate to get to the backyard or to get in and out of a school. Gates in the ancient world were much more than this. A gate was the point of commerce and public policy. It was a way into or out of a city connecting the city to the outside world. This was where politics took place and the leaders in the community could be seen. It was like a town square and more. A gate was also the most vulnerable point in a city wall making attention in this area even more urgent.

Check out a few pictures on the Internet to get the idea. One good place to start is www.bibleplaces.com. If you have access to a color printer, make copies of the gates to show your students. If you have access to a projector, these make a great, quick slide show!

## Life Application

There are several principles from this one passage that can be considered. First and foremost is the concept that this HUGE project was not one that could be done alone.

Is there something God is calling you to do that requires a group effort?

Once this has been discussed thoroughly, consider any of the following as topics for small groups. Notice, these follow along with the questions from the text above.

- When has God provided for you, and then you got back into trouble? What happened next?
- Does your heart break when you hear of people not honoring the Lord? How do you respond?
- Nehemiah confesses sins of his people. How do we individually fit into the sins being committed in our communities? Do we have any responsibility or liability?
- How does your unique position in your community make you ideal to serve the Lord? Are you in a prominent family? Well known on your block? A leader at school?
- Nehemiah is asked a question directly from the king. He would be expected to respond right away and yet, he chooses to stop and pray. What makes it so hard for many of us to stop and pray when responding to questions or considering decisions?
- Nehemiah gets a letter from the king giving his blessing on Nehemiah's vision. The king was the ruler over this area. In what ways do we need to learn to go through the proper authorities to get what we want and believe God is asking us to do? Is it ever okay to skip the proper authorities? If yes, when?
- The leaders in this area liked to be in control. It was to their benefit to have the Israelites no longer honoring God in all they did. Do you think leaders today put people at risk for their own benefit? Do we as Christians have any role in combating such things?
- Nehemiah went to Jerusalem with a few trusted men. He wandered at night assessing the situation. When he told of his plan, he already had people who trusted him in place, had taken care of getting permission, and did his homework on how to accomplish the task. Do you think God still calls His people to huge tasks? What might this look like today?

## Making It Personal

We all have things that God is asking us to do. Some are big and some are not so big. Regardless, He has placed us together. Every task is easier with others to help.

Give your students a few moments to themselves. What task do they have in their lives that they are trying to do by themselves? Remind them that God has given us to one another to make all things more bearable. Invite them to ask the Lord what they need to give up and where they need to ask for help.

Nehemiah had hundreds, if not thousands, working on the wall. Give each student a piece of construction paper cut to be roughly the shape of a rock. Ask each person to write what they need help on and to tape their *rock* to the wall. Together, these rocks will create a small rock wall. While not impressive at first, with each addition, a little more is accomplished, just like in life.

## Service Option

Summer is a great time to get your students together outside of your regular meeting times. This lesson is all about accomplishing something that would be impossible for one person, but absolutely doable for many. Consider getting in touch with your local Habitat for Humanity and sponsoring a workday for the entire church.

Another strong option is to seek someone in your own church who needs extra help around the house. Do you have any single parents? Elderly? Families who have taken in foster children and could use a few extra hands? Approach this person and let them know you are trying to help your students learn to work together on seemingly impossible tasks. Ask if they have a list of things they wish could be done around their house, but know that one person could not do it alone. If they do, allowing you and your teens to volunteer to do these chores would be a huge favor and blessing in teaching this lesson. The person should not feel this is offered out of pity. It is one member of the church family helping others and it happens to be a win-win for both that person and your students! This is also a great way to build relationships in your church that otherwise might never happen.

## Song Connect

"Look After You" by The Fray on *How to Save a Life*

## Quotable Quote

*People who work together will win, whether it be against complex football defenses, or the problems of modern society.*—Vince Lombardi, football coach for the NFL (1913–1970)

# Group Project

*By Amy Jacober*

## Memory Verse
Bear one another's burdens and so fulfill the law of Christ.—Galatians 6:2

## Scripture
Nehemiah 4

## Lesson in a Sentence
Following and serving God is not a solo project.

# Focus

### Water Balloon Volleyball
You will need a volleyball net or a rope over which the balloons can be tossed and a large bucket of filled water balloons.

Stretch a net or rope between two poles or trees just above head height. Split your group into two teams. Give the server of one team a water balloon to start the game. Be careful not to fill the balloons too much as they can break easily. The object of the game is to lob the balloon over the net and try to soak the opposing team. When the balloon bursts on one side, a point is given to the side that threw it, and a new balloon is brought into play. Keep playing while there is still interest and have fun!

Volleyball of any kind cannot be done alone. Water balloon volleyball takes even more teamwork trying to keep it from bursting! Have fun and mention at the end that this was about teamwork.

If you have snacks at the end of this game, make them light and cool. Oranges, fruit pops, celery with peanut butter, or frozen grapes are all good choices.

# Discovery

You've already read through Nehemiah 1—3. Chapter 4 is more of the same only this time with the added complication of having people against you. It's one thing when working with others makes life easier. It is a whole other issue when it is for your own security and protection.

Draw a line down the middle of a dry-erase board. On one side, write AGAINST and on the other side write DEAL WITH IT. Have one person with a strong, charismatic voice to read through the entirety of Nehemiah 4. Ask your students to stop that person each time they hear a way that someone or something is coming against the Israelites, and each time they hear how the Israelites are dealing with this.

For example, in verse 4:1, they were mocked against. Verse 4:4—They were crying out to God letting Him know they were being despised or mocked.

Keep this up for the remainder of the passage.

After you have read the entire chapter, ask "how easy or hard was it for the Israelites to work on and continue working on the wall?" What were the major struggles as you heard them?

## Life Application

It was clear that rebuilding the wall and gates around Jerusalem was no picnic—so much so that they had to work with one hand and hold a weapon in the other. Most of us don't face this kind of physical threat just to carry out God's will, but we do face threats.

Notice in this chapter that it moved from calling names and mocking to actually threatening and harming. Satan does not mess around when he comes after those serving God.

Have you ever felt persecuted? How did you handle this? Have there been times when you have stepped in to help others? Have you ever noticed another Christian needing help but left them hanging? Why?

This passage is all about working together but it does not sugar coat it by saying that life will instantly be easy and wonderful. In fact, life gets hard! Following Jesus with your entire life can be hard, but you are not alone. God is always there to provide for His children in amazing ways!

Consider times when God has provided for you through others in the past. Close by thanking the Lord that even when you are not aware, He has your back.

## Memory Verse Activity

Hand out a stack of craft sticks and a small ball of clay to groups of two to three. Ask each group to create a structure that will be able to bear the weight of a large Bible. Is it possible to make a holder from one craft stick? What would make your structure even more secure?

It is impossible to create a structure with just one stick. It takes several and the more the better! Just like our struggles in life, sometimes we cannot go through it alone. But when we have friends and helpers to share the load, the tasks become easier to accomplish and the struggles are easier to handle.

Ask each student to take a stick and write one thing they could use some help in accomplishing. Trade sticks and ask each student to write the Memory Verse on the other side. Encourage your students to take the sticks home to memorize this verse and also to pray for or offer help for the need expressed by someone else.

# Managing Your Ministry Rather Than Having It Manage You

*By Pamela Erwin*

**66** I don't know where to start. There are no files on anything. I don't know what camps and retreats students have been on in the last ten years. There's nothing to tell me what youth group Bible studies have focused on—nothing. I'm completely overwhelmed."

The young woman on the phone was close to the breaking point after only two weeks in her first full-time youth ministry position. A recent youth ministry graduate from college, her excitement at her first paid position had turned to dismay as she began to realize the magnitude of the task before her.

Allison was now the youth pastor in an urban congregation that, most recently, had little in the way of an organized youth ministry. There were ten to twelve adults who were committed to working with the roughly twenty to twenty-five young people, but there was no organizational structure and regular programming in place. Further, while the children of church members continued to participate in youth activities, neighborhood youth, once a strong component of the youth ministry were seldom present. Expectations were high for Allison to restore the youth ministry program to its former glory. She feared her thirty-hour week job was now going to consume her life. Overwhelmed and without any idea of the best place to start, she called me. We set a time to meet over coffee later that afternoon.

As we talked, it became clear that Allison needed to develop a strategy for building a ministry where there was minimal structure and support. Moreover, she'd have to do it in the context of minimal resources, financial, technological, or people. She felt additional pressure from the expectations of the pastor, parents, and youth, to create a vibrant and energized program of activities and Bible studies. Over coffee, we drafted a plan to help her maintain balance, while factoring in goals to address immediate needs, as well as long-term plans. We came up with some guidelines that would help her stem the panic that seemed to dominate her life.

## Taking Control of Your Schedule

Allison was overwhelmed between immediate pressing needs of planning for Wednesday night youth group activities and Bible study, putting together a monthly activity and service project, mapping out a strategy for the upcoming summer, and developing a long-range strategy. She was expected to accomplish this quickly and in a church where she knew only a handful of adults and young people. She had no idea where or who to go to for help and support. The pastor of the church was supportive, but was of little help in the tasks Allison was facing.

The first principle I suggested to Allison was to develop a budget of her time. Recognizing that she could work 24/7 and still not feel as if she were getting it all done, she began to identify key areas of responsibility and allocate her time in each of these areas. In many respects, Allison's job was a start-up ministry and she knew that she would need to put some long hours in to get things going. Without a time budget, she would be more likely to focus on immediate crises, making it more difficult to build in good structure and long-term strategy for the ministry.

Allison identified five areas in which to budget her time: 1) Relationship building, 2) Study and program planning, 3) Staff and ministry meetings, 4) Long-term planning, 5) Personal Sabbath and renewal.

Allison's job description called for her to work thirty hours per week. We both knew that she would often function in the red, at least initially, but like a financial budget, a time budget would help keep her closer to a realistic expenditure of time, while keeping her on notice where she was spending too much time.

In developing her time budget, I encouraged Allison to let two principles guide her time allocation. First, in a new ministry position, particularly, a start-up ministry, a youth pastor needs to focus on getting to know people and build relationships. Secondly, a new youth pastor should avoid making any major changes in the first six months. It takes time to get to know the culture of a ministry and to learn about the history, heritage, and traditions. Making changes too quickly increases the likelihood that changes do more harm than good.

Based on these principles, Allison prepared a time budget that looked like this:

|  | Hours per week |
|---|---|
| Building Relationships | 4–5 |
| Study Time | 4–5 |
| Program Planning & Administration | 9–10 |
| Staff & Ministry Meetings | 3–4 |
| Long-term Planning | 2–3 |
| Personal Sabbath & Renewal | 2–3* |
| Program Events | 6–7 |
| Total Weekly Budget: | 30–37 |

*Allison planned additional Sabbath and renewal time in her personal time budget.

Using her budget, Allison now had a framework for planning her weeks. First, she built into her schedule regular events such as youth ministry activities, staff meetings, and youth leader meetings. Secondly, she added to her weekly planner times for study and Sabbath and renewal. I encouraged her to build in more than three hours per week for Sabbath and renewal, but to look at the additional time as non-job time. Study and renewal time are typically the first things to go in a busy schedule and it often seems too rigid to make appointments for these kind of down times. But, if we don't discipline ourselves to put them on our calendar, it is much too easy to skip them. These are the very times that will keep us fresh and able to put our best effort into the other aspects of our ministry life.

Once Allison had filled in these pieces, she could then focus on one of the primary objectives of any youth ministry—building relationships.

*Youth Ministry Sourcebook*

## Target Relationships

In her time budget, Allison allocated one-third of her workweek to relationship build-ing. As we continued to talk over coffee, she talked about her desire to build strong relationships with students. Most of us in youth ministry are there primarily because of our desire to build strong relationships with young people. Building relationships is essential, however, longevity and health in a ministry demands we work to build relationships with other groups of people, as well. We identified four groups of relation-ships Allison needed to allocate time for: 1) students, 2) adult leaders, 3) church leaders, and 4) parents. Nine to ten hours per week seemed like a lot of time for building relationships, but as Allison had already begun to realize, you could easily spend that amount of time with students, leaving little time for other relationships. She devised a plan that looked like this:

|  | Hours per week |
|---|---|
| One-on-one time with one student each week | 2 |
| Meetings and conversations with parents | 2 |
| One sporting or school event or outing | 2 |
| Meetings/conversations with adult leaders | 2 |
| Contact/meetings with pastor of church | 1 |
|  | 9 |

## Managing Your Life, Rather than Allowing Life to Manage You

As we began to wrap up our coffee, we talked about Allison's need to prioritize her administrative and planning tasks. She acknowledged that she had already found how easy it was to lose all sense of time with the myriad details involved in youth ministry. On the few occasions that that had happened she found herself working long days and longer nights to fit everything in. I suggested when she was at work in her office that she figure out how much time she had to allocate to a specific task or to administrative details and then set her cell phone to remind her when her time was almost up. That way she had control over her schedule. I also told her that as she developed these skills, she would find she was more likely to stay focused and complete a task in a given time period when she knew that she had a set time and no more. As someone who was so recently a college student, I reminded her to think of her current time management as a final exam. A good test taker always reads through an exam, completing the easy pieces first, and then allocating the remainder of the test period to the remaining tasks. Allison smiled at that. She had always been a good test taker, but had never thought about applying her test-taking skills to ministry. Allison walked out the door of the coffee shop with the same huge ministry responsibilities she had sat down with, but now she had a plan and her job didn't seem as overwhelming.

# For Such a Time as This

*By Amy Jacober*

In this lesson, students will:
- ✔ Learn how God used Esther's unique gift of beauty.
- ✔ Consider ways God may be using them now or preparing them for later.
- ✔ Recognize there will be people and groups out to destroy the kingdom.
- ✔ Understand that we are always called to be wise and bold.
- ✔ Learn to rely on God for all our provisions.

Stuff you'll need:
- ❑ A decree written before students arrive (see Option 1)
- ❑ Baskets (see Option 1)
- ❑ Sports equipment (see Option 2)
- ❑ Poster board
- ❑ Markers

## Memory Verse

And we know that all things work together for good to those who love God, to those who are the called according to His purpose.—Romans 8:28

## Scripture

Esther

## Lesson in a Sentence

God can impact the world in many ways through His followers.

## The Big Picture

As followers of God, we look for ways to share our faith with others. Today's society has become more aware of God through the public profession of Christianity by movie stars, singers, television characters, and athletes. While most of us will not become celebrities of this stature, we can still find ways to serve God in our own lives. Teenagers are involved in numerous activities and scenes where they can witness and teach others about their faith such as parties, classes, after-school work, babysitting jobs, and sports. Esther's story reminds us that any role in life can be used for God's glory and the blessing of His children.

# Focus

## Option 1

Before your students arrive, write a decree nice and large on the entryway. This decree states that they may not worship God and they must empty their pockets, purses, and backpacks of all valuables. A basket should be available to collect MP3 players, cell phones, and wallets. A second basket should be available to collect the Bibles they have brought. If you have a leader who can pull it off, dress as a bouncer with dark glasses posted at the door to enforce this rule.

As the students enter, they should see large sheets of paper taped around the room with titles such as education, fashion, music, sports, boyfriend/girlfriend, or whatever categories suit your community as areas that demand a great deal of attention.

Instruct your students to choose which of these categories are in their lives. They must choose at least two though they can choose more. Write their initials on the category sheets of paper.

## Option 2

Invite your students to a game of volleyball, teens against adults (or whatever sport you want to play . . . this is not the important part).

After fifteen to twenty minutes of play, call a time out. Huddle the adults and then announce aloud to your students that you are altering the rules slightly. Each team may decide what they believe to be the best strategy for winning, even if it breaks the traditional rules. For example, the same person may serve every time if he or she is able to slam it. Be certain the adults are serving or in the position of control to make the point. Play for another fifteen minutes or so. Another great game is kickball. When you alter the rules, allow only those who kick homeruns to kick each time.

Ask your students what happened? What was it like to keep playing when the best players got put in their position? Did anyone get frustrated noticing that the game was no longer quite fair? Remind them that they, too, had the chance to alter their strategy though they most likely did not have a chance to implement it.

Today, we are going to learn about a woman who knew exactly what her strength was and was willing to use it to glorify God and to save her people.

# Discovery

The book of Esther is best considered as a whole first. With ten chapters, it is a difficult one to read straight through as a group.

Assign one of your leaders to spend time in the book of Esther before your meeting. Ask him or her to share a summary of the book with your students so they understand what the story is about. This story is about power, beauty, racism, deceit, and God's ability to overcome it all. Be certain to hit each of these points in the summary.

Divide the students into nine pairs asking each team to take one chapter of the book. If you do not have enough students to create nine groups, consider your leaders taking a group or asking a team to take more than one chapter.

Ask each team to write a main point or lesson to be learned from their assigned chapter(s).

## Teacher's Note:

King Xerxes was a major leader in a military and cultural powerhouse. Persia was a dominant force. Today, this area is known as Iran and still carries political and cultural power and influence in the Middle East and around the world. Depending on your Bible translation, you will see the name King Xerxes or King Ahasuerus.

The book of Esther records the beginning of the feast of Purim, now a firmly established holiday. It is an annual reminder of how God saved His people from a seemingly hopeless situation. Those who were against the Jews, Haman in particular, received justice which was encouraging to God's people. For further explanation of the Jewish holiday of Purim, see http://www.jewfaq.org/holiday9.htm.

## Life Application

Patterned from the billboards seen around the country displaying a message from God, invite your students to create a billboard that conveys the lesson in their chapter. (If you are unfamiliar with these, see www.Godspeaks.org.) Once this is done, give a sheet of poster board and markers in order for them to create their billboard.

This will take at least twenty minutes. Pay attention to time as your students work. Some will jump right in; others will struggle and need your guidance. Be certain to keep them moving.

Once the groups are finished, in order of the chapters in the book, present each billboard weaving the story of the book of Esther.

## Making It Personal

Play "Beauty for Ashes" or another song as you invite your students to consider which lesson best suits them for where they are today. Once the song is through, ask them to share in small groups which lesson fits them and why.

Reread Esther 4:13–14. Encourage the students to ask the Holy Spirit to show them what they should be doing right now to build up the kingdom. Close in prayer, thanking God for His wisdom in being able to turn all circumstances into good.

## Memory Verse Activity

Before your students arrive, write the Memory Verse, Romans 8:28, on a large poster board. If you have a large group, write it twice on two separate sheets. Once your students have arrived, ask a leader to cut the poster board into a puzzle made of the number of students you have present. Hand out a puzzle piece to all the students instructing them to put together the Memory Verse. How does this verse relate to the book of Esther?

## Song Connect

"Beauty for Ashes" by Crystal Lewis on *Beauty for Ashes*

# For Such a Time as This

*By Amy Jacober*

## Memory Verse

And we know that all things work together for good to those who love God, to those who are the called according to His purpose.—Romans 8:28

## Scripture

Esther 4

## Lesson in a Sentence

God can impact the world in many ways through His followers.

# Focus

Bring in the past week's newspapers, news magazines, and headlines. Give your students some time to get familiar with things that happened this past week. Remind them to consider what is happening here at home and around the world.

On a dry-erase board, create a list of what your students decide are the top ten headlines for the past week.

Once you have the list in a visible place, ask your students to name which situation(s) they have difficulty seeing where God may have a solution.

# Discovery

Gather your students together with their Bibles. Remind your students of the entire story of Esther to place this passage (Esth. 4) in context.

Before you read, tell your students to listen for two things: 1) What was the problem? 2) What was the creative solution? Go around the group asking each student to read one verse until the entire passage is read.

### TEACHER'S NOTE:

We read in Esther 4:16 that it is not lawful for Esther to approach the king. This is a huge understatement. When she says, "If I perish, I perish," she is not kidding. The king could summon people to himself, but people were not to approach him. It was perfectly within the right and custom of King Xerxes to have anyone, including his own wife, killed if they dared overstep their place.

## Life Application

Esther finds herself in what seems to be a hopeless situation. Esther was always obedient to what the Lord asked of her. She was a beautiful woman who was willing to risk everything to honor the Lord. Never dreaming she would be used as a leader to save her people, she was simply faithful to who God created her to be.

We are taught to look for ways we can change the world and serve God. Too often, we forget to teach our students to be children of God and allow Him to use them for His glory. In other words, we put the cart before the horse.

- Where do your students believe God can use others to make an impact on the world?
- How can teenagers of today make an impact for the kingdom?
- How does who you are impact what you are able to do?

## Service Option

Every day teenagers are told what they cannot do. Brainstorm with your teenagers on ways to make a difference now in your own community. There is no idea that is too crazy or farfetched! Encourage them to dream and dream big. Once you have the list of brainstormed ideas, carefully consider them. With the help of your students, narrow the list to one or two that are real possibilities. Spend a few moments in prayer asking God for guidance in choosing which option He wants you and your students to do. Once you have prayed for a few moments (you may need to guide your students through this), ask them if anyone heard from God? Does anyone have a sense or a leaning toward one option or the other? Not only is this an exercise in really learning to serve and build up the kingdom right where you are, but in seeking God's direction rather than diving in on your own logic and strength.

Once the option is chosen, set a plan in place to actually follow through.

## Quotable Quote

*Nearly all men can stand adversity, but if you want to test a man's character, give him power.*—Abraham Lincoln

# First—The Good News

*By Amy Jacober*

## In this lesson, students will:
✔ Realize that we must review what we know in order to remember and understand.
✔ Identify what Peter is talking about in his letter and how it applies in our lives.
✔ Encourage one another by sharing faith.

## Stuff you'll need:
❑ Printed copies of your quiz (see Option 2)
❑ Yarn or braided bracelets
❑ Incense or candles (see Ancient Practice)

## Memory Verse
How then shall they call on Him in whom they have not believed? And how shall they believe in Him of whom they have not heard? And how shall they hear without a preacher? And how shall they preach unless they are sent? As it is written: "How beautiful are the feet of those who preach the gospel of peace, who bring glad tidings of good things."—Romans 10:14–15

## Scripture
2 Peter 1:10–21

## Lesson in a Sentence
We are to share Jesus with others every day of our entire life.

## The Big Picture
Evangelism comes in many forms. For some denominations, it is the main focus. For others, evangelism is an afterthought. Getting evangelism in the right perspective is what this week is all about. Sharing Jesus with others is more than a one-time event—it is what we are to do every day of our entire life. Peter reminds Christians to remember what they already know. In fact, he says he will remind them of the truths they already know as long as he is alive. He proclaims Jesus as Lord to his dying day to honor God and to encourage and invite others to follow Him. Peter knew what many of us forget today—that choosing to follow Jesus means choosing for a lifetime. Peter reminds us to keep the gospel as a priority in our lives. Sharing Jesus with others does not need to be a contrived project. Talking about faith should be a natural overflow of what is

important in our lives. Remind your students that sharing Jesus with their friends should be as natural as sharing every other important part of their lives.

# Focus

## Option 1

### One, Two, Three, Look!

This is a super easy game requiring no set up and no equipment. Have your entire group stand in a circle shoulder to shoulder. Assign one person as the leader. With the players having their eyes closed, the leader yells out "One, Two, Three, Look!" The players look to the left or the right. If they find themselves looking face to face, they are out. If the person they are looking at looks the other way, they stay in for one more round. Close the circle in as people are eliminated. Play until you have the final two. If your students are still having fun, play another round or two.

This game is more about luck than skill, preparation, or any intentional action. Too often this is how we live with our faith. We are really not doing anything wrong, however, we are not intentionally focusing on the Lord and His plans for our lives.

## Option 2

So you really passed grades one through six, huh? Create a list of at least fifteen questions that would reflect this knowledge. Be certain to include social studies questions that show where you live. If you need help, spend a little time checking out textbooks from students who are in the children's ministry—you know, fourth through sixth graders who have social studies, science, and English textbooks. This does not need to be anything difficult, just standard information from grades passed before the age of those in your youth group. Ask your teenagers to take the quiz on either a handout or by PowerPoint presentation.

For example:

**Q:** What is the capital of Washington?
**A:** Olympia

**Q:** How many counties does Arizona have?
**A:** 13

**Q:** Who was our forty-second president?
**A:** William Jefferson Clinton

**Q:** What is the largest organ of the human body?
**A:** skin

**Q:** How many ounces are in one pound?
**A:** 16

**Q:** What is an isosceles triangle?
**A:** A triangle with two sides of equal length and two congruent angles

**Q:** What is a pronoun?

**A:** A word used to replace a noun or noun phrase designating things asked for, previously mentioned, or understood from the context.

**Q:** What wonder of the world is found in Egypt?

**A:** Pyramids

**Q:** Name one natural wonder of the world.

**A:** Grand Canyon, Northern lights, Mount Everest, Victoria Falls, The Great Barrier Reef, The Harbor at Rio de Janeiro, Paricutin Volcano

**Q:** How many atoms of hydrogen are in the formula for water?

**A:** 2

Grade your quizzes and have a few treats on hand as prizes for anyone who was able to get 100%!

Ever feel like you need to review things you have already learned and mastered? Review keeps things fresh in your mind and builds a better understanding of the knowledge. In Scripture, we are encouraged to review the meaning of following Christ and sharing Him with others.

# Discovery

Take your students outside. Ask for three volunteers. Have three lines drawn parallel for about thirty to forty feet on the ground (chalk is an easy way to do this!) The lines should be at least four feet apart from one another. Ask each student to take four to five steps on the lines.

Ask if it was easy to stay on the line. The answer will obviously be yes. They can walk on a line.

Now, blindfold each student. Ask them to finish their walk by trying to stay on the line without looking.

They will stay on the line for the first few steps but then they will veer to the left or right. Pay attention so that they do not run into each other. Ask if there is anyone else who would like to try this. Continue until each person who wishes gets a turn.

We accomplished the ability to walk in a straight line a long time ago. But if we don't keep our attention on where we are going, something simple can cause us to lose our way. Peter talks about this with regard to our Christian walk. He refuses to stop sharing Jesus with people, knowing that we can easily get off course.

While still outside, ask someone with a nice, loud voice to read 2 Peter 1:12–21.

Peter is reminding us to remember the gospel, both for ourselves and to share with others.

## Life Application

Return to your meeting room and ask students to divide into small groups. Have available at least three different translations of Scripture for these groups. Ask them to reread 2 Peter 1:12–21 from the different translations.

As they read, ask them to keep these questions in mind:

- For whom is this letter intended?
- What, in general, is Peter saying in this letter?
- How often do we take the gospel for granted?

Give a sheet of paper and pen or pencil to each group. Ask them to make a list of the things they think today's Christians need to be reminded of. Their list may be similar to Peter's or completely different.

Once the lists are made in the small groups, compile the lists on a dry-erase board and talk about what your students have created. Where do we need reminders? Why is it so easy to forget what we once knew?

While one leader is going through this process, have another leader busy working on a letter to your group in particular. Have this leader incorporate some of the elements listed by your students encouraging them to remember what they have known. Read this letter aloud after your group discussion. If you contact your students by e-mail, this is a great reminder to send midweek!

## Making It Personal

Is there anything you need to be reminded of? We all have something! Check the list on the dry-erase board. Do any of those fit you specifically? If not, what does?

Give your students a piece of yarn (or if you are really crafty, make braided bracelets in multiple colors for your students). Ask each of them to take a few moments to themselves praying and asking the Lord to remind them of a truth they need to recall. After they have prayed, tell them to find another student to tie the yarn on their wrist. They are to tell that person what they hope to remember and use the yarn as a reminder. Follow up with your students by asking them weekly to report what they needed to remember.

## Song Connect

"Awake" by Seventh Day Slumber on *Finally Awake*

## Quotable Quote

*I think that at the supper I neither receive flesh nor blood, but bread and wine; which bread when it is broken, and the wine when it is drunken, put me in remembrance how that for my sins the body of Christ was broken, and his blood shed on the cross.*—Jane Grey

## Ancient Practice

Incense has been used for centuries as a way to offer up prayers and have a tangible action as a reminder. The smoke is a reminder of God being present in a cloud and prayers being carried up to heaven throughout biblical tradition. A few such examples are as follows: Exodus 30:4–38; Psalm 141:2; and Luke 1:1–8. Another option is to use a candle since smoke is also created in this manner. Be aware that some people are sensitive to incense or smoke and this could take away from the lesson you are trying to teach. Candles are a great option for active participation. Give each of your students a tea light to use as a reminder of what they need to recall, beginning with the good news of Jesus Christ.

# First—The Good News

*By Amy Jacober*

## Memory Verse

How then shall they call on Him in whom they have not believed? And how shall they believe in Him in whom they have not heard? And how shall they hear without a preacher? And how shall they preach unless they are sent? As it is written: "How beautiful are the feet of those who preach the gospel of peace, who bring glad tidings of good things."—Romans 10:14–15

## Scripture

Matthew 28:16–20; Romans 10:14–15

## Lesson in a Sentence

We are to share Jesus with others every day of our entire life.

# Focus

Ask each of your leaders to dress as a character such as a convenience store worker, high school student, softball coach, piano teacher, or auto mechanic. Be sure these are people teenagers would actually come into contact with and that at least two of them are high school or junior high students. If you know that you will not have enough leaders, this is a great week to ask other adults in your church to come to youth group as special guests to help out! Each character will have an index card stating who they are and whether or not they are open to hearing about Christianity. Remind your characters that they don't need to be obnoxious, but to play their part as realistically as possible. Options would be to have the following: someone who used to go to church but walked away, someone who has never heard of Jesus, someone who thinks Christians are judgmental and mean, or someone who is really curious and willing to talk.

Split your youth group into as many groups as you have characters—ideally, no more than three students per group. Let your students go through a rotation of visiting several characters. Ask them, as best they can, to share the gospel. You may want a whistle or something to indicate when it is time to move to the next character. Allow at least five to ten minutes with each character.

After a few rotations, call your students back together. Ask them to describe their experience. Was it easy? Difficult? Frustrating? Why?

Once your students have shared, ask each of the characters to share briefly their perspective of the experience.

# Discovery

In their same groups, have your students read Matthew 28:16–20 and Romans 10:14–15. Give each group time with these first three questions.

- What is Jesus commanding?
- What message, specifically, are believers being told to share?
- How do these two passages work together?

After a few moments, offer the following questions to guide discussion.

- What struggles do we have with sharing our faith today? Why do so many of us hesitate?
- When is it easy to talk about Jesus? When is it hard?
- Do you think we have any kind of responsibility to share with the people we know? Why or why not?
- What good ways can we share faith? What ways should be avoided? Why?

## Life Application

Do you think these passages apply to teenagers? Why or why not? What would this mean for you personally?

Ask each group to spend a few moments asking God to show them with whom they should share their faith. Pray for one another as God calls us where we are to share Jesus in our everyday lives and conversations.

## TEACHER'S NOTE:

This can be a tricky lesson if you have some students present who may not know the Lord. Be sensitive to this fact, allowing for open honest conversations, and praying for the Spirit to lead as the gospel is shared multiple times in this one meeting. Some of your students may not be able to articulate their faith as you would hope, but that does not mean that God is not at work in their lives. They may not yet be saved but are interested in talking with others about what God is doing. This allows them to join in fully while still being honest about where they are in their faith walk.

## Extra! Extra!

Sharing faith for many of us can be a scary and intimidating thing to do. We live in a world where Christians are often viewed as harsh, judgmental, angry, and arrogant. We also live in a world where our teenagers are hearing about tolerance and acceptance of others all the time. Many of them have no idea how to begin talking about their faith or a relationship with Jesus. A great Web site for help comes from Youth for Christ and can be found at www.3story.org.

# What Does the Bible Really Say About Drinking?

AUGUST 17 2008

*By Amy Jacober*

In this lesson, students will:
- ✔ Learn that God has a strict opinion on drunkenness.
- ✔ Discuss the many ways drinking alcohol impacts the body and mind.
- ✔ Relate the principles that can be applied to drugs as well as drinking.
- ✔ Develop a plan to say no to drinking and/or drug use.

Stuff you'll need:
- ❏ Paper
- ❏ Pens or pencils
- ❏ Butcher paper
- ❏ Markers
- ❏ Dry-erase board
- ❏ 3x5 Index cards

## Memory Verse

Wine is a mocker, strong drink is a brawler, and whoever is led astray by it is not wise.
—Proverbs 20:1

## Scripture

Ephesians 5:15–21; Proverbs 23:29–33

## Lesson in a Sentence

God does not approve of drunkenness because He loves and cares for us.

## The Big Picture

Drinking is a huge issue in today's society, especially with teenagers. Whether they have tried drinking or not, the glorified images, the sexy and explicit commercials, and feel-good messages are bombarding young audiences every day. Drinking is glamorized in music, movies, and television. The impact and consequences of being drunk, however, are far less notarized. The negative effects on lives and families are not good for the news media ratings, therefore kids get the wrong impression about drinking. Church denominations have various views and positions on alcohol. Talk with your pastor to determine how to handle questions your students will undoubtedly have. This lesson offers a look at what Scripture says about drinking. Educate your students on the negative effects of alcohol and drugs, but emphasize what is written in Scripture and what God has to say. Furnishing facts and tools for students to use in their everyday life situations can go a long way in positive decision-making and wise choices. This lesson could very well save someone's life!

# Focus

## Option 1
### Name That Slogan
Divide students into teams of three to four. Allow two minutes for each team to come up with as many slogans for alcoholic beverages as they can. (This is not to promote alcohol but rather to point out how well the advertising industry has conditioned our society. Even if someone doesn't drink and is not impacted by alcohol, it is often a surprise to see how aware they are of its presence.) Have them share their lists.

- Were any of you surprised at how many of these you knew?
- Why do you think these were so easy to name?
- Do these advertisements appeal to you? Do they encourage you to try drinking?
- How do you avoid "trying" alcohol and drugs with friends?

## Option 2
### Testimony
Stories are amazing ways for people to connect. Many students have been warned against drinking and drugs before. They also know that the Bible warns against these habits as well. What they may not know is how easy it is to slide from trying something, to allowing it to ruin your life. If you know of someone in your community who has a history of alcohol or drug addiction in his or her past and is now sober or clean, ask them if they would mind sharing their story. Ask them to focus on the ease with which a person can go from trying something or experimenting, to addiction. If the person is comfortable and willing, allow your students to ask questions at the end of the presentation. Nothing makes a better impression than listening to someone who has "been there and done that" and lived to proclaim a positive outcome. The more information you can arm your students with, the better their chances are of being able to stand up against the temptations that surround them every day.

# Discovery

Break into groups of three. Give each group a sheet of paper and ask them to make two lists. On one list, write what God wants us to do, and on the other list, write what God wants us to avoid according to Ephesians 5:15–21.

- How strong is the argument for or against drinking in this passage?
- Why do you think Christians have become so strongly against drunkenness?

Now turn to Proverbs 23:29–33.

- Is this still a good description of a drunk today?
- If yes, how? If no, how would you change it?
- What message does this passage send about drinking?
- How do you like the comparison of wine to a serpent?

## TEACHER'S NOTE:

This would be a good opportunity to discuss the laws of our country regarding drugs and alcohol. Scripture warns against drunkenness for anyone. It does not strictly forbid drinking, but it does forbid drunkenness. Many students are frustrated and feel lied to when they have been told that the Bible says to never drink. This does not mean that it is okay for teenagers to drink. The law states that you must be twenty-one years old. Until you are twenty-one, this is a nonissue. You will, however, be confronted with alcohol many times before turning twenty-one. This lesson is about looking honestly at what Scripture says regarding drinking, and guiding students to make wise choices.

On a large piece of butcher paper or on a dry-erase board, brainstorm together as a group to devise "a plan" to avoid getting drunk or being encouraged to use drugs. This needs to go beyond just saying don't drink. How, specifically, can you avoid being in situations where you will be tempted to get drunk or experiment with drugs? Let the students be as creative as they can to come up with ideas to use as weapons in this fight. Make no mistake—Satan is out to take as many prisoners as possible in this all-out war to win our young people, not to mention the adult population. You never know what words or phrases from this list might be just what a student remembers that will give him or her the courage to say no. Anything that can be a deterrent to temptation is one more step we are making toward living the Christian life God wants us to live.

## Life Application

You have just read two Scriptures regarding drinking.

- How is drinking viewed today?
- Is it more accepted now than in biblical days?
- If we know there are so many negative aspects to drinking, why is it still such a problem?
- What about drugs? The Bible does not address every drug we have today directly. Do the same principles apply?
- Do you see drugs or alcohol as the bigger problem faced by teens today?

Make a list on a dry-erase board of all the reasons you think people try drinking, or continue to drink, even when they know it is illegal and not good for them (rebellion, curiosity, self-medication, fun, etc.).

- Do you think God is just trying to keep us from having fun?
- How do we balance this with God's warning that sorrow, complaints, wounds, red eyes, hallucinations, and perverse thoughts come with drinking?

## Making It Personal
- Have you ever been tempted to get drunk or try drugs?
- How did you handle the temptation?
- How could you use "the plan" we have created? Would any ideas stand out as ways to say no?
- Will you take this "plan" home with you and memorize the ideas?

Today's Memory Verse is Proverbs 20:1. I have yet to meet the person who wants to be known as a fool, but I have known plenty of people who act the fool. Getting drunk or doing drugs is foolish. It breaks God's heart, but not because He is mean and judgmental. Rather, He knows how much this will mess up your life. Pray with your students that God will give them wisdom in making choices when faced with choices regarding alcohol and drugs. Ask that He arm them with the tools they need to stand up against temptations.

## Song Connect
"Jesus Walks With Me" by Kanye West

## Quotable Quote
*Drinking makes such fools of people, and people are such fools to begin with, that it's compounding a felony.*—Robert Benchley

## Extra! Extra!
When students have finished devising the "Plan," all ideas should be printed on paper and handed out to the students at the next meeting. Give each student a 3x5 index card and let them copy the ideas that are most helpful to them on that card to be kept with them for reference.

# What Does the Bible Really Say about Drinking?

*By Amy Jacober*

## Memory Verse

Wine is a mocker, strong drink is a brawler, and whoever is led astray by it is not wise.
—Proverbs 20:1

## Scripture

Luke 21:33–36

## Lesson in a Sentence

God does not approve of drunkenness because He loves and cares for us.

# Focus

### Izzy Dizzy

We are going to have a relay race. Break into teams of six to ten each. Find an area large enough for running, preferably outside, unless you have a gym or student center you can use. Have the teams line up behind a line. At least twenty yards away, have a baseball bat for each team. One person will be the official counter and will be holding the bat vertically on the ground as students run around it. Begin the race by having the first person in each team run to the bat, place their forehead on the bat while the end of the bat is on the ground, and run around in ten circles. Once the circles have been run, send the person back to his or her team. Once they have crossed the line, send the second player. Keep going until the entire team has played.

- Why was it so hard to run in a straight line after running in circles?
- While this was just a game, can you imagine making yourself feel this way on a regular basis by choice?
- What other things are hard to do when you are really dizzy?
- Do you get sick at your stomach? Headaches? Blurred vision? Loss of memory?

These are all conditions that occur when a person overindulges in drinking or drugs. Sometimes, the effects can be much worse, including lifelong disabilities and even death. The next time you are tempted to drink for fun, remember the way you felt after this game. That should be a deterrent.

Your students will be dizzy after circling the bat. It may seem easy to run back to the group but place a few spotters around (people to help guide) to be certain your dizzy runners do not run into each other!

You may have some students who become extremely dizzy after this. Keep some water on hand and be certain to allow time for sitting down to recover.

# Discovery

Jesus is not going to care if you are simply dizzy from running around. He does care if it is from drinking—so much so that He has strict warnings against this habit.

Read Luke 21:33–36.

Answer the following questions:

- Jesus said a long time ago that His words would not pass away. But the world has changed a lot since then. Do you think these words still mean something to us today (v. 33)?
- What does it mean to be on guard? How do we avoid being wasted and/or drunk (v. 34)?
- Do you think this is a temptation that can come to anyone (v. 35)?
- Are you supposed to have to do this on your own (v. 36)?

## Life Application

- Why do you think Jesus warns us against drunkenness?
- How would you feel to be wasted or drunk in front of Jesus?
- What would you tell a friend if you saw him or her drinking? Would you be willing to sacrifice your friendship to tell him or her what you thought about drinking?

**TEACHER'S NOTE:**
Verse 34 says the day will come suddenly like a trap. This can be misunderstood if you only look at the few verses mentioned here. In context, Jesus is talking about His return. He is warning us to not be caught wasted or drunk when He returns. Since we do not know when His return will be, we must be on guard at all times.

Jesus cares enough for us to not try and trick us, but to offer plenty of warning. Think of a time when someone warned you about something coming up . . . this could be to avoid a teacher who wasn't fair, or to tell you about traffic to avoid. It doesn't need to be anything major—just a time when you avoided something bad because of a warning. Jesus' warning to avoid being drunk falls in this same category. He knows what is best for us and the heartache we will suffer if we disobey. He tells us to not be wasted or drunk—not to keep us from having fun, but because He loves us and cares for us.

# Extra! Extra!

The origin of **Alcoholics Anonymous** began with a Christian perspective. The language of the 12-step program makes this very evident. If you think it would be appropriate, share this with your students, letting them know the most successful program to break addiction was created with God in mind.

# And the Leader Is . . .

*By Amy Jacober*

---

In this lesson, students will:
- ✔ Discuss service and leadership.
- ✔ Consider their role as a servant leader in the kingdom.
- ✔ Recognize that leaders don't always look like what we expect.

Stuff you'll need:
- ❑ Dry-erase board
- ❑ Dry-erase markers
- ❑ Magazine pictures glued or taped onto papers
- ❑ Slips of paper
- ❑ Pens or pencils
- ❑ Hat or bucket

---

## Memory Verse

But God has chosen the foolish things of the world to put to shame the wise, and God has chosen the weak things of the world to put to shame the things which are mighty.
—1 Corinthians 1:27

## Scripture

Exodus 15

## Lesson in a Sentence

Leadership is birthed through character and opportunity.

## The Big Picture

Leaders can sometimes be the most unlikely of people. It is not unusual to find their track record is filled with failures and struggles. However, once they have succeeded, most people forget about the failures in the past. We all have a picture in our minds of what we consider a leader to be. If you are tall, considered good looking, and an extrovert, studies show that others would consider you to be a good leader. While this is not intended to be a slam on tall, good-looking, extroverted people, it takes a lot more than what is on the outside to be a leader. Even in ministry, it is not unusual for the biggest troublemaker in a youth group to grow up and return as an amazing youth volunteer or youth pastor. Miriam was under slavery and when freed, she was in the shadow of a very famous brother. On top of that, she had her own issues that would seem to disqualify her, but God saw otherwise. Just like Miriam, your students can become leaders in spite of their own failures and with God's blessing.

# Focus

## Option 1

What does a trucker look like? A movie star? Basketball player? Dentist? Teacher? Construction worker? Pastor? We all have images in our minds of what these people should look like. Before your youth meeting, go through several magazines and cut out pictures of people from all walks of life holding different jobs and enjoying their hobbies. (This is also a great task to delegate to a student. Be certain to give them plenty of time and instruction.) Write a list on a dry-erase board or poster of each job/hobby that is demonstrated in the pictures. Tape the pictures around the room with a number beside each one. Give each student a piece of paper. Ask the students to number the paper to match the pictures and write their guess of what the person does. Check their guesses and give a prize to the person with the highest number of correct answers.

For a twist on this, invite a few adults from the church with unique hobbies. Write a list of those hobbies on a poster and ask your students to guess which person matches which hobby. The funnier the better—a mom who dirt bikes, a grandfather who dances competitively; any hobby will work. Create a game-show atmosphere complete with MC and prizes!

## Option 2

On small slips of paper, write the name of each person present. Place these in a hat, bucket, or whatever you can use to draw them from. Separate your students into partners or small groups. Ask each group to draw one slip of paper for each person in their group. If they get their own name, put it back. Once each group has a few names, welcome them to the yearbook simulation! It's the day when you get to decide what each person is most likely to do or be in the future. If you have an old yearbook with this section, bring it in to show your students. If not, explain that in many yearbooks the students guess what their classmates will be doing later in life. Encourage them to be as creative as possible. If you have a more hands-on group, offer basic art supplies and ask them to design their own yearbook page for that person.

Have each group share their prediction and tell why they chose this one. Get ready to laugh! Make sure the predictions are kept clean and that no one gets hurt by what is predicted.

# Discovery

Ask your students to name some of their favorite worship bands and/or to describe who they think of when they think of a worship leader.

Today, you are going to check out one of the very first, if not the first worship leader we know, Miriam. She missed out on the privilege of the finest education; her brother Moses got that. But still she was a prophet and a leader. In particular, she has the honored position of leading God's people in praise after one of the most memorable events in history.

Set the scene by having one of your leaders explain what took place in Exodus 14 when the sea was divided and the Israelites were delivered.

Separate your students into at least three groups. Group one is to read Exodus 15:19–21 and then Exodus 15:1–18.

- What does this say about Miriam?
- Why was she dancing and leading music?
- What do you notice about the comparison between 15:1 and 15:21? (There is a common thought that Miriam actually began the worship first; however, it is not recorded this way. The longer song of Moses begins with what his sister most likely had already said.)

Group two is to read Exodus 12:1–16.

- What is happening here?
- What was Miriam saying? Do you think she was out of line?
- What happens to her?

Reread Exodus 12:15. What did the people do?

(Miriam was important! She had screwed up but this did not mean she was out for good—just a short time and then she was restored. The people did not move without her.)

Group three is to read Exodus 15:20, Micah 6:4, and Numbers 20:1.

(This is good for a younger group or a group that struggles to focus since there are few verses.)

## Teacher's Note:

If your students are not familiar with the story of Miriam, give them a quick overview from Exodus 2. This is the same young woman who followed her brother as he floated in the Nile. All baby boys had been ordered to be killed but Miriam, following her mother's lead, refused to accept this fate for her brother. She was young at the time probably between the ages of fourteen and seventeen. Being an Israelite in Egypt did not help her situation. The Pharaoh had long forgotten the good relation with Joseph, and Miriam's people were seen as a threat. This was also a patriarchal society with women in very distinct roles. She could not change her age, her gender, or her ethnicity and it seems she didn't need to. God raised her up as a leader and she was remembered along with her brothers.

## Life Application

Who do you consider to be a leader today? Not just someone who is famous but someone who is actually a leader? (This can be a national leader or someone from your school or church.)

- What do you notice about this person?
- What do you like about their leadership?
- What do you dislike about their leadership?
- Do you think it is possible to be a leader and to honor God at all times? If yes, how? If no, why?

Ask each group to think of a few ways where you, as a group, can be leaders in your church or community. This may be a recycling program, raising money for AIDS awareness, organizing a monthly prayer meeting with other youth groups, or any variety of things. Teenagers are amazing and have much to offer right now.

## Teacher's Note:

At this point in time, being a leader seems to be equated with money and fame. Just ask your students what they want to be when they grow up. If this is an issue in your group, be certain to point out to your students that many, if not most, of the influential and powerful leaders throughout history are known by only a few. This does not make their contributions any less amazing. Need some examples—ask them to name the president of Canada, or the members of the Supreme Court, or any of the Nobel Peace Prize winners of the past year. Another angle for discussion would be the flood of stories about those who struggle due to their fame. What seemed fun and exhilarating at first, leaves many celebrities lost and in destructive lifestyles.

## Making It Personal

Ask your students to reflect on what they have heard. Give two to three minutes of silence and invite students to pray, asking God what leadership role He may have planned for their lives.

Before your final closing prayer, ask your students if any of them felt any leading from God. If not, let them know that this was a very short time to pray and encourage them to go home and repeat their question to God regarding what the Lord may be calling them to be.

## Web Connect

Check out the Web site http://www.myspace.com/lc2lc. A young man began a campaign while he was in the seventh grade focusing on ending human trafficking. The campaign is called "Loose Change to Loosen Chains." At the time of this publication, he is still in high school. This is a great example for your teens that not only can they dream big right now but they can make a difference in their communities and world.

## Connections

Miriam was not the only woman to lead in worship after a great battle. Read Judges 5 and 1 Samuel 18:6–7 for other examples.

# And the Leader Is . . .

*By Amy Jacober*

## Memory Verse

But God has chosen the foolish things of the world to put to shame the wise, and God has chosen the weak things of the world to put to shame the things which are mighty.
—1 Corinthians 1:27

## Scripture

Matthew 10:1–4; 16–23; Mark 3:13–19

## Lesson in a Sentence

Leadership can come from the most unlikely sources and combinations.

# Focus

Choose any active team sport or game that your group enjoys. This may be volleyball, kickball, fingerblaster battles, or any other game. Choose two people as team captains. If your group is mixed junior high and high school, choose one of the younger ones as captain. Ask each captain is to put together their team by choosing teammates. Instruct each team to take a few moments to strategize, having the captain lead the discussion.

Spend some time playing the game. You may even want to set up a mini-tournament with the best two out of three games. When the game is over, point out that while each person was needed, there was a captain. In some cases, the captain will remain prominent throughout the game. Whether this is the case or not, the teams were chosen by a leader and then intended to work together.

At the end, ask a few if they were going to create their own all star team, both from people they know and either college or professional athletes, who would they choose and why? Would they rather have a superstar or a team player? Someone who is consistent or someone who is hit or miss but when they are on, they are amazing?

# Discovery

Once you get everyone back together from the game, tell them that for a few moments, just as they created their own dream team for a tournament, they are now to create a dream team to serve with Jesus.

In groups of two to three, they are in competing consultation firms suggesting which group Jesus needs to choose. They should consider occupation, age, social status, gender, and any other categories they choose. Their focus can be in the past or who they would suggest that Jesus choose if He were here today. Ask each group to offer a rationale for their choice of a team. (For example, they wanted people who were charismatic, powerful in the world, prayer warriors, or a balance of personalities.) Have each team list their choices on butcher paper to be hung throughout the room after sharing with the entire group.

See who Jesus really chose!

Turn to Matthew 10:1–4 and Mark 3:13–19. Write the names of the disciples on either a dry-erase board or butcher paper to be hung in a prominent place. As you list each of these, ask your students what they know about each one. Write a word or two to remind them who was chosen.

- Simon Peter—fisherman, brother of Andrew (Matt. 4:18–19)
- Andrew—fisherman, brother of Peter (Matt. 4:18–19)
- James—fisherman, brother of John (Matt. 4:20–22)
- John—fisherman, brother of James (Matt. 4:20–22)
- Philip—Slow to catch on (John 14:7–9)
- Bartholemew—an apostle
- Thomas—doubts, needs physical proof of Jesus' death/resurrection (John 20:25–26)
- Matthew—tax collector (Matt. 9:9)
- James—son of Alphaeus (Matt. 10:9)
- Thaddaeus—an apostle
- Simon the Zealot—(Mark 3:18)
- Judas—known for betraying Jesus (Matt. 26:14–16)

Jesus' team is a far cry from what most of us would put together for such an important assignment. To complicate matters even more, check out what they have to look forward to on this job.

Ask a strong reader to read aloud Matthew 10:16–23. Read it aloud a second time and ask your students to count how many times something bad or difficult that is going to happen is mentioned.

## Life Application
Involve your students in a discussion on leadership today. Consider using some of the following to guide your discussion.

- After looking at what Jesus Himself says can be expected, would you take the job?
- How do these kinds of struggles play out today?
- These are the leaders Jesus has chosen. What can we learn about the difficulties of leadership from this passage?
- What kind of person is suited to live up to these expectations?
- Ask each student to consider what he would be willing to endure to do what Jesus asks.
- What kinds of things does Jesus ask teenagers to do today?
- What are the consequences, positive or negative?

- What things are you willing to spend time on or to be a leader in—School? Soccer? Music? Stealing? Cheating? Online communities?
- The same skills are used for both positive and negative leadership. What is more important—being a leader for something positive that matters or simply being a leader?

Close by rereading Mark 3:13 and the list of those chosen by Jesus. This passage states that Jesus chose those whom He wanted. He never discusses why their skills, finances, personality, or social status were beneficial. Leaders come from the most unlikely of places. Jesus proved this by His choice of disciples, friends, and most importantly, those who would carry on kingdom work after He ascended to heaven.

## Song Connect
"Least of These" by DecembeRadio on *DecembeRadio*

# Apollos: We All Have a Role in God's Work

*By Rick Bennett and Amy Jacober*

## In this lesson, students will:

✔ Understand the roles Apollos and Paul had in the church in Corinth and the faith of the Christians there.

✔ Understand that every action they take while attempting to share the love of Christ with others matters (not just the attempts which get results).

✔ Be able to identify with Paul and Apollos.

## Stuff you'll need:

❏ DVD of *Lord of the Rings: Return of the King* (special edition)
❏ Note cards
❏ Pens
❏ Large writing surface (chalk board)

## Memory Verse

For we are God's fellow workers; you are God's field, you are God's building.
—1 Corinthians 3:9

## Scripture

1 Corinthians 3:1–9

## Lesson in a Sentence

As followers of Christ, it is our faithfulness in sharing our faith that matters, not who gets credit for the work or the results.

## The Big Picture

Competition and rivalries are a natural part of life. However, there is no place for competition and rivalry in the Christian community.

# Focus

On a chalkboard, write the names of these heroes or characters:

1. Batman
2. Sherlock Holmes
3. Fred Flintstone
4. Han Solo
5. Harry Potter
6. Lone Ranger
7. Peter Pan
8. Snoopy

Ask the students to give the names of the sidekick for each character (answers):

1. Robin
2. Dr. Watson
3. Barney Rubble
4. Chewbacca
5. Ron Weasley
6. Tonto
7. Tinkerbell
8. Woodstock

If your group is active, you can split into teams and play a game by seeing which team can guess the sidekicks first.

Ask the students to give the names of other famous sidekicks and main characters from film or literature. Ask which sidekick is their favorite and why.

Ask students to describe the main characteristic of a sidekick (some answers may include: loyalty, companionship, intelligence, resourcefulness, taking care of the main character, or saving the main character).

Introduce students to the "Lord of the Rings: Return of the King" characters of Frodo Baggins and Samwise Gamgee.

In the film, *Frodo,* the main character, is given the task of returning a ring to its rightful place to stop an evil character from taking over the kingdom. Samwise is to travel with Frodo and help him, at all costs (which could mean his own life). In this scene, Frodo is almost there but can no longer carry the burden. Samwise is unable to carry the ring for Frodo, but he is able to carry Frodo. ("Lord of the Rings: Return of the King," special edition—disc 2, chapter 66. The scene lasts from 1:15:28—1:17:44.)

Ask students to discuss the differences in the tasks of the characters. Which character is more important to the story and why? Could Frodo accomplish his task without the help of Samwise?

The main point to get across is this: While Frodo (or any main character) is the leader, he is not able to accomplish what he is called to do without the sidekick saving him or helping him.

Ask the students which character they identify with (main character or sidekick) and why.

You may use other sidekicks and main characters or choose another movie. Other film scenes could include Batman and Robin, Han Solo and Chewbacca, or whomever you choose.

# Discovery

Choose a student to read 1 Corinthians 3:1–9. Ask students which person they know more about, Paul or Apollos. Invite students to tell the rest of the class what they know about each one.

Read Acts 18:24–28. Who was Apollos?

Return to 1 Corinthians 3:1–9. Explain to students that the church at Corinth was being torn apart by divisions and factions. These factions focused on who the people felt was the true leader of the church (Paul, Peter, or Apollos), and which one they chose to follow.

Have you seen similar actions in school, church, or society? Have you seen groups that should be getting along who are torn apart by the same behavior? Why does this happen? This could lead to great discussion, so be mindful of time and direction.

Imagine a group of people deciding that in order to get the ring destroyed, Frodo was the most important one to follow, while another group decided that since Samwise had to carry Frodo, he should be the one they follow? Why would this be wrong?

(Answer: Since both characters were needed to accomplish the same task, there should be no rivalry.)

The same is true in the church. According to Philippians 2:1–11, we are to have the same purpose. We are on the same team. There should be no competition between people as to who is the more important person as we follow Christ. All are needed and all are useful (but in different ways and at different times).

## Life Application

Give each student a note card and pen. Ask students to write down two to three persons they look up to (spiritually). Can you rank their importance? Why or why not? Should you rank their importance spiritually?

How have these leaders impacted you? Have they used different means? Have they impacted you in different ways? Do you look up to them for different reasons (for middle school students you will need to be more specific)?

Read the passage once more and ask how it applies to these leaders.

## Making It Personal

Look at the list of the persons you follow. What would happen if that person disappointed you? Would it change anything?

This is one reason it was so important to Paul that everyone follow Jesus and not individual teachers. He understood that people can disappoint their followers or mess up in ways that destroy a person's faith, if the followers have put their faith in the leader above anything else.

Who do you put your trust in? Who is your leader? If it's not Jesus, what would happen to your faith if your chosen leader disappointed you, or another leader with different and better teachings came along?

Ask students to pray for their leaders and to follow Jesus above all else. Ask students to put aside their factions and divisions to follow Jesus.

To end the session, sing the hymn, "I Have Decided to Follow Jesus."

## TEACHER'S NOTE:

It is important to understand the culture surrounding the church at Corinth. It was common practice for first-century Jews to follow closely the teachings of a particular rabbi on rabbinical school. If one followed a particular rabbi's teachings, the teachings of other rabbis were dismissed, especially in areas of difference, no matter how inconsequential. Rivalries among teachers and schools were quite common.

Paul's message concerning the equality of all servants below the teachings of Christ was a radical concept for the church at Corinth. There are many parallels today in politics, education, and the church. It may be interesting to discuss these with a mature group.

## Song Connect

"I Have Decided to Follow Jesus" (hymn)—A number of Christian and secular artists have redone this song.

"I Will Follow" by U2

## Extra! Extra!

Promote this lesson with a headline that sounds more like a wrestling or boxing match. Here is an example:

### Head to Head Tonight!
# Paul of Tarsus *vs.* Apollos of Alexandria

In this corner we have Paul, former Pharisee and writer of much of the New Testament *vs.* Apollos, knowledgeable in the Scriptures and a good debater. It should be an easy match for Paul.

## Memory Verse Activity

On the back of the note card with the names of leaders, ask each student to write down the Memory Verse.

For we are God's fellow workers; you are God's field, you are God's building.
—1 Corinthians 3:9

During the week, ask them to pray for those leaders to be like Paul and Apollos as they lead.

# Apollos: We All Have a Role in God's Work

*By Rick Bennett and Amy Jacober*

## Memory Verse
For we are God's fellow workers; you are God's field, you are God's building.
—1 Corinthians 3:9

## Scripture
1 Corinthians 12:4–31

## Lesson in a Sentence
As followers of Christ, it is our faithfulness in sharing our faith that matters, not who gets credit for the work or the results.

# Focus

***Popsicle Pushup Game***
Now if you tell your students this name, they will be looking for a treat! Since it is August, feel free to bring a few for after the activity.

This game gets its name from the old Popsicle stick picture frames many of us made as kids. Ask four students to be in a group. In this group, they are to lay on the ground making a square, head to feet. Once they get the basic shape, ask each person to place his or her feet on the upper back (just behind the head) of the person at their feet. It will look like an interlocking square with each person having their feet on top and their back below someone else. Ask them to do one pushup. It takes teamwork but it can be done! If they get it easily, ask for five. This is a great activity to remind us that all people have something to contribute and when one person chooses not to, the activity fails.

# Discovery

Ask your students to list on a dry-erase board the things they think are most important in serving God. Push them to be specific! Once these are listed, ask if they think there is a top five of importance? Write the rank order or make stars next to these really important ones.

On a set of index cards, write the following: one part per card. Do this for at least four sets.

- Right Hand
- Left Hand
- Right Eye
- Left Eye
- Right Ear
- Left Ear
- Nose
- Right Foot
- Left Foot

Separate into at least four groups (or the number of groups to match the number of sets of cards that you made). Place all of the cards in a bag and mix them up. Ask someone from each group to draw out nine cards. On a large sheet of paper, ask each group to draw a picture of a person having the number of parts they drew, no more and no less. For example, they may draw three feet, three eyes, and no hands. They may draw two noses and one eye. Whatever it is, instruct them to draw their person according to the parts chosen.

Look at the drawings. What's wrong? Seems silly, yet we are always wishing to be someone or something other than what we were created to be.

In those same small groups, read through 1 Corinthians 12:4–31.

- What is this passage talking about?
- Is there any one part that is better than another?
- How does the analogy between the physical body and Christ's body fit together?

## Life Application

Have each person name at least one thing they do well. If your group knows one another well, ask each person to share something about the others as well.

All of us are needed in God's kingdom. There is no one role that outshines all the others.

Can you think of a time when someone was truly skilled but a complete jerk for their arrogance or mean spirit? Sadly, these examples are not few and far between. This is the opposite of what God is calling His followers to be.

Consider what your youth group, your church, your school, and community might look like if people stopped positioning themselves to be seen as better than others and simply served out of their giftedness. What would change? What would stay the same?

Close with a prayer asking the Lord to help us all set aside our pettiness with one another, learn to cooperate, and stop denying that we each have something to offer.

### TEACHER'S NOTE:

This is unnatural for most of us since we have been taught a false humility. This should not encourage arrogance, but rather acknowledge that God has gifted each of us for His service. When we deny that we do anything well, we deny God at work in our lives.

# What Kind of Friend Are You?

*By Randy Prosperi*

In this lesson, students will:
- ✔ Be able to discuss the godly friendship of Jonathan and David.
- ✔ Examine their own friendships to find out if there are actions or attitudes that need to change.
- ✔ Prayerfully ask if there are qualities they need to change or improve.
- ✔ Determine if there are friendships in which they need to ask forgiveness or make something right.

Stuff you'll need:
- ❑ Large pieces of poster board
- ❑ Markers
- ❑ Individual small pieces of paper for each student
- ❑ Pens or pencils for each student
- ❑ Colored paper cutouts of little dresses and pants and shirts that the students can write on and use as bookmarks

## Memory Verse

Therefore, as God's chosen people, holy and dearly loved, clothe yourselves with compassion, kindness, humility, gentleness and patience.—Colossians 3:12 NIV

## Scripture

1 Samuel 18:1

## Lesson in a Sentence

Does the way I treat my friends reflect the fact that I am a Christian?

## The Big Picture

Friendships can be difficult at times. As Christians we are to treat our friends in a way that honors Jesus. Many times this doesn't come naturally to us. Instead we allow jealousy, competition, gossip, and anger to creep in. When conflicts arise, we choose to lash out or ignore rather than deal with the issue by choosing truth in love.

We must examine how we treat those closest to us, asking God to give us the grace to treat them as He would. We must ask Him to reveal any jealousies or resentments that we have against our friends. We should guard the words we say to or about them.

We may need to choose to forgive a friend for something that they did or maybe we should ask them to forgive us for something that we said or did.

Friendships often reveal the good and bad in our own hearts and give us the opportunity to choose to respond as Jesus would. Is there an action or attitude regarding a friendship that you need to change?

# Focus

Divide students into groups of four. Give each group a large piece of poster board and a marker. Ask them to write down the characteristics they look for in a good friend. Give them plenty of time to create their list. When it looks like the majority of the groups have finished, then get everyone's attention so the groups can share with each other. Stand at the front of the room with a new piece of poster board and call on each group to share their list. After you have all of the groups' lists compiled into one big list, ask the students to choose the top three characteristics of a good friend. If there is a lot of variance in the answers, take a vote. On the big poster board circle the three characteristics that students chose as most important to them.

# Discovery

Ask if any student can describe the character traits of David and Jonathan. After that student attempts it, ask others if they have anything to add. If no student offers to answer, ask the group some questions that might jog their memories on who David and Jonathan were.

Read 1 Samuel 18:1 and 20:16–42.

- Why was their friendship unlikely?
- Based on verse 16, describe their friendship.
- Detail the plan that the friends concocted in order for David to find out if he was in danger from Jonathan's father, Saul.
- What did their plan reveal about the safety of David?
- Has there ever been a time when you devised a plan to protect a friend? Maybe you protected their reputation or guarded them from physical harm. If you can share the situation without naming names or divulging the person, please tell a little bit about it.

Now is the time when you have the opportunity to share with the group. Think of a time when a friend took a risk for you. Maybe it was to help you out of a sticky situation or maybe he or she stood with you when no one else would. Share this story with your group, making sure to highlight how your friend's actions reflected the character of Christ. Don't be afraid to be vulnerable. Students need to see you as someone real who has encountered some of the same issues they have at times.

- What would you have done knowing that your own life could be in jeopardy if you protected your friend David?
- How did protecting David assure that Jonathan would lose the opportunity to be king one day? What does that reveal about his heart?
- What would it mean for you to be a better friend? Is there something that you could increase, such as encouragement or support? Is there something you could eliminate, such as gossip or jealousy?

## Teacher's Note:

When dealing with personal issues such as friends, be sure to ask students to use discretion when they share answers or personal stories. It could be tempting for students to use the share time to *vent* or hurt someone else's reputation so be sure the students are careful in the way they answer the questions.

## Life Application

Ask students to think of a way a friend sacrificed for them. Now ask them to think of a meaningful way to thank their friend. They may want to write them an e-mail or send a card. Tell the students that if it seems awkward to do this, they could always reference the lesson and tell the person this is part of *homework* that they received.

## Making It Personal

Give pieces of paper and pens or pencils to each student. Ask the students to spend a few minutes thinking about how to be a better friend. Now ask them to write their ideas on the pieces of paper. You may want to offer some suggestions such as forgiving someone, or making amends for a previous action. Maybe they need to ask a friend to help them stop gossiping. Whatever it is, assure students that they will be the only ones who will see their sheets of paper. Now ask them to write an action plan for making their commitment a reality. If they need to talk to a friend about something, ask them to write down the exact time they will do that. If they have decided to stop a certain behavior, they may want to write some practical ideas for how they intend to stop, and what behavior they will replace it with. Now ask them to tuck the paper somewhere they can look at to remind them of their commitment.

## Memory Verse Activity

Give each student a marker and one of the cutout bookmarks. Ask them to write the Memory Verse on the bookmark and then place it somewhere they will see it, such as their Bible or a schoolbook. When they see their bookmark, they will be reminded of the *clothes* they should be wearing each day—compassion, kindness, humility, gentleness, and patience.

## Service Options

You may want to remind students that we are called to be a friend to the friendless. You could give the students an option to serve this week. Ask a senior citizens' home or homeless shelter if they could use your group's help. If so, tell your students about the opportunity to share, explaining to them that God calls us to serve those less fortunate and those who can never repay. Discuss Luke 14:12–14 with your students before you go to serve.

# What Kind of Friend Are You?

*By Randy Prosperi*

## Memory Verse

Therefore, as God's chosen people, holy and dearly loved, clothe yourselves with compassion, kindness, humility, gentleness and patience.—Colossians 3:12 NIV

## Scripture

John 15:12–13

## Lesson in a Sentence

When we look at the example of Jesus, we are challenged to be self-sacrificing in our relationships with friends just as He was.

# Focus

The world we live in today is a "look out for yourself first" society. Ask students to think of ways this message is conveyed in our culture. Ask them to share specific places where this message is displayed such as music or magazines. Next, challenge students to rethink the message the world gives and choose to place serving others above being served by them.

# Discovery

Ask one student to read John 15:12–13. Ask the following questions:

- Who is talking in this passage?
- What are some practical ways we can accomplish verse 12?
- Will we ever be able to live up to the sacrifice of Jesus?
- What was Jesus talking about in verse 13?
- While we most likely won't be called to literally die for a friend, what are some ways we can accomplish verse 13?

## Life Application

Divide students into groups of three or four. Ask them to think of some practical ways they can put someone else ahead of themselves this week. Give them some ideas. They may want to let someone in front of them in the lunch line at school or choose to straighten up a part of their house for a family member. Or they might want to help a friend in a practical way, such as helping them with some work they need to do. After the groups have had time to brainstorm, let them share their best ideas with the whole group.

## Making It Personal

Ask students to think through the ideas that were listed above and to choose one way they are going to put others in front of themselves this week. Encourage them to surprise someone by serving him or her, if possible. They may even want to keep their act of serving anonymous.

## Connections

Even as Jesus suffered on the Cross, He was compassionate toward others. Luke 23:32–34 says that He even prayed to His Father on behalf of those crucifying Him. Read this passage with the students and discuss the unending compassion and sacrifice of Jesus.

# Leadership, Wisdom, and Skill

*By Amy Jacober*

---

In this lesson, students will:
- ✔ Identify characteristics of a wise leader.
- ✔ Consider how to develop wisdom.
- ✔ Learn that experience breeds wisdom.
- ✔ Learn that knowledge and wisdom are not the same things.

Stuff you'll need:
- ❏ Clay
- ❏ Toothpicks
- ❏ Dry-erase board and markers
- ❏ Paper
- ❏ Pencils

---

## Memory Verse

He who is faithful in what is least is faithful also in much; and he who is unjust in what is least is unjust also in much.—Luke 16:10

Whoever can be trusted with very little can also be trusted with much, and whoever is dishonest with very little will also be dishonest with much.—Luke 16:10 NIV

## Scripture

Judges 4

## Lesson in a Sentence

Wisdom, leadership, and skill are gifts from God to be developed and used for His glory.

## The Big Picture

Ever met a kid who seems wise beyond his or her years? Ask a few questions and you'll find out some major life-altering experience is in his or her background. Wisdom, leadership, and skill are developed through experience. Each of these can be used to honor God or oneself and one must make a choice. Another choice is to recognize these qualities in others.

# Focus

## Option 1
### Who's the Leader?

Make a circle with chairs as your students come into the room. Once everyone is seated, ask for a volunteer to leave the room. Once the volunteer is gone, ask for a second volunteer to be the leader. The leader will lead everyone in the circle in some kind of action—stomping feet, scratching their head, twiddling their thumbs, whatever. Once the volunteer returns, the actions begin. Every few seconds, the leader changes the action. The first volunteer watches and tries to discover which person is the leader. Once guessed, the first volunteer sits down and a new volunteer is sent outside. Repeat this activity for several rounds.

What made it easy or difficult to guess the leader? How difficult was it for those who led? What made it easy or difficult for you?

Leadership takes skill. Some people are good at leading and some are not. Regardless of where you start, the more experience you have, the more effective a leader you will become.

## Option 2
### Bridge to Nowhere

This activity takes teamwork, skill, leadership, and thought. It will feel pointless to many of your students but if you present it well, they will get into it!

Divide into groups of no more than four (more than four will make it too easy for one person to sit out and watch their team). Give each team a piece of clay that is about the size of a football and a handful of toothpicks (50–60). Have a large surface where each team can work. The object is to build a structure that extends the farthest out from its clay anchor. DO NOT give any extra clay since they must pinch from the one they have to stick the toothpicks together. Create a starting line with a piece of tape on the table. Each group may place their structure as close as possible to the line without crossing over. Have a measuring tape on hand to determine which structure went the farthest. The structure must hover above the table without touching, with the exception of its base. The longest structure wins!

While this seemed like a silly little activity, it took leadership, teamwork, skill, trial and error, and a great deal of thought. Check out the Memory Verse, Luke 16:10. How does this connect with the activity you just did?

# Discovery

This is going to take a little background work to get your students caught up. Have two of your leaders take turns reading the following passages with intensity and strength. Explain to your students that this is a time after the Exodus and God has provided for His people and now calls them to follow all that He has commanded.

- Judges 2:1–10
- Judges 2:11–18
- Judges 2:19–23
- Judges 3:7
- Judges 3:12
- Judges 3:15
- Judges 4:1–3

Anyone seeing a pattern? God provides; the people do what they want; the people fail.

The book of Judges is a series of passages reminding us of years and years of God calling for obedience, providing a leader, and over time the people falling away. Judgment comes, God calls for obedience through a leader and over time, the people fall away.

In small groups, read Judges 4. Deborah is a prophetess. She was chosen by God to help get the people back on track. Ask the students to pay special attention to Deborah to see what we can learn from her. She is in charge; she is humble; she is wise; she is obedient; she tries to raise up others; she is willing to do what it takes to get Barak to lead as he should; she is not a doormat and takes credit when it is hers; and she points to the Lord at all times.

## Life Application

With the help of your students, list the characteristics of Deborah on a dry-erase board.

- What struggles do you think teenagers go through today? What struggles did your grandparents suffer? Your parents?
- Do you think life changes much from generation to generation?
- How is your life easier or harder than the previous generation?
- Do you think you have anything to learn from those who came before you?
- What do you enjoy learning from those God has placed over you (parents, teachers, youth leaders), and what gets on your nerves?
- What would it take to have someone like Deborah around today?
- How do the leaders you know measure up? Are they wise and humble? Willing to do what it takes to lead as God directed?
- What do you want the legacy of your generation to be?

## Judges 5 Option

If you have a creative group, check out Judges 5. This is the song of Deborah and Barak in commemoration of their victory. They recount what God has done and offer praise and hope for the future. Ask your students to divide into groups and write their own song thanking God for what He has done, offering praise, and looking forward to the future. Give each group time to work on this song as a prayer offering to the Lord. Close with each group sharing their song aloud.

## Teacher's Note:

Judges had a much broader leadership during this time in history than our judges of today. They were military leaders, civil administrators, and judges in matters of dispute and law. They were placed in the position to help deliver the Israelites and restore their obedience to the Lord.

A point of interest: The song of Deborah is considered one of the earliest poems in all of Scripture.

## Making It Personal

Deborah was calling an entire people to follow God's ways. She was placed in a position of leadership and required to courageously use her wisdom to help the Israelites.

What wisdom do you have? Is it wisdom if it doesn't change your life? Wisdom must be accompanied by courage to act. This may mean choosing not to fight with your brother or standing up for someone at school. Knowing the right thing and not doing it is useless. Information without action is just that—information, not wisdom. Wisdom knows action is required and wisdom knows best when, where, and how to use the information.

Is there an area in your own life that needs to change? Do you have the wisdom and courage to make that change?

Spend a few moments asking God for wisdom in a difficult situation in your life. This could be a difficult math test. It could be how to speak up about an abusive household. Give your students plenty of time and remind them that you are available if they need to talk.

# Leadership, Wisdom, and Skill

*By Amy Jacober*

## Memory Verse

He who is faithful in what is least is faithful also in much; and he who is unjust in what is least is unjust also in much.—Luke 16:10

Whoever can be trusted with very little can also be trusted with much, and whoever is dishonest with very little will also be dishonest with much.—Luke 16:10 NIV

## Scripture

Luke 2:40–52; 1 Corinthians 1:25

## Lesson in a Sentence

Wisdom, leadership, and skill are gifts from God to be developed and used for His glory.

# Focus

This activity focuses on choices and how we make them. Before you meet, type the following questions and add a few of your own. Make enough copies of the list of questions for each of your students.

Adjust the list to your own needs but use the following example as a starting place. Think of situations that may speak directly to your students.

No one wants to be told what to do! Look over this list and consider all of the choices you may one day face. Circle the choice you would make and briefly tell why.

1a. A full ride scholarship to a four-year college requiring a minor in literature.
1b. A partial scholarship to a community college on the sport of your choice.
2a. A minimum wage job at your favorite store at the mall.
2b. A job that pays $3/hour above minimum wage cleaning rooms at a hotel.
3a. A prom date with the hottest guy or girl in school.
3b. A prom date with one of your best friends.
4a. A guaranteed A in chemistry with a little help from a stolen test paper.
4b. Most likely a C in chemistry no matter how hard you study.
5a. Letting your parents know about your *MySpace* knowing you have to keep it clean.
5b. Creating a separate *MySpace* so you can say and post whatever you want.
6a. Going to a sports camp for two weeks.
6b. Going on a family vacation to Hawaii.

Most choices are not between good and bad. Most choices are between two things that are either both neutral or both good. Which soda you drink, what shirt you wear, if you call or text are everyday decisions. Regardless, we must make choices. As you rely on God, learn to be decisive. Practice in the small areas so that when the big, meaningful choices come along, you are more prepared.

# Discovery

Ask one of your students to read aloud 1 Corinthians 1:25. In large letters on either a dry-erase board or butcher paper, write this verse as they are reading.

After you have written 1 Corinthians 1:25 in a prominent place, hand out index cards and markers to each student. Ask them to write their own copy of the verse and keep it out.

In groups of three read Luke 2:40–52.

- Why would the Bible ever talk about Jesus growing in wisdom; He was God after all wasn't He?
- What can we learn from Jesus' growing in wisdom?

Now read Proverbs 3:13–18.

- What does wisdom bring?
- How is wisdom personified?

How do these three passages relate to one another? What does looking at all three of them teach us about wisdom?

## Life Application

Life is full of choices. Every day, thousands of choices are made without even paying attention—what cereal to eat, text to answer, song to listen to, or friend to talk with at school. Most of these do not require much wisdom or thought, or do they?

What wisdom is required in the everyday choices you make?

What decisions cause you to stop and think (to ditch school or not, to say yes to a date, to delete a song that you know is degrading to others, and so on)?

On tough decisions, how do you decide? (Talking with friends? Praying? Pro and con lists?)

What do we do with the idea that God's foolishness is greater than our wisdom? What's the point of even trying then? How might God guide us in these decisions?

Remind your students that they know more now than when they were in first grade, or third grade, or even fifth grade. What does this say about how much more they will know in their twenties, thirties, or sixties? Hopefully, wisdom is gained with each new experience in life.

Ask each person in a group of three to share one decision they have ahead of them. Ask each group to pray for one another for wisdom and guidance from the Lord for the pending decision. The prayers do not need to be eloquent or perfect. Students are simply asking God to guide the person as he or she weighs the decision to be made.

## Song Connect
"What It Means" by Jeremy Camp on *Beyond Measure*

## Quotable Quotes
*To understand reality is not the same as to know about outward events. It is to perceive the essential nature of things. The best-informed man is not necessarily the wisest. Indeed there is a danger that precisely in the multiplicity of his knowledge he will lose sight of what is essential. But on the other hand, knowledge of an apparently trivial detail quite often makes it possible to see into the depth of things. And so the wise man will seek to acquire the best possible knowledge about events, but always without becoming dependent upon this knowledge. To recognize the significant in the factual is wisdom.*
—Dietrich Bonhoeffer

*Science is organized knowledge. Wisdom is organized life.*—Immanuel Kant

## Extra! Extra!
See You at the Pole™ (SYATP) is coming up in two weeks! You may have been doing this for years or it may be your first time. Whichever it is, teenagers typically need a reminder and some encouragement. Check out the Web site at www.syatp.com for resources and more information. It is a student-initiated, student-organized, and student-led event. It is all about students meeting at their school flagpole to pray—for their school, friends, teachers, government, and their nation. See You at the Pole is not a demonstration, political rally, or a stand for or against anything.

# Mysterious Communication SEPTEMBER 21 2008

By Sharon Koh

In this lesson, students will:
✔ Learn that prayer is a form of communication that we cannot fully comprehend.
✔ Understand what it means to wrestle in prayer like Epaphras.

Stuff you'll need:
❏ Masking tape and a flat area of floor (preferably carpet)

## Memory Verse
I call on you, O God, for you will answer me; give ear to me and hear my prayer.
—Psalm 17:6 NIV

## Scripture
Colossians 4:12–13

## Lesson in a Sentence
God understands and cares about the things we pray for.

## The Big Picture
Prayer is defined as *talking with God,* but for many, this is an abstract concept. How does it work? Can God really hear my thoughts? When is it God's turn to speak? Why doesn't He say anything?

# Focus

### Human Checkers
This game works almost exactly like the board game, Checkers, but it is life-sized. First, draw a checkerboard on the floor using the masking tape (8 squares x 8 squares). Make sure every other square is black. Adjust the size of the squares according to the room size, but make sure they are each large enough for a student to stand in.

Place the students in two teams and tell them that there is one new rule: No talking. The two teams have to challenge one another at Checkers *without* verbal communication. Then, let them have five minutes alone with their team to figure out how they are going to communicate during the game.

# Discovery

After playing Human Checkers, ask the students to describe how their teams communicated. Sometimes, teams have one person do the thinking for the whole team and other members of the team just follow instructions. Even if this is not the case, the team would have needed to figure out some form of nonverbal communication among themselves (hand signals; eye contact; head nods, etc.). Oftentimes, the communication needs to go back and forth because team members cannot see what all the other players see in front of them. So, they have to communicate in all directions. Make sure the students notice that it was indeed *possible* to communicate without talking.

Turn the conversation to the topic of prayer and invite students to consider how prayer works. Let them speculate how God can hear our thoughts.

Make the point that, if students in a simple game of Checkers can figure out how to communicate, is it not possible that God (who is all-powerful) has figured out a way to hear our thoughts? Perhaps it is better to occupy ourselves with the comforting thought that God does hear our prayers rather than wonder too much about things we cannot explain.

As an illustration of someone in the Bible who is known for his praying, bring up Epaphras. Ask the following questions of the students:

1. Read Colossians 4:2—6. What do we learn about prayer from these examples of prayer? What kinds of prayer exist?
2. Read Colossians 4:12—13. What is Epaphras known for? What did he pray for?

## Life Application

Ask students to consider what it means to wrestle in prayer. Ask them to think about things that they have really wanted God to do in their lives. Remind them that God uses one of three answers to our requests: *yes, no,* or *wait.* It is in the category of *wait* that we get to wrestle with God. We can ask God, "why?" and sometimes He doesn't answer us for years. So, we ask again, and again, and again.

Other times, we pray for other people (as Epaphras did). He was commended for wrestling in prayer that the Colossians might stand firm in the will of God. We need to learn to be persistent and faithful in the prayers that we pray on other people's behalf.

## Making It Personal

Let students write some of the things they would like to wrestle with God in prayer for this week. Keep the list so that you can ask them what it was like to wrestle in prayer over these things. Keep in mind that some of their responses will need further discussion. ("I prayed and I prayed, but nothing happened!")

## Options

The life-sized Checkerboard works with the game of Chess as well. It is much more complicated to play Chess without verbal communication, but it is even more fun.

## Song Connect

"Father, Spirit, Jesus" by Casting Crowns on *Lifesong*

# Wrestling with God— The Parable of the Persistent Widow

*By Sharon Koh*

## Memory Verse

But if from there you seek the LORD your God, you will find him if you look for him with all your heart and with all your soul.—Deuteronomy 4:29 NIV

## Scripture

Luke 18:1–8

## Lesson in a Sentence

God honors the faithful and persistent person of prayer.

# Focus

Wrestling is big business in the world today! Do you know any of these people?

Bring in a clip from any wrestling show or ask your students if you can borrow one of their videos. While much of this is scripted and well . . . fake, you still have to be in good physical shape. You can fake really hurting someone but you cannot fake holding someone over your head. You are either strong enough or you are not.

Ask your students to consider what is and is not fake about wrestling. Keep a running list on a dry-erase board. Why is wrestling so popular? Be certain this does not become the all-consuming conversation of your meeting time. For some groups, wrestling is HUGE! For other groups, there may be no one who is into it. The interesting third option is: when you think you have no one who is into it and learn just how many of your students can name all of the wrestlers and what is currently happening!

# Discovery

Read Luke 18:1–8. Jesus is teaching how we should pray. What does the persistent widow pester the judge with? What is her request?

The widow's request is one of the key things to note about this parable. She represents someone with little-to-no status in her society. The judge is someone who has a lot of power and status but no reverence for God. Her repeated request is for "justice against my adversary." Eventually, the judge gives in and grants her what she is asking for, and Jesus summarizes the point of the parable in verses 7 and 8.

Earlier, we looked a little at the idea of *wrestling* with God in prayer. This parable gives us an illustration of someone who wrestled in prayer. Her request is for justice and her behavior is deemed *faithful*. This is the kind of person that Jesus is looking for when He returns to the earth.

Learning to wrestle with injustice in prayer is a significant part of maturing as a Christian who is going to be about God's kingdom business on earth.


## Personal Application

Invite students to consider specific requests *for justice* that they can pray for consistently. Are they aware of unjust situations at school? In today's current events? Within their church community?

# Gideon: Using the Least of the Least

By *Matthew and Dianne Madsen*

In this lesson, students will:
- ✔ Become familiar with the story of Gideon.
- ✔ Be challenged to see themselves as God sees them, and follow His battle plan for their lives.

Stuff you'll need:
- ❏ "Warrior Search"
- ❏ Paper
- ❏ Pens/pencils
- ❏ Magazines
- ❏ Newspapers
- ❏ Mirror
- ❏ Flashlights
- ❏ Trumpets made of construction paper cones (can use real trumpets, if available)
- ❏ Bibles

## Memory Verse

. . . but God has chosen the foolish things of the world to shame the wise, and God has chosen the weak things of the world to shame the things which are strong.
—1 Corinthians 1:27 NASB

## Scripture

Judges 6:12; 7:1–25

## Lesson in a Sentence

When God is in control of our lives, we are assured of victory in any situation.

## The Big Picture

Gideon had the odds stacked against him—he was the youngest son of a weak clan. He was even hiding out from the enemy when the angel of the Lord found him. But God saw in Gideon what Gideon didn't see in himself—a mighty warrior. The Scripture passage chronicles the process through which God prepared and provided for Gideon resulting in victory.

Our students may often feel that the odds are stacked against them—trouble in school, rough times with family, peer pressure, or problems with relationships. When we allow God to be in control of our lives, we will be assured of victory.

# Focus

*"Warrior Search"*

Ask the students to draw their concept of a warrior or find pictures of warriors in magazines, newspapers, or books. They can choose any era they like and use their imagination. For younger students, you could gather pictures of various people (i.e. bankers, teachers, construction workers, soldiers, etc.) and ask them to choose the ones they think are the warriors.

What is God's idea of a warrior? Do we have the same image of a warrior that God has? Hold up the mirror in front of the students. This is what a warrior looks like to God . . . YOU! You don't have to have certain weapons, clothes, or skills. In our lesson today, we're going to take a look at an unlikely warrior, in an unlikely war, which resulted in an unlikely victory.

# Discovery

Print out a copy of Judges 6:12 and 7:1–25 for each student. After reading the Scriptures, let the students act out the story. Assign students to be God, Gideon, and all the other primary characters in the story. Use construction paper to make trumpets and flashlights for torches. Ham it up and have fun!

## Making It Personal

Play a recording of the song "When You Are a Soldier" by Steven Curtis Chapman after giving these instructions:

Take a few minutes to think about the different battles you are facing in your own life and list them on your construction paper bookmark. After writing them down, pray about them and keep this bookmark on the page of today's Memory Verse.

". . . but God has chosen the foolish things of the world to shame the wise, and God has chosen the weak things of the world to shame the things which are strong" (1 Cor. 1:27 NASB).

Remember that no matter how weak you may feel, God will be by your side to help you through the battles of life.

## Life Application

The following can be read or paraphrased:

Gideon's very name meant *warrior*. What made him such a feared opponent was not his proficiency on a trumpet; it was not the size of the clay jars that he broke; nor was it his ability at handling a flaming torch. What made the difference between the Gideon that we see hiding from the enemy and the Gideon that we see leading his people to victory is his relationship with God.

Judges 6:12, "The angel of the LORD appeared to him and said to him, 'The LORD is with you, O valiant warrior'" (NASB).

Just as God promised to be with Gideon through the battle ahead, God promises to be with us in our battles also. While we might not be facing the entire Midianite army, we do have battles of our own—battles that result in casualties. For some of us warriors the battles are fought at home. Still others see the hostile environment of their school campus as their battlefield. Believers in Christ have nothing to fear.

In Judges 6:14, God says to Gideon, "Have I not sent you?" God sent Gideon into battle and stayed by his side. God has also sent you into battle. Just as God strengthened and protected Gideon, He will strengthen and protect you.

It is crucial for us as Christians to seek the guidance of the Holy Spirit so that we know we are going where He sends us. A soldier could find himself in a heap of trouble if he reported to the wrong battlefield, or if he didn't know his part in the battle plan. As warriors in God's army, we need to remember to consult our Commander in Chief to ensure that we are fighting the war the way He wants us to fight. It doesn't matter how big or how bad the enemy is that we are facing.

"What then shall we say to these things? If God is for us, who is against us?" (Rom. 8:31 NASB).

## Extra! Extra!

History is filled with stories of military battles that were won against seemingly insurmountable odds. If you are familiar with any of them, such as: the Spartan defeat of the Persian Empire, World War Two's Battle of the Bulge, etc. . . . you no doubt are aware of the impact these stories can make. Use these illustrations to connect the truth in the Scriptures with your students by having a special guest (perhaps a war veteran) tell the underdog story to your students.

# Gideon: Using the Least of the Least

*By Matthew and Dianne Madsen*

## Stuff you'll need:
- ❏ Three 3x5 index cards for each student
- ❏ One pen/pencil per student
- ❏ At least one Bible for every four students in your group (in case some were left at home)

## Memory Verse
". . . but God has chosen the foolish things of the world to shame the wise, and God has chosen the weak things of the world to shame the things which are strong."
—1 Corinthians 1:27 NASB

## Scripture
Hebrews 11

## Lesson in a Sentence
This chapter, called the "Hall of Faith" is full of warriors for God. Would you make the list?

# Focus

On each of three of the 3x5 index cards, ask the students to identify their top three personal heroes. These can be sports personalities, rock stars, or anyone that they admire as a role model. Now, ask them to flip the card over and identify the characteristics that caused them to choose that person.

This could be expanded into a game (if there's time). Have the youth group try to guess who each student selected, based solely upon the characteristics and traits listed.

# Discovery

Break up into small groups with no more than four in a group. Each group will read through Hebrews 11 together. After the group has read the chapter, ask them to sum up the chapter's common thread of faith in terms that they can explain to their friends at school. Then ask each group to narrow the list of those mentioned in the "Hall of

Faith" to three personal favorites and have them share with their group why they selected those particular people.

## Life Application

Gideon was mentioned in the Hall of Faith—along with many other biblical heroes. Though he was only part of a larger list, he was mentioned. By being faithful to God and learning to be the person God saw him to be, he was able to make a difference in the life of Israel!

When we live out our faith, there is no end to the influence and impact we can have on the world. Living our faith every day, in every circumstance is not easy. It's challenging for young and old alike; it's even a challenge for your pastor!

We all have different stories for our lives. We come from different backgrounds; grew up in different families; and have different circumstances in life that we deal with. But there are many things we have in common. As Christians, we have the Holy Spirit to help guide and direct us. The Holy Spirit came upon Gideon (Judg. 6:34) and empowered him to do God's will. All the members of the Hall of Faith were led by God. None of them had an easy life. Noah built a huge boat in the desert and was mocked for it. Joseph was sold into slavery by his brothers. Moses wandered in the desert and there are plenty of other stories of hardships endured by people of the Bible. We are not promised an easy life when we live as a warrior for God and follow Him in faith. But two things we know for sure: we'll never be bored and the retirement plan is out of this world!

## Extra! Extra!

Dear Teacher, you are taking on a great responsibility—to teach young people the things of God! Thank you for your dedication, perseverance, and willingness to be used by the Lord to instruct these students in the Word of the Lord. You need to remember that you, too, are a warrior to be mightily used by the Lord. Your students need you to be a warrior for them . . . a prayer warrior, a warrior of living for the Lord, and maybe even a warrior to stand in the gap for them. Continually pray that God will give you wisdom and guidance as you teach your class and there will be many victories to be won!

## Memory Verse Activity

Write the Memory Verse on a piece of cardstock (or other sturdy paper). Cut into puzzle pieces, but keep out a piece of the puzzle before giving it to the students. Let the students put the puzzle together. They will quickly learn that there is a piece missing. Produce the missing piece and say, "just as it doesn't make sense to put together a puzzle with missing pieces, it doesn't make sense to call ourselves Christians and then follow what the world says and does. We need to follow what God wants for our lives. Sometimes His directions may be hard to understand, or seem strange (as those in today's lesson), but God knows what is best for us. He can see the big picture, and He is worthy of our trust!"

## Ancient Practices

In Judges 7:13, a dream that indicates Gideon's triumph over the Midianites is shared. In this dream a loaf of barley bread tumbled into the camp and hit the tent of the Midianite, and the tent fell. This bread—a simple, common, everyday food of the poor— is another reminder that Gideon was nothing special on his own. He was the youngest son of the family; his clan was a weak one; and his people were under persecution by marauders. He did not have the pedigree of a warrior. But God saw potential in Gideon. In Judges 6:12, Gideon is greeted as *valiant warrior*. This isn't because of anything special about Gideon himself, but the potential that he had to be a great warrior when he let God have control of his life and followed God's commands.

## Quotable Quotes

*Faith grows only in the dark. You've got to trust Him where you can't trace Him. That's faith. You just take Him at His Word, believe Him, and grip the nail-scarred hand a little tighter. And faith grows.*—Lyell Rader

*Faith is like a toothbrush. Every man should have one and use it regularly, but he shouldn't try to use someone else's.*—J. G. Stipe

## Service Options

As a way to connect your students with other generations, let them write letters or make small gifts of thanks (i.e. bookmarks, journals, etc.) for people in your church who have served in the Armed Forces. Gifts can also be distributed to local VA hospitals or care facilities.

## Something Else

Big Idea Productions, the makers of "VeggieTales" has a video called, *Gideon the Tuba Warrior* that is a cute retelling of the Gideon story. Kids and adults alike enjoy "Veggie-Tales," and viewing this video may provide a different take on the story while providing a few laughs along the way.

# Don't Forget the Junior Highers!

*By James W. Mohler, Ph.D.*

The mere thought of junior high students causes some to break into a sweat. Those of us who actually like working with these students are considered saints by those in the church who don't understand them. Yet, junior high ministry may be the *most strategic* ministry in the church!

Junior high ministry looks very different in various churches. But those that don't understand the uniqueness of this important ministry tend to make one of two major mistakes: 1) they tend to make junior high a part of the children's ministry, and simply upgrade the children's program to reflect older children; or 2) they will combine the junior high ministry with the senior high ministry, or simply offer a senior high ministry "lite" for the junior highers. Both of these approaches neglect the unique opportunities for junior high ministry.

Junior high students are at an important time of change in their lives as they enter that wonderful and scary time of life known as *puberty*. Someone once said that puberty is when God turns a perfectly normal child into Silly Putty. *Everything* changes about them. The most obvious changes are the physical ones, but they also greatly change in how they think, how they experience emotions, and how they process their moral values.

The process of thinking changes from concrete thought to the beginning of abstract thought. Suddenly young teens are able to look in a mirror and notice themselves in new ways. Boys in elementary school don't care about bathing, combing their hair, or how they dress. Often they don't even notice the mirror in the bathroom. Yet, sometime in late elementary to junior high school they begin to notice new odors emanating from their bodies, and they begin to take *at least* one shower every day. They stop and notice their hair, and spend several minutes getting just the right look. Girls begin this process a bit earlier than the boys, but it is no less dramatic in it's nature. Both girls and boys begin to notice themselves and be concerned about what others think. Looking in the mirror becomes a required daily ritual. They start to look forward to receiving clothes for Christmas. Their self-esteem begins to depend more on how they think others perceive them than simply on their own achievements.

As their thinking skills begin to develop, young teens are able to begin to process their faith in new ways as well. As children, they believe most everything a trusted adult tells them. But now they begin to ask more questions, and begin to try to figure out how their faith is different from others around them. They try to figure out *how* what they believe fits in with their peers. It is a great opportunity to assist students to learn to ask the right questions, where to go to find good answers, and to discover what faith can mean in their lives.

Relationships also change in junior high. The child-parent relationship often goes through a rather dramatic change, one that startles many parents. Younger children see their parents as adults who know about or can do almost anything. But a junior high student's parent often doesn't know much at all! Younger children like to have their parents around, but early adolescent students often feel embarrassed when parents are present around their friends. This natural maturing process takes place because of the change in cognitive thinking structures.

These young adolescent students also make friends for different reasons than when they were younger. Children often have a few good friends based upon similar interests (sports) or because they are in the same classroom at school. Junior high students begin to develop new and multiple friendships, and not always with people one would expect. Often, as a young person *tries on* several personalities to figure out their own sense of self, they will develop some friendships that might not be the most beneficial. Junior high is an important time to assist students in understanding how friendships impact their lives and their faith.

When we approach junior high ministry as an advanced part of a children's ministry, we miss the distinctiveness of puberty as it begins. This is not to say the children's ministries are unimportant. They are *very* important. But they are usually not designed for the changes a junior high student is experiencing. In addition, it is always tempting for those in charge of a children's ministry to include the junior highers as a part of the larger group of children. Junior highers want to be treated as young men and women, desiring that separation from the younger kids.

On the other end, doing junior high ministry as a scaled-back senior high ministry is equally challenging. It assumes that the young teen is ready to attack the world with a maturity that many of them do not yet have. Many high school teens have figured out what they like to do . . . most junior high teens are beginning to explore what they like to do. Junior high kids need more structure than high schoolers, and need more choices provided to them.

Young teens enter puberty at various times, and basically it is unpredictable. Some girls begin puberty as young as age nine or ten. Some boys don't begin puberty until as late as age sixteen. Thus junior high groups have the unique challenge of trying to minister to some young teens who still act like children, and others who are as mature as some college students. This variety in maturity forces us to see ministry to this unique age group as vital to the success of reaching students with the gospel before they reach adulthood.

One more thing: My experiences with junior high kids are that they are, like Silly Putty, still very moldable. During this transition in their lives, young teens are looking for adults outside of their homes who will truly care for them. They want to be challenged, to have growing opportunities to experience life, and to learn to serve. They want to have crazy fun, but they also want others to acknowledge that growing up is actually happening.

Early adolescence may be the most important time for youth ministry. It is at the time when young people experience the greatest level of change outside of infancy. It is a time when young people make choices that will affect them for the rest of their lives. In youth ministry, we must acknowledge this uniqueness and prepare to minister to, and with, them in ways that can acknowledge the tremendous changes occurring in their lives, helping them transition from childhood to the challenging waters of adolescence. Don't neglect this important ministry!

# Gatekeepers: All That You Do, Do for God

*By Rick Bennett*

In this lesson, students will:
- ✔ Know what the gatekeepers did and why it was important to the people of Israel (and more importantly, to God).
- ✔ Be able to name things they do that seem mundane or inconsequential and discuss how they are important to God and others.
- ✔ Walk away with a sense that everything they do is an act of worship.

Stuff you'll need:
- ❑ Note cards (two for each student)
- ❑ Pens or pencils
- ❑ A box or hat for note cards
- ❑ Chalkboard or butcher paper
- ❑ Postcards or Thank You cards for each student
- ❑ Heart-shaped piece of paper or construction paper for Memory Verse

## Memory Verse

Whatever you do, work at it with all your heart, as working for the Lord, not for men.
—Colossians 3:23 NIV

## Scripture

1 Chronicles 9:17–34; Colossians 3:23

## Lesson in a Sentence

Because God has a purpose for everything we do, we must have a good attitude toward work, no matter how mundane it seems, because it is one way we worship God.

## The Big Picture

The gatekeepers of Jerusalem were chosen by God for this task. While this job was not one of prestige, it was so important to God and His people, that we are given the details of their jobs in the book of 1 Chronicles. Gatekeeping was difficult and not very rewarding financially, however, it was necessary in order for temple worship to be carried on. In our churches today, we need people to preach sermons, teach classes, usher, clean the church, and mow the grass. All of these tasks are important in order for worship in the church to be effective. We must take seriously whatever task we are called to do, because our work is another way of worshiping God.

# Focus

Give each student two blank note cards. Ask the students to take the first note card and write on it a job that does not seem important to them (it can be a job title or a task). Then ask each person to take the second note card and write down something they have to do (ask them to mention something beyond basic chores or homework) that seems mundane or inconsequential.

Put the note cards in a hat or box and shake it up. Ask for a discussion of two or three things that were written on the cards and why they feel these jobs or tasks are not important (tell the students you will come back to the note cards later).

Note: If you are working with middle school students or those who may not focus on their own note cards, it is possible to use a chalkboard or butcher paper and have a brainstorming session about jobs that seem inconsequential and things the students must do that are inconsequential. You may find it helpful to allow them to discuss homework and household chores if they have a hard time coming up with other ideas.

# Discovery

Read the story of the gatekeepers in 1 Chronicles 9:17–34 (also read 9:1–3 for context). Be careful with whom you choose to read verses 17–21. (There are some names which are hard to pronounce and some students could be embarrassed by this.)

After an initial reading, ask someone to go to the chalkboard or butcher paper. Look closely at verses 22–33 and write down the details of the Scripture.

Focus first on the tent (gates, directions, rooms, etc.). Draw a diagram of the tent as students tell you the details they see in the Scripture.

Then focus on the duties or responsibilities. Write down the names of those listed and what their job descriptions are. Now write the others (not listed by name) and their duties.

Discuss which of these duties seem important to the students and which ones seem mundane or unimportant. Brainstorm why each of these tasks or duties is important (you will want to do some further study in order to know some of these details).

Now discuss some of the less than glamorous duties that are needed in your local church and tell why they are important.

Finally, read Colossians 3:23. Ask students how this verse fits in with the previous passage. Ask students to discuss how it changes the work done by the gatekeepers and people in your local church when seen as "working for God, not men."

## Life Application

Come back to the note cards. Shake up the box once more and ask each student to pick out one card. Have them read the card to the rest of the group. Ask each student to tell how that job or task (preferably a job someone else wrote down) is important to others or to God (big picture). If a student seems stumped, use this time for brainstorming regarding the task. Allow discussion for each topic. If you have a small group, there may be time to go through each card in the hat.

Make sure this question is asked when discussing each note card: "How does this job, task, or duty change with a change in perspective, from work for others, to work for God?"

## Making It Personal

Gather the note cards once more and redistribute them so that each student gets his or her card back. Ask each student to consider the job or task they saw as inconsequential. Encourage the students to take time this week to thank a person doing a mundane job, for his service to others and God.

Ask the students to write their commitment on the back of the note card. If time permits, hand out blank postcards or thank you cards to each student. In teams or individually, ask students to write thank you cards to people they know who have mundane jobs. Ask the students to mention in their cards some of the things they learned tonight. Please go over cards with students to make sure they are appropriate and affirming.

If they feel frustrated about their jobs or duties during this week, ask the students to remember the verse they learned and thank God for the opportunity to work for Him.

### TEACHER'S NOTE:

Feel free to look at commentaries or study Bibles for more information on the gatekeepers. Here are some basic notes from the *NIV Study Bible* and other commentaries regarding the gatekeepers:

1. The gatekeepers were responsible for the security of the House of God (temple). These gatekeepers do not have the responsibility of protecting the city.
2. The chief gatekeeper was responsible for keeping the gate used by the King.
3. Twenty-four guard stations were manned in three shifts during the day (similar to shift work done by police officers in many cities today). Seventy-two men were needed each week. With a total of 212 men, each would be needed every third week.
4. The Levites were responsible for the temple precincts, opening the gate each morning, closing it at night, along with chambers and supply rooms. They also prepared baked goods (Ex. 25:30).
5. One of the responsibilities of the gatekeepers was to keep those deemed unclean from entering.

## Connections

Paul sees everything we do as an act of worship, including eating and drinking. He believes it is our attitude that must change. This is discussed in 1 Corinthians 10:31 and Romans 12:1 during the Midweek session.

## Song Connect

"Meant to Live" by Switchfoot

"(Everything I Do) I Do It for You" by Bryan Adams

## Memory Verse Activity

This is a simple verse to memorize. Give each student a heart-shaped piece of paper (or let them cut it out). Ask each student to write the Memory Verse on the card and place it where they will be able to see it during the week while doing those things they feel are mundane.

Ask students to take out the card and thank God for the opportunity to work for Him during the week.

## Ancient Practices

Throughout church history, Christians have sought to redeem the mundane tasks of life and see them as spiritual acts of worship (Rom. 12:1). One practice used by many ancient church leaders, including the Celtic Church was prayers for all tasks. Celtic prayers have been found for Christians to speak during tasks such as milking a cow, making butter, walking, herding cattle, fishing, harvesting crops, and kindling a fire.

Here is an example of a prayer of blessing for the kindling of fire. Feel free to read it aloud to your students.

*I will kindle my fire this morning*
*In presence of the holy angels of heaven,*
*God, kindle thou in my heart within*
*A flame of love to my neighbor,*
*To my foe, to my friend, to my kindred all,*
*To the brave, to the knave, to the thrall.*

*Without malice, without jealousy, without envy,*
*Without fear, without terror of any one under the sun*
*But the Holy Son of God to shield me.*

# Gatekeepers: All That You Do, Do for God

*By Rick Bennett*

## Memory Verse

Whatever you do, work at it with all your heart, as working for the Lord, not for men.
—Colossians 3:23 NIV

## Scripture

1 Corinthians 10:31; Romans 12:1

## Lesson in a Sentence

Whatever we do, we must consider it an act of worship and respond accordingly.

# Focus

On a chalkboard or butcher paper, write these categories.

*Act of Worship*

*Not an Act of Worship*

*Maybe an Act of Worship*

Now ask students to brainstorm activities, duties, jobs (pretty much anything), and list what they say under each category. Ask them pointed questions and allow them to discuss what makes any topic go into a specific category.

After completion of the brainstorming session, erase the second and third categories. Replace each with *Act of Worship*.

Read this definition of worship.

The word *worship* simply means "to ascribe worth or value to something." Everything we do ascribes worth to something. The question then becomes, what does it ascribe worth to? God or something else?

# Discovery

Read the Memory Verse and the Scriptures. Ask students to notice what Paul is speaking about in the Corinthians passage (hint: eating). Ask students if they consider eating to be an act of worship? Why or why not? Did Paul consider it an act of worship? Why?

Allow them to come up with an answer on their own.

Now go back to the list and discuss why each thing on the list is an act of worship. Ask students how they should change their behaviors in each action if it is an act of worship. How does looking at work or homework as an act of worship change how you approach it? How does this change what we eat and how we eat? How does this affect everything?

## Application

Ask students to come up with simple prayers of praise and thanksgiving for each action they have to do during the week, including chores, homework, etc.

Encourage the students to write down at least one of these prayers and commit to saying it during the next week.

## Extra! Extra!

You may have heard the story of Brother Lawrence, so-called author of *Practice of the Presence of God*. He was a simple cook in a French monastery in the seventeenth century. Monks, visitors, and others noticed that throughout his career, he spoke very little and complained none regarding his menial tasks. He turned everything into a spiritual act of worship, no matter how unimportant the duty seemed to others. He knew he was doing everything for God's glory and responded accordingly.

He understood and shared that what we do is not what matters, but how we do it that matters (our attitude). His story of simply following Jesus in all actions, no matter how small, led to the writing of one of the classics of Christian literature.

## Quotable Quotes

*I am a little pencil in the hand of a writing God who is sending a love letter to the world.*
—Mother Teresa (1982)

*When I am operating, I feel the presence of God so real that I cannot tell where His skill ends and mine begins.*—Attributed to a famous surgeon

# Coaching for Life

By *Whitney Prosperi*

In this lesson, students will:
- ✔ Learn the biblical principles of mentoring.
- ✔ Study two examples of mentoring from the Bible.
- ✔ Identify someone they can personally mentor.
- ✔ Identify an older Christian who can mentor them.

Stuff you'll need:
- ❑ Construction paper
- ❑ Markers
- ❑ A piece of paper for each student
- ❑ Pens

## Memory Verse

Don't let anyone look down on you because you are young, but set an example for the believers in speech, in life, in love, in faith and in purity.—1 Timothy 4:12 NIV

## Scripture

Titus 2:3–5

## Lesson in a Sentence

We should constantly invest in younger people's lives while finding older believers to invest in our own lives.

## The Big Picture

We each have the opportunity to make a difference in the lives of the people we know. You may not realize it but there are younger people who look up to you. Do you take the opportunities you have to help them know and understand Jesus better? What you say can make a huge difference. How you act can influence the choices they make in their own lives. Do you take time to reach out to those younger than you so that you can help them?

Just as we should seek out those younger than us, we should also find those who are older than us who have a close relationship with Jesus so they can help us grow. Do you have people like this in your life? If not, find someone who will be a coach to you in your faith. This person will make a huge difference in your Christian walk.

# Focus

Ask students to remember the different coaches they have had over the course of their lives. They don't have to be sports coaches. They can describe coaches of any kind, including those people who helped them with a school subject, after school activity, or develop a particular skill. Divide students into groups of three and have them list the characteristics of good coaches on big pieces of construction paper. After the groups finish, let them come back together and ask groups to share the qualities they listed. Next, vote as a group to determine the top three characteristics of a good coach.

# Discovery

Ask who can explain the meaning of mentor. Once you have someone willing to share, write the definition in a place where all can see it. Now ask students to think of examples of mentors in the Bible. Give them a chance to explain their answers.

Read Titus 2:3–5.

- Why is it so important for the older generation to live according to God's Word?
- In what ways do the older generations affect those who are younger?
- What is the potential for good effects? For bad effects?
- In what ways have you been trained by a mentor?
- How is a mentor a type of life coach?

Remember a time when you were taught by a mentor and share this with the students. Preferably, share a story from when you were younger. Explain the ways that this mentor changed you—attitudes or actions. Make sure you focus on the fact that this was just an ordinary person with a desire to help you.

Has anyone ever helped you in a mentoring type role? If so, what did they do and how were you changed?

You may want to give students some ideas as they think about their answers. Maybe it was a teacher, youth minister, older friend, or family member.

Now you'll want to give students some principles for finding an appropriate mentor. Ask them to list some and then add others they don't list.

- The same gender as they are.
- Older and more mature in the faith.
- Someone who lives life according to God's principles.
- A person who is willing to spend time coaching you.

Now look back over the list of requirements for a good mentor and ask students to explain reasons why each of these characteristics is necessary.

Next ask one student to read 1 Timothy 1:1–2. Explain the mentor, or coaching, relationship that Paul and Timothy shared.

Describe what you think Paul must have been like? (Encourage students to share even though they do not know for sure what he was like.)

- What do you think Timothy was like?
- What benefit did Timothy gain from this relationship? How about Paul?

## Teacher's Note:

In the discussion about mentors and life coaches, some students may talk about their parents and how they have helped guide their faith. Encourage the students to talk about their experience but also remember that not all students will share. Be sensitive to the differing backgrounds of the students in your group.

## Life Application

Ask students to think of several people they know who might serve as a mentor to them. Now ask them to list these people on a sheet of paper. Encourage students to pray over this list asking God to give them wisdom as to whether they should ask any of these people to serve as their mentor.

## Making It Personal

We can choose to make a profound difference in the lives of those younger than us. Ask students to list two people they can choose to influence who are younger than they are. Give them some ideas as they are thinking about their two people. They may decide to invest in a younger neighbor, student from church or even a brother, sister, or cousin. After they have decided on two people, give the students some practical ideas on how they can make a difference in the young persons' lives. (They may need some more time to think about their two people and that is perfectly fine. They can think about it at home.) You may suggest they meet with that younger person for a common activity, talk on the phone, send them e-mails, or encouraging notes. Encourage your students to let God guide them in their creativity as they invest in this other person's life.

## Memory Verse Activity

### Memory Verse Idol

Divide students into groups of four and ask them to write a song or rap that has the words of the Memory Verse in it. Ask them to perform their creation in front of the group. Give an award to the group with the most creative or catchy tune.

## Connections

Have the students brainstorm about different coaching/mentoring relationships found in the Bible. Give them some time to find the passages to support their answers and ask them to share with the larger group.

## Service Options

Is there a need in the children's ministry at your church? If so, talk to the person in charge if that area and ask them how your students can help meet that need. They may get the opportunity to help out with childcare. (If so, you'll want to make sure that students go through the appropriate channels such as background checks and training.) Maybe there is an opportunity for them to serve as referees at children's sporting events put on by the church. Maybe your students could teach a backyard Bible club for children in a nearby neighborhood. If you give your students the opportunity to serve children younger than themselves, they will learn the enjoyment and satisfaction in helping and reaching out.

# Coaching for Life

*By Whitney Prosperi*

## Memory Verse
Don't let anyone look down on you because you are young, but set an example for the believers in speech, in life, in love, in faith and in purity.—1 Timothy 4:12 NIV

## Scripture
Ruth 1:16

## Lesson in a Sentence
We should constantly invest in younger people's lives while finding older believers to invest in our own lives.

# Focus

Ask students to pair up with a partner. Now let them rehearse a conversation with an older person where they ask the person if he or she would be willing to serve as their mentor. One student is to play the older person and the other is the student seeking a coach or mentor. After one student gets to practice, let the other student take a turn.

# Discovery

Assign a student to read Ruth 1:16. Ask the following questions:

- Does anyone know the background of Ruth and Naomi's relationship?
- Describe the circumstances they found themselves in.
- Being aware of the culture of that time, why do you think this was extremely hard for them?
- What promise did Ruth make to her mother-in-law?
- What impact do you think this made on Ruth? Naomi?

## Application
Divide students into groups of three. Ask students to think of all of the benefits that come from a mentoring relationship—for both people involved. Now ask them to determine the most important benefits.

Challenge students to look for opportunities to invest in younger people's lives. Ask them to pray that God would open their eyes for ways to meet people they can mentor—and also those who can mentor them. Let them know they don't have to be especially talented or outgoing. Instead all they have to do is be available to get involved in someone else's life.

## Teacher's Note:

A student may ask that you mentor him or her. If you have time to commit and if you think it is an appropriate fit, go for it! If not, be prepared to point the student to someone that you think would be willing. You may even want to talk to some adult leaders ahead of time and ask them if they would be willing to mentor some of these students. If they are willing, be ready with their names, phone numbers, and e-mail addresses so students can easily contact them.

## Connections

Mentors are found throughout the Bible. Jesus modeled the mentoring ministry in that He poured into the lives of twelve who later poured into many others. Today His message is spread across the globe because of those twelve followers. Second Kings 2:1–2 tells about Elijah and Elisha who also followed the mentor/mentored pattern. If you have time, explore some of the other mentor models that are found in Scripture.

# Defending the Defenseless

## Jehosheba: Standing Up for Those Who Cannot Stand Up for Themselves

*By Sharon Koh*

In this lesson, students will:
- ✔ Learn to recognize situations in their lives when someone is being oppressed.
- ✔ Gain courage to do something about those situations when they present themselves.

Stuff you'll need:
- ❏ Active imaginations and skit-writing abilities

## Memory Verse

Blessed are the poor in spirit, for theirs is the kingdom of heaven. Blessed are those who mourn, for they will be comforted. Blessed are the meek, for they will inherit the earth. Blessed are those who hunger and thirst for righteousness, for they will be filled. Blessed are the merciful, for they will be shown mercy.—Matthew 5:3–7 NIV

## Scripture

2 Chronicles 22:10–12

## Lesson in a Sentence

God blesses those who show mercy and stand up for others who cannot stand up for themselves.

## The Big Picture

In life, there are times when people are being bullied, oppressed, molested, or emotionally beaten down. We are not the person responsible for these hardships being placed on others, but if we are witness to the situation, we should not turn a blind eye or walk away to keep from getting involved. God expects us to have courage and boldness to stand up and protect our fellow brother or sister. We should always demonstrate the love of God and look for ways to help others, especially in their times of need.

# Focus

Divide students into three groups. Each group will be responsible for putting together a skit to be presented to the other two groups.

Group 1: Based on 2 Chronicles 21:1—24:15, put together a skit that shows the sequence of events in this section. Be sure to include the following characters: Jehoshaphat, Jehoram, Ahaziah, Athaliah, Joash, Jehosheba, and Jehoiada. (Feel free to include as many other characters as you feel are necessary.)

Group 2: Based on a modern day scenario in the local high school, put together a skit in which someone is being bullied or threatened into doing something they do not want to do. In this skit, show the tragedy of what happened when nobody stood up for the person being bullied.

Group 3: Based on a modern day shopping mall or supermarket scenario, put together a skit in which someone is being oppressed. In this skit, show the beauty of what happens when someone stands up for the person being oppressed or picked on.

# Discovery

Read 2 Chronicles 22:10–12.

1. Who is Jehosheba? Daughter of whom? Wife of whom?
2. How is she related to Joash?
3. Who is Athaliah? What evil deed did she try to do? Why?
4. Jehosheba and her husband Jehoiada, preserved Joash's life and hid him from harm in the temple when he was just a year old. Joash later became king (at seven years old!), and during his reign, he was able to do many good things in the temple. What were these things (2 Chr. 24:1–16)?

## Life Application

Allow students to reflect on their day-to-day, week-to-week lives. Ask them if they are ever in situations where they see a need to stand up for someone. Ask them to describe these situations. If students are willing to talk about it, ask them to share how they responded to the situation. Then, ask the group to consider other ways they could have responded to the situation—more positively? More negatively?

## TEACHER'S NOTE:

If students are curious to read about other things that took place in King Joash's life, direct them to 2 Chronicles 24:17–27. He did not live a perfectly good life. In fact, the latter part of his life was less than ideal, particularly in regards to his treatment of Jehoiada's son. This is the complexity of human nature. No one person is entirely good or entirely evil, but capable of many things, and very much in need of God's grace and mercy. This is not the focus of today's lesson, but nevertheless, it does come up in the context of this story in Scripture.

# Just as Guilty

*By Sharon Koh*

## Memory Verse

Blessed are the pure in heart, for they will see God. Blessed are the peacemakers, for they will be called sons of God. Blessed are those who are persecuted because of righteousness, for theirs is the kingdom of heaven. Blessed are you when people insult you, persecute you and falsely say all kinds of evil against you because of me. Rejoice and be glad, because great is your reward in heaven, for in the same way they persecuted the prophets who were before you.—Matthew 5:8–12 NIV

## Scripture

Obadiah (entire book, especially verse 11)

## Lesson in a Sentence

Standing aloof is just as bad as participating in the crime.

## The Big Picture

In the book of Obadiah, God condemns Edom (Esau's descendants) for "standing aloof" while violence took place against his brother, Jacob (Israel and the descendants of Israel). God says that "you were like" one of the strangers who came and devastated Jacob's land (with its capital in Jerusalem) because they stood by and did nothing to stop the devastation.

# Focus

We as Christians are taught that we are to love one another as God loves us. In doing so, we should always be alert to situations where we might show the love of God to someone who is being abused, bullied, or any other form of oppression, by standing up for them.

# Discovery

Read the book of Obadiah. Pay careful attention to verse 11. What is God indicting Edom for doing? Why?

## Making It Personal

Ask students to reflect on situations in their lives when they saw someone being picked on and they did nothing about it. Have them consider what they would do if they could go back and change history. How could they respond differently? How would they respond differently?

# Fearless Faith

*By Amy Jacober*

---

In this lesson, students will:

- ✔ Learn that trusting in God's plans will bring about success in life.
- ✔ See what happens when faith is abandoned.
- ✔ Compare their personal goals with goals set by God.
- ✔ Be shown that following the crowd isn't always the best course of action.

Stuff you'll need:

- ❏ Paper and pens
- ❏ Items for an obstacle course
- ❏ Inexpensive prizes for games

---

## Memory Verse

Many are the plans in a man's heart, but it is the LORD's purpose that prevails.
—Proverbs 19:21 NIV

## Scripture

Numbers 14:6–9

## Lesson in a Sentence

Trusting God allows us to experience the best that God has for us, even when other people only see the impossible.

## The Big Picture

Trusting God is about exercising faith and choosing the best no matter the circumstances or popular opinion.

# Focus

## Option 1

Focusing on goal setting, ask your students the following question: "If you make a list of goals for your life five years, ten years, twenty years from now, what would you write down? College, job/salary, marriage, children, house, cars, office, power/prestige? Don't forget character goals such as integrity, love, joy, peace, faithfulness, and compassion."

Next get them thinking about God's goals for their lives by asking, "What if you could somehow see God's list of goals for you five years, ten years, twenty years from now? Which do you think would be the best for you? Why?"

# Option 2

Try one of those blindfolded obstacle courses where one student is blindfolded and has a guide who can only *speak* directions; they can't be led by holding hands. Then, let everyone else yell out directions trying to distract the follower. Design the course so they have to walk around the room, inside and outside of chairs, around plants and tables, etc. Discuss the difference in trusting the guide's voice, who wanted to help you get through the obstacles, as opposed to the other loud voices that wanted you to fail in your efforts.

# Discovery

The response of the Israelites to the report from the spies of a *problem* in the Promised Land was countered by Joshua and Caleb's report and their faith. Joshua and Caleb had been a part of the same group of spies and had seen the same land, fruit, and people. So, what was the difference in the points of view?

First, the spies saw the great opportunity but feared the giant people. Caleb and Joshua saw the same inhabitants and yet had a greater faith in God. The ten spies' perspective sounds crazy once you remember where and what the Israelites had been through on their journey from Egypt. Think about all they had experienced and witnessed. They had seen the most powerful army of their time defeated by God in the Red Sea. They had been following God's presence in the form of fire during the night and a cloud by day. Furthermore, they had the manna and quail miraculously appear to sustain them when they had nothing. Now they stand on the border of the Promised Land and are scared to go in?

Fear has a way of immobilizing us and shaking the heart of our faith. The spies saw the incredible goodness of the land but were overwhelmed by the thought of how they would possess it. Instead of trusting God, their thoughts distorted how they saw themselves: "We seemed like grasshoppers in *our own* eyes." Fear works that way. It affects the mind in such powerful ways that reality becomes blurred and history becomes insignificant. After hearing the report, the people were influenced the same way they had wept and grumbled. As a result, they really believed it would be better to go back and die in Egypt! Yet, God had rescued them and promised them life.

Joshua and Caleb must have been amazed at the quick reversal of divine momentum. They tore their clothes, which was a sign of mourning and grief. Then they exhorted the people to see God at work. Clearly their perspective was grounded in God's promise. In the end, the doubt of the people affected their ability to hear from God, and Joshua and Caleb were heartbroken. Both of them had seen in the land how God desired to bless the Israelites. Now poised on the border, the long-held promise had the potential to be fulfilled. Caleb and Joshua's response was based in faith; faith in God and His Word so they would move to take action.

Faith also causes you to see circumstances differently. When the ten saw themselves as insects, Joshua and Caleb had a vision of something different. Why? Because they knew what God could do and believed He would do it for the Israelites if they would have faith. While the spies could only see the impending doom of the present, Caleb and Joshua acknowledged it but saw beyond the present to the future and what God was going to do. Caleb voices it this way, "We will swallow them up . . . eat them like bread . . . their protection is gone . . . God is with us." How easy is that? Eating bread! Most bread cannot resist your teeth, unless it is day-old bread from the school cafeteria, right? Not once in the report from the doubting spies is God or His plan mentioned.

Another result of the scouts' report was the "follow the crowd mentality." The Israelites were easily swayed by the ten spies. There is a lot to consider when you are making life's important decisions. Consider who is speaking, their integrity, what you know of their spiritual life, etc. Caleb and Joshua are the only ones who were mentioned by name of the twelve who went into the land. Joshua had been by the side of Moses in many situations and don't forget the times in the Tent of Meeting (Ex. 33:7–11). Caleb is with Joshua and that shows his wisdom. (You can find the commentary on Caleb's life in Numbers 14:24; 32:12; Deuteronomy 1:36; and Joshua 14:14 NIV.) The people follow the ten and murmur against their leaders, Moses and Aaron, but Caleb doesn't seem to doubt in spite of the giants or popular opinion. He completely trusts that God will lead them and He will make a way for them to possess the land He promised. The Scripture says the night after the report, the people wept, indicating that the complaining spread quickly so that the whole group sided with the ten spies. That kind of negativity led them to want to go back to Egypt! They didn't even want to try to see the great land, the land flowing with milk and honey. Those resources indicate the land's richness of life in part because in the harvest of both honey and milk nothing is killed; they are totally renewable! Still the people didn't see it and their display of rebellion was ultimately a display of ingratitude toward God.

Caleb and Joshua exhort the people not to rebel or be afraid. It is bad to be afraid of a human enemy but rebelling against God and His plans is much worse. Our culture continually sends so many messages at us. It is easy to get caught up in what everyone is doing, wearing, or saying. Popular opinion confuses the real identity of the enemy at times. The people and rebellious spies turned against God's appointed leader, Moses. Be sure you can clearly define the enemy and then trust what God can do. They missed the fact that Moses, Aaron, Caleb, and Joshua were on their side but instead they wanted to choose a new leader.

Think about your present circumstance; your parents, teachers, and pastors can be helpful leaders in life's tough decisions. It is usually the voices of the few that we need to listen to, especially those that are reminding us of God and His promises. Don't let circumstances or faithless friends determine your response to God's promise. It is wise to slow down, consider several viewpoints, and get some advice before you determine your actions. Check to see what God's Word says and consider a spiritual perspective. When you do, you'll be pleasing God and then you'll experience a part of life that is incredible (Ps. 37:4).

Finally, hope has to be a counterpart of fear and faithlessness. Seeing the future and having hope is critical to life. Hope in God's plan gave Caleb and Joshua motivation to take the land. Hope that God is for us wakes us up every morning. Hope is the anchor for our soul (Heb. 6:19). What do you hope happens?

# My Plans, God's Plans . . .

*By Amy Jacober*

## Memory Verse

Many are the plans in a man's heart, but it is the LORD's purpose that prevails.
—Proverbs 19:21 NIV

## Scripture

Acts 16:6–10; 16–34; Philippians 1:3–4

## Lesson in a Sentence

When our plans don't work out the way we want, our tendency might be to complain and miss God's plans because we are disappointed. Watch for God at work in all of life's situations, good and bad, because there can be something eternal that you would miss.

## The Big Picture

Don't stop and pout when you don't get your way. Believe that God is in control and has something better in mind.

## Focus

Play any game that provides some light competition such as a race, trivia, or something with points. Tell the students you have a small prize for the winner but instead, award it to someone who didn't finish first or score the most points. You are trying to illustrate how our assumptions or expectations are not always met.

## Discovery

A quick read through the book of Philippians finds Paul almost giddy with joy at all that is happening in his life and the life of the Philippian church. But looking back at Paul's life and travels at the time of writing, he is in jail. Add to that the fact that he would have never made it to Philippi because it was not originally a part of Paul's plan.

Read Acts 16:6–10.

Paul kept trying to go to Asia. His plan was to spread the gospel to the people of that land. I believe one would say that spreading the gospel is a *good* plan. However, God had a different plan and it was revealed in a night vision calling Paul in another direction, to Macedonia. According to verse 7, this change in direction was clear to Paul and Luke since the Spirit would not allow them to enter Asia. Thankfully Paul was not as stubborn as I am when there is something I want. Paul and his group waited in the city. They kept doing what they knew was right, and then God showed them the next step.

Read Acts 16:16–24.

Almost as soon as they get to the city, Paul experiences some success through several conversions of key people. That quickly changes, however. He and Silas are beaten severely and put in jail! Talk about uncomfortable. Is that a part of God's plan? Yes, it seems so. At this point I think I would seriously question God's will. But in jail, locked up with other criminals, they start singing. Then, God shows up and shakes the doors open and the chains off. That is pretty good confirmation of God's plans, don't you think? Ultimately, in verse 29 the jailer wants to be saved and includes his whole family!

If not for this brief time in Philippi, the church probably wouldn't have been birthed there. And, if you think back to Paul's turning from Asia and going into Macedonia, history would be much different, too. Many Bible scholars believe that if Paul had continued to Asia, Christianity would not have spread to America.

In the first lesson about Joshua and Caleb, the Israelites chose not to follow God's leading into the Promised Land. The people of Israel end up spending forty years in the desert before getting another chance to enjoy God's plan. Here Paul's obedience leads him to some short, painful suffering, but his life impacted history.

Now, as you read Philippians 1:3–4, Paul writes that he is thankful *every time* he thinks of the Philippians and that he also prays with *joy* as he remembers his time in the city. Paul had spent about as much time in jail as he did walking around. It had been painful but fruitful. On the other side of God's plans, there is gratitude and joy. I don't think that is always true about following only the plans of man. Often there are regrets and mistakes that accompany stubbornness in the heart. So, Christians must keep their relationships with Jesus so fresh and alive that it is possible to hear His voice, to follow His lead and discern the best.

# Extra! Extra!
Read Psalm 33:11.

- In what ways do you see God's plans standing firm in your life? Name some that have stood forever?
- What do you/will you tell those around you and those who come after you about God's plans?

Read Proverbs 16:3.

- Committing to the Lord shows total dependence. Is this true about your life?
- Is it God's approval that we strive for, or do our plans slowly change to mirror His? Looking for God's approval might leave you working and wondering, whereas doing what is on God's heart will ultimately result in success.
- If God is committed to you, why do you still worry?

Read Proverbs 16:9.

- Contrast what people plan against what really happens?
- What role do motives play in your plans?

Read Matthew 6:33.

- Living for and under God's rule, according to the way His kingdom functions, changes things. What are some of those?
- What things of the world do you want if you are living for God's kingdom?
- How can we continually show that we are seeking first His kingdom if we have some of those things?

# Being a Peacemaker

*By Amy Jacober*

## In this lesson, students will:
- ✔ Understand that God believes they can make a change.
- ✔ Identify places of injustice or inequality.
- ✔ Learn how God worked through others in the past.
- ✔ Be encouraged to consider their part in injustices in the world.

## Stuff you'll need:
- ❏ *Blood Diamond* DVD
- ❏ Newspapers
- ❏ News magazines
- ❏ Tape

## Memory Verse
Be anxious for nothing, but in everything by prayer and supplication, with thanksgiving, let your requests be made known to God; and the peace of God, which surpasses all understanding, will guard your hearts and minds through Jesus Christ.
—Philippians 4:6–7

## Scripture
1 Samuel 25:1–42

## Lesson in a Sentence
Being a peacemaker takes courage and risk.

## The Big Picture
Peace is a big topic in our world today. Regardless of where your group and leaders are politically, we can agree that God calls us to be risk takers for peace. God may be calling for peace in your home, your neighborhood, between friends at school, or even in your church. In this lesson, we meet Abigail who was willing to lay down her own life to prevent a conflict that would have left many dead. While our call to obedience may not be this extreme, we are called to seek reconciliation to the best of our ability. This may include standing up for those who have no voice, or choosing not to retaliate when we could easily do so. Peace is God's desire in spite of the sinful, broken world we know today.

# Focus

## Option 1

Show a clip from *Blood Diamond*. There are several scenes depicting helping others at great risk to oneself. While much of the movie walks through the journey of a man motivated by greed and self-interest, there are moments of redemption and it is ultimately his actions that lead to change. Remember, this is a fiction movie based on real situations. Do not take what is depicted as reality but the principles do transfer. There are also many graphic scenes in this film. Be certain the one you choose is suitable for your group.

As an optional activity, consider hosting a movie night where you rent this film and watch it in its entirety with your whole group. The points of discussion are many, including God's provision for the poor, those with power taking advantage, how every day someone wants to enslave others, and how God can use the most unlikely of sources to bring redemption.

## Option 2

This one is really funny and actually proves the opposite of what you want for tonight. It is the straight-legged race. God may believe we can do all kinds of things (and we can) but there are some things that are just not biologically possible.

Tell your students that you are going to have a race. This doesn't need to be very far but at least fifteen strides of a normal run. Line all your students up on one side and point out the finish line at least fifteen yards away. Before the race begins, set the rules. Each person may race but they must keep their arms stuck at their sides and they may not bend their knees. The first few steps are easy but after that, it all falls apart. It feels weird and is even funnier to watch. If you don't believe this, try it on your own before your students arrive!

# Discovery

This story can seem a bit long for the language in conversations and speeches. To help move your students along, offer a short play straight from Scripture. If you have a creative edge, change the language to match phrases your students might use. Once they have seen this story, invite your students to turn to 1 Samuel 25:1–42 to read it on their own.

| | |
|---|---|
| NABAL | MESSENGER #2 |
| ABIGAIL | NARRATOR |
| DAVID | SERVANT |
| MESSENGER #1 | |

NARRATOR: David, you know, that redheaded future King?! This is the point in the story where he's still running from Saul but he is far from alone. With all of his boys, he's hanging out in the desert of Moan. It was the time of year to shear the sheep and David was kind enough to keep an eye on things to be certain no one took advantage of a wealthy guy named Nabal. David's no fool. He knew to take care of those who had money. Nabal on the other hand was a fool, literally. The name Nabal means *fool*. You thought your middle name was bad! Back to David and the fool. So David, after helping a brother out sends a few guys to see Nabal.

MESSENGER #1: Greetings to you in the name of David. In other words, our man says "what's up!" Some of your guys crashed with us and we wanted to remind you that we treated them good. Knowing that you've got it going on here, we'd like to get in on some of this. Nothing big, just some food and a place to crash.

NABAL: Who did you say you were with?

MESSENGER #2: That would be David, son of Jesse. The one who treated all of your shepherds with respect.

NABAL: David? No, doesn't ring a bell. You know, there are all kinds of people running around always trying to take what doesn't belong to them. Heck if I'm going to hand over what I've got to a bunch of desert rats from who knows where!

SERVANT (listening to the whole conversation; when the messenger leaves, the servant runs over to Abigail): Now I don't want to give it up on someone but that fool, I mean your husband just blew it. When we were out in the desert we were cared for and protected day and night by people we barely knew. The leader of those people was David. David just asked to join the festival and for a little food along the way and Nabal not only said no, but insulted them without a thought.

ABIGAIL: You are a good servant. I will do what I can. Help me gather two hundred loaves of bread, two jugs of wine, sheep, grain, raisin cakes, fig cakes, and donkeys to carry it all. Get help and we will all head out to try to make amends. I'll deal with Nabal later. I'm always having to clean up after that man!

NARRATOR: Meanwhile—the messengers meet David.

MESSENGER #1: David, the good news is that we made it and delivered your message!

MESSENGER #2: The bad news is that the guy was a jerk, refusing to give anything to us, insulting us as he sent us away.

DAVID: Ingrate! Grab your swords. We'll show him who insults those who gave protection. (Almost mumbling under his breath): I look after all his land out here in the desert, protecting and caring for all he has and I get treated like this?! We'll see who the desert rat is. He'll be lucky if there is even one man left alive when we're through.

NARRATOR: While Abigail was on her way with servants and gifts, David and at least 200 men were on their way to teach Nabal a few manners. They meet on the road.

ABIGAIL (upon seeing David, she falls to the ground; keeping her head down she says): You must be David. I can't tell you how sorry I am for what happened. That man shoots off his mouth and never thinks of what might happen. If you must, take it out on me but leave those back at home alone. I did not see your messengers when they came and if I had, our household would have welcomed you with open arms.

May God give you everything you deserve. May the Lord bless you and make all of your enemies a fool like my husband. You may not know it yet but big things are in your future and you don't want unnecessary blood on your hands. Please walk away with these gifts and trust that God will give Nabal what he deserves.

DAVID: I don't know how to explain it except for God, but your words have taken the fight out of me. If it weren't for you, the men in your household would be gone. May you be blessed, "bringer of peace." Go home and deliver your message of peace letting Nabal know what almost happened.

NARRATOR: When Abigail made it back home, Nabal was partying. She thought about trying to talk to him but he was too drunk and having a good time. She waited for the morning and dropped the news. For once, Nabal had no comment. Ten days later, he fell over dead.

## Life Application

Do you think Abigail was just as much a fool as her husband? Just in a different way?

When have you known someone to take a great risk in order to bring about peace?

Imagine you worked for six months, every week, every day helping someone out with their homework. In fact, you helped so much that you started to fall behind on your own work. What would you do at the end of six months if they not only didn't thank you, but if they pretended to not know you, saying you weren't the kind of person they would hang with?

Bring in newspapers and news magazines from the past week. Give students ten minutes or so to go through them looking for headlines, specifically ones where an injustice or sort of peace or reconciliation is mentioned. Ask them to cut these headlines out. Have tape available and on one wall, tape all of the stories about war, injustice, and any other story that would be about conflict of some kind. On another wall, ask your students to tape any stories about peace, reconciliation, or helping others in some way. Look at the two walls. Which one has more stories?

Sadly, in the world today we hear more about people hurting one another than good things happening. Why is this?

Would you be willing to take a great risk toward peace if it meant that you might never get credit for it?

What if it might cost you greatly, either financially, friendships, or even your life?

Abigail was clearly concerned for her household. This would not have been the norm that a master (or wife of the master) would put her own life at risk to protect servants.

What do you think God calls us as Christians to do today that might be similar?

God was clearly directing Abigail. She was obedient and bartered peace in what seemed to be an impossible situation.

How might God empower us to do something similar?

## Making It Personal

God believed in Abigail and her ability to bring peace to her household. Even more, God worked in the life of David, allowing him to move from anger to calm. He recognized God's words through the mouth of a woman coming to plead for her household. David not only recognized God's words, but he was humbly willing to change.

Choose a quiet song for meditation at the close of your meeting. Invite your students to look back at the wall and all of the headlines. Ask your students how God might be calling them to step toward peace in some area of their lives or the lives of others? Can they dream of a time when there are more headlines about peace and helping others than of war and injustices? Close with a time for students to share if they desire.

# Being a Peacemaker

*By Amy Jacober*

## Memory Verse
Be anxious for nothing, but in everything by prayer and supplication, with thanksgiving, let your requests be made known to God; and the peace of God, which surpasses all understanding, will guard your hearts and minds through Jesus Christ.—Philippians 4:6–7

## Scripture
Philemon 4–22

## Lesson in a Sentence
Being a peacemaker takes courage and risk.

# Focus

**Steal the Bacon**
Split your group into two even teams. The teams line up shoulder to shoulder facing one another with roughly ten yards between. Number each player on the two teams 1, 2, 3, 4, and so on. Be certain to start on opposite ends for the numbering. In other words, if you have twenty students, numbers one and ten would be facing each other, numbers two and nine would be facing each other and so on. Place a ball, a sock, or whatever (representing bacon) in the center of the two groups. Call out a number and the first to get to the *bacon* and cross back over his or her line wins a point. If the person who steals the bacon is tagged before crossing his or her line, no team earns a point. Play to ten points (or whatever seems suitable for your group). Don't forget, you always want to stop a game before the students want it to end.

We all have things that belong to us. When one of our possessions goes missing, sometimes conflicts are created. Some movies are based on the disappearance of items such as jewelry or art. Sibling brawls are common if a favorite T-shirt or MP3 player can't be found. Almost all of us have heard or said "don't touch my stuff" in a heated conversation when something has gone missing.

# Discovery

Get your students ready to hear a letter. You may want to create a little ambience by having the lights low, drinks served, and a few candles lit. Have pillows or beanbags to offer several options for them to get as comfortable as possible. As soon as they are settled, tell them that you have a letter to read. They are to assume the role of a slave owner and are hearing from an old friend who is now in prison.

Read Philemon 4–22 from *The Message*. After you have finished reading, hand out a copy of the letter to each person. Allow a few moments for them to reread this letter.

- Who was Onesimus?
- What, specifically was Paul asking Philemon to do?

In biblical times, there were masters and servants. This is slightly different from the idea of modern slavery. When a slave went missing, it was not to be taken lightly. While not quite an abolitionist move, in his letter, Paul is calling for the freedom of Onesimus. Even more, he calls for Philemon to recognize this man, not as his servant but as a brother in Christ—an equal.

## Life Application

There are many ways to be involved in seeking peace. Earlier this week you considered ways that you might get involved—in your own homes, friendships, schools, and communities.

There are still others around the world who need to hear from those of us who are blessed to be living free at this moment. If not us, who will speak to them?

Consider prayer requests from any number of groups. For one that goes with this lesson well, look to www.stopthetraffik.org.

If you need other suggestions, consider the following. Each one will have links to other organizations, all needing prayer.

- www.persecutedchurch.org
- www.worldvision.org
- www.compassioninternational.org

In closing, give each student a piece of fair trade chocolate. Let them know that many of the products they get or use every day are linked to slave labor across the world. When the demand goes down, the supply will also. You may not be able to free children in slavery around the world today but you can make a difference a little at a time. And who knows, one day someone in your room might be changing the world. (If you are uncertain if your chocolate is fair trade, ask your grocer. While at one time this was difficult to find, it is more and more prevalent as the demand rises offering living wages to people around the world.)

## Song Connect

"Does Anybody Hear Her?" by Casting Crowns on *Lifesong*

## Quotable Quote

*If you want to make peace, you don't talk to your friends. You talk to your enemies.*
—Moshe Dayan (1915–1981)

## Extra! Extra!

This next week is the International Day for the Persecuted Church. Remind your students of the need to remember those suffering around the world. Go to www.persecutedchurch.org to learn more.

# Stephen: Forgiveness in the Most Difficult Times

*By Chuck Hunt*

**In this lesson, students will:**
- ✔ Understand the way to forgiveness is love.
- ✔ Know that Jesus forgives us.
- ✔ Understand that Jesus' forgiveness means that we should do the same for others.
- ✔ Be given an opportunity to forgive and be forgiven.

**Stuff you'll need:**
- ❑ Decision cards
- ❑ Pens
- ❑ Half sheets of paper
- ❑ White board and markers

## Memory Verse

Therefore I say to you, her sins, which are many, are forgiven, for she loved much. But to whom little is forgiven, the same loves little.—Luke 7:47

For this reason I say to you, her sins, which are many, have been forgiven, for she loved much; but he who is forgiven little, loves little.—Luke 7:47 NASB

## Scripture

Acts 7:54–60

## Lesson in a Sentence

Our ability to forgive is directly related to our ability to see ourselves as loved by Christ, who makes us whole.

## The Big Picture

Forgiveness is not just a discipline that we are called to act out. There is a reality of forgiveness that we often forget in the midst of our pain. When we have been wronged and hurt by someone, our pain is usually related to the fact that we care about the person or persons who have wronged us. If we didn't care, our pain would not be as intense. It is this same caring that allows us the ability to forgive.

# Focus

There are so many opinions about what forgiveness looks like, it may be helpful to get your students to express those opinions out loud without fear of ridicule. Create an opinion night that allows the students to express their ideas.

Divide students into groups. Add a leader to the group, only to progress the discussion. The leader is not allowed to interject thoughts or opinions during this time. Give the groups *decision cards* (strongly agree, agree, disagree, and strongly disagree). Do not give them a "not sure" or "I don't know" card. This will not help them state their opinions. The rules are simple:

1. Show them a statement (whiteboard, PowerPoint).
2. Give them five minutes to discuss the statement and decide together what response they want to give.
3. On the count of three, make all of the groups hold up their card so everyone can see.
4. Go around to each group and have a spokesperson explain why the group came to that decision.
5. Other groups need to respect their decision even if their own decision is opposite.

Here are some statements that you could use:

1. Human beings are mammals (example).
2. Forgiveness is the response to an apology.
3. Forgiving is forgetting.
4. Murder is unforgivable.

Read Acts 7:54–60.

- "Stephen forgave because he knew Christ loved him."
- "Stephen forgave because he loved those who were stoning him."
- "You can forgive because Christ loves you."

At the end of the discussion section, give a talk based upon the reason why Stephen was being stoned.

## Quotable Quote
*Dance like nobody's watching; love like you've never been hurt. Sing like nobody's listening; live like it's heaven on earth.*—Mark Twain

# Discovery

The quote by Mark Twain says, "love like you've never been hurt."

Ask your students to explain the benefits of living that way? What are the risks?

Hand out a half sheet of paper that has the phrase "I love you because . . ." on the top, and "I forgive you because . . ." in the middle. The students may take as many sheets as they want and write notes to anyone they need to forgive for hurting them. The key is that if they write "I love you because" first, they will usually write "I forgive you because I love you." This is the whole point of the lesson.

These are optional elements that may be woven into a lesson. Some will appear as highlighted boxes. Others will simply become a part of the text. A few will make appearances at the end of the actual lesson. They are NOT all to be in every lesson, rather a sample of items that may accompany the essentials.

## Teacher's Note:

This is one of my favorite lessons. One of the interesting facts in this story is that everywhere else in the Bible, Jesus is *seated* at the right hand of the Father. This is the only place where Jesus stands at the right hand of the Father. The connection is that Stephen is standing to defend Christ and Christ is standing for Stephen or "if you stand for Christ, He will stand for you."

## Connections

Jesus forgives.

Jesus said, "Father, forgive them, for they do not know what they are doing." And they divided up his clothes by casting lots.—Luke 23:34 NIV

## Song Connect

"Who I Am Hates Who I've Been" by Reliant K, *MmHmm*

## Extra! Extra!

## Option 1

### Love Unhurt

In the book of Job, Satan contends that no one serves God except for selfish reasons, but God disagrees and presents Job, a righteous man who fears God and shuns evil, as an example to counter Satan's claim. In order to prove to Satan that Job's loyalty is not based on material reward, God permits Satan to take from Job all of the material benefits Job has received and to afflict him with a most severe and excruciating pain. Through all of this suffering, Job never complains. His wife urges him to curse God and die to end his suffering, but his only response is, "The LORD gave and the LORD has taken away; may the name of the LORD be praised" (Job 1:21 NIV).

"... and suddenly a great wind came from across the wilderness and struck the four corners of the house, and it fell on the young people, and they are dead; and I alone have escaped to tell you!" Then Job arose, tore his robe, and shaved his head; and he fell to the ground and worshiped (Job 1:19–20 NKJV).

# Questions

1. Job loved God despite having his life torn apart. Have there ever been times when you felt God had abandoned you or wronged you? What was your spiritual response? How does it compare to Job's response?
2. What is your general attitude/response toward people who have hurt you (revenge, forgiveness, ignoring them, etc.)?
3. What are some benefits that might come with loving as if you had never been hurt?
4. Job's wife urged him to curse God and die so that his suffering would end. Instead, he risked and endured more suffering but still praised God. What are the risks of loving unhurt, and are you willing to take them?
5. What steps can you take to enable yourself to be willing to take the risk of loving more freely?

# Option 2

The Nooma Video Series has a video called *Luggage*. This may be a great discussion starter for your students.

# Quotable Quotes

*I have found the paradox, that if you love until it hurts, there can be no more hurt, only more love.*—Mother Teresa

*If you give it [Love], you don't need to give anything else, and if you don't give it, it doesn't matter much what else you give.*—Anonymous

# Making It Personal

## Improv

Materials needed are precut slips of paper, pen, and two baskets.

Ask the group for a list of ten to fifteen emotions or states of mind or disciplines (rage, forgiveness, panic, love, excitement, joy). Write each down on a small slip of paper and put in a basket. Then ask the audience for household chores, sports, or other types of distinctive actions. Write each of these on a small slip of paper and put in a separate basket. Divide the kids into groups of three to four. Each group will take turns acting out an *Improv* scene while the other groups watch. The advisor pulls one emotion and one action from the baskets and shouts it out. One of the teams begins acting out the chore, using words and actions, and conveying the emotion. Every thirty seconds or so, the advisor calls out a different emotion. The actors change emotions immediately, carrying out the same chore. Each group should get one action, and then two to three emotions to act it out with. After two to three emotions, move on to the next group and pull another action with emotion from the baskets.

# Stephen: Forgiveness in the Most Difficult Times

*By Chuck Hunt*

## Memory Verse

Therefore I say to you, her sins, which are many, are forgiven, for she loved much. But to whom little is forgiven, the same loves little.—Luke 7:47

For this reason I say to you, her sins, which are many, have been forgiven, for she loved much; but he who is forgiven little, loves little.—Luke 7:47 NASB

## Scripture

If your brother sins against you, go and show him his fault, just between the two of you. If he listens to you, you have won your brother over.—Matthew 18:15 NIV

## Lesson in a Sentence

In order to forgive, we need to be willing to hear and be heard.

# Focus

In the Dr. Seuss book *The Sneetches and Other Stories,* read the story about The Zax. It is a story that shows how ridiculous it is when two people are immovable and unwilling to hear the other. Pride is the issue in the story.

# Discovery

### Marco Polo

This is the same game that you would normally play in a swimming pool but if you play it on an open field, it has the same effect. After playing for awhile, ask the students who are not *it* to stop responding and be silent. After the game, ask the student who was *it* to come up and describe his experience. The point is that if you live in a world where no one will hear you, you generally give up. It is the same way with forgiveness. If you are dealing with someone who does not want to hear you, it makes you want to give up.

Divide students into groups and ask them to read Matthew 18:15–18. Focus on verse 15 and discuss what it feels like when someone doesn't hear you.

## Quotable Quote

*We know that if we really want to love we must learn to forgive. Forgive and ask to be forgiven; excuse rather than accuse. Reconciliation begins first, not with others but with us. It starts with having a clean heart within. A clean heart is able to see God in others. We must radiate God's love.*—Mother Teresa

## Application

We need to be prepared to forgive whether or not we have been heard. In fact we need to forgive before we even accuse someone of sinning against us. That act will allow our pain to be heard.

## Connections

Matthew 6:9–15 (Focus on verses 14–15.)

# Grieving with God

*By Sharon Koh*

**In this lesson, students will:**
- ✔ Gain an understanding of the biblical mandate to love the poor.
- ✔ Discover ways they can serve others in need.

**Stuff you'll need:**
- ❏ An expectation for a meal (if your group does not regularly have one, invite them to "A Taste of the World" banquet for the day of this lesson. Ensure that students arrive at the event *hungry.*
- ❏ Rice (cooked)
- ❏ Rice and beans (cooked together)
- ❏ Steak and potatoes
- ❏ Utensils to eat only the steak and potatoes

## Memory Verse

"Then the righteous will answer him, 'Lord, when did we see you hungry and feed you, or thirsty and give you something to drink? When did we see you a stranger and invite you in, or needing clothes and clothe you? When did we see you sick or in prison and go to visit you?' "The King will reply, 'I tell you the truth, whatever you did for one of the least of these brothers of mine, you did for me.'—Matthew 25:37–40 NIV

## Scripture

Lamentations 2:11–12; 3:48–51; 4:9–10

## Lesson in a Sentence

God's heart breaks for those who are hungry and in need. By tending to those in need, we identify with God.

## The Big Picture

Hunger and poverty are two things that weigh very heavily on God's heart. He grieves for those who are in need (Lam. 2:11–12). As Christians, we want to care about the things He cares about and grieve with God over things that break His heart. So, it is important for us to care about the hungry, the poor, and those in need.

# Focus

Divide students into the following proportions (preferably before they enter the room so that assignments can be random): 75%, 20%, 5% based on the size of your group.

In a group of fifty students, you would have thirty-seven students in the first group, ten students in the second group, and three students in the last group.

Students are grouped according to worldwide income proportions (but don't let them know this until the end of the banquet). Seat them in their groups—group one on the floor with mats; group two on chairs with no table; and group three with a table and chairs.

Serve group three the full meal of steak, potatoes, dessert, and drink—within sight of the other two groups.

Serve group two rice and beans cooked together and water to drink (the lack of utensils will require them to use their hands).

Require group one to get up and get their food and water from a remote location (a ten-minute walk away).

After the meal, have different members of each group share with the whole group how their situation made them feel (embarrassed to be the only ones getting real food; angry at the simplicity of their meal; grateful for what they have, etc.).

Tell the students they were divided according to global proportions. This is how the world's levels of income are distributed. They are experiencing a small-scale representation of how people around the world live daily.

# Discovery

Read Lamentations 2:11–12; 3:48–51; 4:9–10.

1. According to these passages, why is God in so much pain and sorrow?
2. Who are the people that God grieves for?

Now, read Matthew 25:37–40.

1. What does Jesus ask His followers to do about the needs they perceive around them?
2. When they do these things, who are they really giving to?

## Life Application

Let students reflect on their day-to-day, week-to-week lives. Ask them if they personally know people who have less than they do. Ask them to consider how they can give to or share with these people. Next, ask students to consider people all around the world that they don't know, and ask them to consider ways to give to or share with those who are truly starving and in need.

## Making It Personal

Ask students to consider what they would like to do in response to today's lesson. Let them write their commitments on a piece of paper so they will have a reminder.

## Teacher's Note:

It is important to allow students to see both *near* and *far*. Is there someone in the school who would appreciate shared food or clothing? Are there local facilities such as a Rescue Mission/Salvation Army/Goodwill/Soup Kitchen where they can contribute items? Then, ask students to consider Web sites such as www.compassion.com or www.worldvision.org where the group can make a donation or sponsor a child together on a regular basis. This helps make the action steps from this lesson very concrete in the lives of students.

# Grieving with God

*By Sharon Koh*

## Memory Verse

"They also will answer, 'Lord, when did we see you hungry or thirsty or a stranger or needing clothes or sick or in prison, and did not help you? "He will reply, 'I tell you the truth, whatever you did not do for one of the least of these, you did not do for me.'
—Matthew 25:44–45 NIV

## Scripture

Matthew 25:31–46

## Lesson in a Sentence

Jesus closely ties our eternal destination with our treatment of those in need around us.

## The Big Picture

There are negative implications for neglecting those in need. God desires for His children to be helpful and caring for others who are less fortunate.

# Focus

Remind the students of the commitments they made during Sunday's meeting. Ask the students to report on any ideas they have had regarding people they know who might need help, support, or friendship. Let them discuss things they might have done this week to work on their commitments.

# Discovery

Read Matthew 25:31–46. Ask students to note what behavior is rewarded and what behavior is condemned. What is the reward/punishment? Allow students to wrestle with the seriousness of this teaching of Jesus. Do not make excuses for how difficult the teaching is. Ask if this reading has an impact on the way they view the commitments they made to help others in need.

# Extravagant Worship

*By Sharon Koh*

---

In this lesson, students will:
- Consider the times when they feel inhibited in their worship of Jesus.
- Gain a greater freedom to stand up for their faith.
- Learn how to express themselves in worship.

## Stuff you'll need:
- ❑ *Unashamed Love* CD by Lamont Hiebert

---

## Memory Verse

Therefore, I tell you, her many sins have been forgiven—for she loved much. But he who has been forgiven little loves little.—Luke 7:47 NIV

## Scripture

Matthew 26:6–13; Luke 7:36–50

## Lesson in a Sentence

The extravagance of our worship is proportional to our gratitude to God for the forgiveness of our sins.

## The Big Picture

Jesus tells a parable about two men in debt. The one with the greater debt is more grateful when it is forgiven. This is because his relief is proportionally greater. Likewise, Mary of Bethany pours out her gratitude in the face of scorn and mocking. Why? Jesus says that her "beautiful" gesture indicated the extent that her heart longed to worship Him. When faced with the gravity of where our sin could have taken us, we also can find ourselves pouring out extravagant worship at the feet of our Savior.

# Focus

If your youth group has a worship leader who can work with you on this lesson, this will be a little easier. If not, perhaps you can have a guest worship leader come in or you can use a worship CD. Begin the session with a time of musical worship. If possible, include the song, "Unashamed Love." Allow students to sit or stand—whichever is most comfortable for them during this time.

# Discovery

Read Matthew 26:6–13 and answer the following questions:

1. Why were the disciples indignant? What was the basis for their irritation? Their own pride? Condemnation of the woman?
2. What did Jesus see in her actions that touched His heart?
3. Did Jesus actually tell them to disregard the needs of the poor?
4. Why did He praise her for what she did?

Now, read Luke 7:36–50.

1. What is the attitude behind Simon's remarks?
2. What exactly did the woman do? How did this show her utter abandonment in her worship of Jesus? What was said of her when Simon showed his distaste?
3. Explain Jesus' parable about the two men who owed money.
4. Jesus explains why her worship is so extravagant. What is the reason that Jesus offers?

## Life Application

We do not always think of ourselves as sinners. We are more likely to allow ourselves to be Simon in this story. We scorn other people for their displays of foolishness, and we disregard the debt that we owe Jesus for our own lives.

It is absolutely essential for us to consider the magnitude of our own debts that have been forgiven. This is why confession has been such an integral part of the worship experiences of churches through the centuries. With confession comes the realization of what forgiveness means, and with that realization comes an outpouring of worship.

## Making It Personal

Allow students some time for reflection—to silently pray about the things for which they have been forgiven and their gratefulness to the Lord. Perhaps you can allow them some time to write things down. This helps to focus thoughts.

Ask students to form a circle and face outward, so they can't see each other. Play the music again. This time, urge them to imagine they are alone and worshiping in front of God. Ask them to express bodily what they are feeling inside while they worship (e.g., kneeling, turning palms upward, bowing heads, lifting hands, etc.).

**TEACHER'S NOTE:**
Even though students have been encouraged not to look at each other during the second set of musical worship, they will probably try to peek out of the corner of their eye. It is important that you, as the teacher, feel free to express yourself extravagantly. Allow yourself to get down on your knees and raise your hands, if that is what your spirit wants to express.

## Song Connect

"Take It to the Streets" by Matt Redman on *Beautiful News*

## Extra! Extra!

The concept of worship has exploded in the last twenty years. For a Web site with a variety of accessible resources, go to www.worshiptogether.com. Discussions, free songs, new music, and more can all be found here.

# Unashamed Love

*By Sharon Koh*

## Memory Verse

I will praise you as long as I live, and in your name I will lift up my hands.
—Psalm 63:4 NIV

## Scripture

2 Samuel 6:12–16

## Lesson in a Sentence

David is a good example of someone who worshiped God extravagantly in the face of scorn.

# Focus

Ask students to think of a time when they felt too shy to stand up against something they knew was wrong. Encourage those who are willing to share. It may be that one or two leaders need to begin this process.

# Discovery

The context of 2 Samuel 6 is that someone (Uzzah) had died because he was not reverent enough in his treatment of the ark of the covenant. Therefore, David is filled with fear and trembling when he undertakes moving the ark again. This time, the ark will be moved to the City of David.

They were so afraid of showing disrespect to the ark that they sacrificed every six steps of the way! When the ark was entering the city, there was so much earnest worship and joy that David danced in a "linen ephod" (*his underwear*). His ex-wife, Michal, "despised" him when she saw this behavior (2 Sam. 6:12–16 NIV).

## Application

The story of David dancing in his underwear is a vivid example of extravagant worship, but sometimes our expression of loyalty to God is not so radical. Sometimes, the allegiance that we express to the One we worship is in terms of what we stand up for.

Many Christian students have heard derogatory remarks made about Christians and their God at school. Other students have witnessed bullying or mocking of other students. Others know of cheating taking place around them. Perhaps a form of "extravagant worship" would be to stand up by saying something against these things.

## Making It Personal

Ask students to talk about how they would have liked to respond to the situations they thought of earlier in light of this lesson.

# Preparation for the Coming — November 30, 2008

*By Rick Bennett and Amy Jacober*

In this lesson, students will:

- ✔ Understand the importance of preparation and anticipation for the Coming of the Messiah.
- ✔ See that preparation for the holidays spiritually will allow them to think of the holiday differently.
- ✔ Learn something about the anticipation of Jesus' Coming and why it is important to them today.

Stuff you'll need:

- ❏ Greenery for decorating the church
- ❏ Dry-erase board and markers

## Memory Verse

Prepare the way for the Lord, make straight paths for him.—Mark 1:3b NIV

## Scripture

Mark 1:1–3; Luke 1:26–38

## Lesson in a Sentence

We must prepare ourselves in advance for Christmas and Jesus' birth as Israel was instructed to do preceding His birth.

## The Big Picture

We need to prepare ourselves spiritually so that we can focus on the real meaning of Christmas. We may find ourselves thinking about things we want as gifts, how much money we will spend, and the many pressures surrounding the holiday, instead of remembering the glorious event that occurred with the birth of Christ. If we prepare ourselves spiritually for the Coming of Christ, we will enjoy the season of Christmas with hearts filled with the love that was intended by the birth of Jesus.

# Focus

## Option 1

Consider a *hanging of the green* for your church. Many churches spend a great deal of time decorating and getting ready for the holiday season. This year, the first Sunday of

Advent falls in November, giving plenty of time to transition from Thanksgiving to Christmas.

Advent means *coming*. It is a term of expectation such as the arrival of a special guest. In this case, the special guest is God Himself. We expect the birth and all of the excitement that comes with a new baby, while never forgetting this Child is coming for a specific role—to die on a cross for the sins of the world.

Christian tradition offers the origin of the *hanging of the green,* but it is not a biblical mandate. Holly, ivy, pine, or any other evergreens indigenous to your area can be used. The greens are a reminder that they are never changing; green even in the dead of winter, signifying life. This symbol is our reminder of the everlasting life that Jesus offers. Holly is a favorite as it embodies the reminder of everlasting life coupled with the pain of the pointed leaves and deep red berries foreshadowing the blood shed on the Cross.

The evergreen Christmas tree is another popular symbol that reminds us of the tree of life. Christmas trees were first used in Germany beginning with symbolic decorations and later transitioning to various other decorations. A great activity for the entire church is to set up a tree with no decorations. Then invite the congregation to place items on the tree that symbolize a gift they received from God in the past year. It could be a baby rattle if they had a child or grandchild, a hospital ID bracelet if they were sick and are better, a graduation invitation for a child that graduated, a toy plane for a trip someone was able to take, or a toy house for a new home. It could be just about anything! Encourage the congregation to bring the items the following week and to be as creative as possible.

Another common item for a *hanging of the green* is not green at all! It is the poinsettia. While these plants come in a variety of colors, the traditional is deep red. It is a plant native to Mexico and has been used for centuries as a reminder of the star of Bethlehem due to its unique shape.

Decorating the church can be great fun! Have a short time of explanation, crank up the music, and get to work!

## Option 2
Advent offers us a time to prepare for the birth of Jesus.

- Ask students what they are doing to prepare for Christmas?
- What are they looking forward to?
- What are they dreading?
- How do they prepare when a guest is coming over? Do they rent a movie or the latest video game? Do they clean their room? Take a shower? Of course, the preparation depends on the guest, but we all do certain things when we are expecting visitors.

# Discovery

Read Mark 1:1–3 and Luke 1:26–38.

- What warnings were people given for the Coming of Christ?
- What preparations do you think they needed to make based on these passages?

- What do you imagine Mary and Joseph were like?
- What do we know about them from Scripture?

## Life Application

Mary and Joseph and the Israelites were told of the coming of Emmanuel.

- How is what they were told different from what we are told today?
- What made it similar?

## Making It Personal

On a dry-erase board, make a list of major areas of life such as family, school, sports, friends, work, dating, volunteering, social justice, and prayer. Ask your students to choose one area of their life that needs a little attention as they look toward the Coming of Jesus. Where do they personally need to do a little housekeeping to have their heart, mind, and soul ready to celebrate the birth of Christ?

As you softly play a Christmas CD in the background, encourage your students to spend a few moments in prayer asking the Lord to show them what part of their lives need work. Hand out a piece of red ribbon wide enough to write on. Give each student a pen or marker so they can write on the ribbon the area in their lives that needs attention. Give each student a piece of greenery on which to tie their ribbon. This will remind them to focus on their area of need as well as the everlasting life Christ brings.

## Song Connect

"Oh Come, Oh Come Emmanuel" (traditional hymn). Finding a contemporary version is easy. Try Sufjan Steven or Robbie Seay versions (both found on iTunes).

"He Is Coming" by Andrew Osenga

## Ancient Practices

*An Ancient Prayer to be read responsively*

- In the wasteland may the Glory shine.
  **In the land of the lost may the King make His home.**

- Let us wake to Christ's summons, urgent in our midst:
  **He comes to bring judgment nearer than we know.**

- Let us wake to the truth that His power alone will last:
  **The worlds that scorn Him will vanish like a dream.**

- Let us wake to the truth that His glory can be seen:
  **In all the deeds that sweeten, in all the thoughts that heal.**

- Let us wake to the truth that His reign is yet to come.
  **That routs out the world of evil; that fulfills the world of good.**

- The earth is becoming a wasteland:
  **Breath of the Most High, come and renew it.**

- Humanity is becoming a battleground:
  **Child of Peace, come and unite it.**

- The world is becoming a playground:
  **Key of Destiny, open doors to our true path.**

- The world is becoming a no-man's land:
  **God-with-us, come and make Your home here.**

- The planet is becoming a graveyard:
  **Spring of Christ, come with buds of life.**

## Quotable Quote

*Advent is concerned with that very connection between memory and hope which is so necessary to man. Advent's intention is to awaken the most profound and basic emotional memory within us, namely, the memory of the God who became a child. This is a healing memory; it brings hope. The purpose of the Church's year is continually to rehearse her great history of memories, to awaken the heart's memory so that it can discern the star of hope. . . . It is the beautiful task of Advent to awaken in all of us memories of goodness and thus to open doors of hope.*
—Joseph Cardinal Ratzinger, *Seek That Which Is Above,* 1986

## Extra! Extra!

December 1 is recognized as AIDS Awareness Day. AIDS is a real issue in the lives of our teenagers, as well as the world. This is an important lesson to continually remind one another that we need to be prepared ahead of time to prevent the spread of AIDS and to realize the struggle around the world for those who have no choice. While there are many options, consider www.one.org as one Web site attempting to end AIDS.

# Preparation for the Coming

*By Rick Bennett and Amy Jacober*

## Memory Verse

Prepare the way for the Lord, make straight paths for him.—Mark 1:3b NIV

## Scripture

Isaiah 40:1–8

## Lesson in a Sentence

We must prepare ourselves in advance for Christmas and Jesus' birth as Israel was instructed to do preceding His birth.

# Focus

Create an obstacle course for your students. This can be an intense, grueling one or one that is simply crawling under tables and over chairs. Make it as simple or elaborate as you are able. Regardless of the intensity, be certain to have at least ten elements to go through. On each element, tape one of the following words or phrases in an envelope: not trying in school, fighting with parents, sneaking out, lying on your myspace.com Web page, texting or IMing when you are grounded, drinking, looking down on others, being materialistic, exhibiting poor sportsmanship, and lying. Feel free to adjust or change any of these as best suits your group.

After each person has gone through the course, ask what would have made getting from the beginning to the end easier? (This is obvious . . . if there had been no obstacles!)

Check out the Memory Verse, Mark 1:3b. It asks for the way to be prepared for the Lord, and to make the paths straight.

Some of us put up all kinds of obstacles for God, making it hard to get together.

Ask your students to go to the obstacles and pull off the envelopes. Then ask them to read what is in each.

Let your students know that these are just some of the obstacles we place between us and God.

# Discovery

Ask your students to turn to Isaiah 40:1–8. Let each student take one verse until all eight are read.

What stands out in this passage?

Reread Mark 1:1–3. Remember this from the last time you were together?

Isaiah was prophesying the coming of the Lord to this world. He is a reminder to the people that they are to make a straight path.

Reread Isaiah 40:8.

- What does this mean today? How does this help us to read Scripture?
- What do you like about this?
- What do you dislike?

## Life Application

Spend a few moments considering the obstacles offered earlier in this lesson. Do any of these apply to you? If not, can you identify the obstacle that is keeping you and God apart? Where do you need to make a straight path for God?

A symbolic way of doing this is to take small segments of string and have them tossed in the middle of the floor. Play a song or two offering time for your students to reflect. When and if they are ready, ask them to take a piece of string, straighten it out, and tape it to the wall. The end result will be a row of straight strings reminding your group of the straight path they chose.

God wants nothing to be an obstacle between you and Him. In fact, that is the very reason He stepped out of heaven and walked this earth.

## Service Option

Create an Advent calendar for others. You may choose to adopt a local assisted-living home, a homeless shelter, or another class at church. Advent calendars needn't be complicated. They are simply calendars that count down to Christmas Day beginning on the first of December. These can vary from having a verse a day or some Christmas symbol such as a star, sheep, or a manger. Feel free to be creative and do what suits your needs. If you do choose this activity, be certain to have all of your materials organized beforehand. If you need help, search Advent Calendar Templates on the Internet where you will find a variety of options.

# Jesus in the Flesh

*By Rick Bennett and Amy Jacober*

In this lesson, students will:
- ✔ Learn what the Incarnation was.
- ✔ Begin to understand the implication of the Incarnation.
- ✔ Consider the position of humility that God Himself took and how this changed the world.

Stuff you'll need:
- ❑ Unusual snack to experience

## Memory Verse

The Word became flesh and made his dwelling among us. We have seen his glory and, the glory of the One and Only, who came from the Father, full of grace and truth. —John 1:14 NIV

## Scripture

John 1:1–18

## Lesson in a Sentence

The Incarnation is the greatest miracle for Christians; we must understand it and its implications.

## The Big Picture

The Incarnation is one of the key doctrines that separates Christianity from other religions and makes Christmas so important. Every year at Christmas, we are reminded that Jesus loved us enough to step out of heaven to live with us and save us. The Incarnation was an extreme act of humility because Jesus came to have a relationship with us! Jesus knew when He came to earth that His Father had a purpose for His life. He would come into the world as a baby, would lead a humble life, and would die a horrendous death at the hands of the very people He came to save. He did all this for us! Christmas is a time for a great celebration. It is the time when Good News came in the flesh.

# Focus

What experiences do you and your students bring to the group? Has someone been scuba diving? Is someone able to skate on a rail? Has anyone traveled to other countries?

Have one or more of you lived through a divorce in your family or suffered the loss of a loved one? We each have experiences that allow us to relate to others.

Consider a food item that is not common to your area. It may be a tamale, fruitcake, or shoofly pie. What the item is does not matter, just that it is not common. This exercise is designed to let your group experience something new and different for themselves.

Describe to them the food item you've chosen for this exercise. After a few moments, bring out samples for them to try.

God understood the principle that we need to experience things in order to relate. We are able to relate better to those with similar experiences. Think about a time when you met another person who skates, has seen the same movies, or likes basketball. With little time together, you already have a whole vocabulary and many experiences to share.

# Discovery

Read John 1:1–18 for answers to the following questions (you may want to write these on a dry-erase board and have them work as teams!):

- What or Who is the Word?
- What does this say about where Jesus was in the beginning?
- What did John come to do?
- According to verse 14, what did the Word do?

## Life Application

This entire passage is about Jesus coming to the earth. Explain to your students that this is called the Incarnation.

Verse 14 is really the crux of this lesson; Jesus came and dwelt among us. Another way to look at this Word is that He tabernacled. He hung out and spent time.

Ask your students why they think God would do this?

If, after a few minutes, you receive no answer, say the following: "He chose to be fully human while being fully divine so that we might better relate to Him."

## Making It Personal

What does it mean to you that Jesus would be willing to step out of heaven just so you could relate better to Him?

Christmas is an amazing time of hope. We all need to know we are not alone, and others do hear and see us. We have something to offer and others can be blessed by what we give to them.

While living among us, Jesus suffered sadness, was scared, angry, hurt, and had others misunderstand Him. He also laughed, sang songs, shouted, celebrated with friends, and everything in between.

Where in your life do you long for someone to relate to you? Where do you feel misunderstood?

Spend some time thanking God for His willingness to relate to you even when you fail to recognize it. Close in prayer asking the Lord to reveal Himself clearly to your students. Thank Him for the Incarnation and His willingness to come to earth to establish a relationship with us.

## Service Option

Most people enjoy the holidays. For others this can be a depressing and difficult time. Encourage your students to offer help to those in their neighborhoods or church who may need an extra hand preparing for Christmas. You may even want to organize this offering for you and your students to help set up trees, hang lights, bake, or any other needs you find in your church or neighborhood. These are ways for your students to practice the very thing Christ did. They step out of their comfort zones and into the world of others.

## TEACHER'S NOTE:

Songwriter and biblical scholar, Michael Card, has this to say about the idea of Immanuel (God with Us):

> The implications of the name Immanuel are both comforting and unsettling. Comforting, because He has come to share the danger as well as the drudgery of our everyday lives. He desires to weep with us and to wipe away our tears. And what seems most bizarre, Jesus Christ, the Son of God longs to share in and to be the source of the laughter and joy we all too rarely know.
>
> The implications are unsettling. It is one thing to claim that God looks down upon us from a safe distance, and speaks to us. But to say that He is right here, is to put ourselves and Him in a totally new situation. He is no longer the calm and benevolent observer in the sky, or the kindly old caricature with the beard. His image becomes that of Jesus, who wept and laughed, who fasted and feasted, and who, above all, was fully present to those He loved. He was there with them. He is here with us.

## Connections

Philippians 2:5–11 gives us the implications for the Incarnation.

Prophecies of the Incarnation include Matthew 1:21–23, which is a retelling of the prophecy in Isaiah 7:14.

## Song Connect

"A Child Has Been Born for Us" by Jill Paquette

"God with Us" by Don Chafer

## Ancient Practices

An ancient prayer about the Incarnation by St. Augustine of Hippo to be read responsively.

Maker of the sun,
**He is made under the sun.**

In the Father he remains,
**From his mother he goes forth.**

Creator of heaven and earth,
**He was born on earth under heaven.**

Unspeakably wise,
**He is wisely speechless.**

Filling the world,
**He lies in a manger.**

Ruler of the stars,
**He nurses at his mother's bosom.**

He is both great in the nature of God,
**And small in the form of a servant.**

## Quotable Quote

*He was touchable, approachable, reachable. And, what's more, he was ordinary. If he were here today you probably wouldn't notice him as he walked through a shopping mall. He wouldn't turn heads by the clothes he wore or jewelry he flashed.*

*"Just call me Jesus," you can almost hear him say.*

*He was the kind of fellow you'd invite to watch the Rams-Giants game at your house. He'd wrestle on the floor with your kids, doze on your couch, and cook steaks on your grill. He'd laugh at your jokes and tell a few of his own. And when you spoke, he'd listen to you as if he had all the time in eternity.*
—Max Lucado "The Word Became Flesh" from *God Came Near*

# Incarnation

*By Rick Bennett and Amy Jacober*

## Memory Verse

The Word became flesh and made his dwelling among us. We have seen his glory and, the glory of the One and Only, who came from the Father, full of grace and truth. —John 1:14 NIV

## Scripture

Philippians 2:1–11

## Lesson in a Sentence

The Incarnation is the greatest miracle for Christians; we must understand it and its implications.

# Focus

News about celebrities is never difficult to find. Either go to the Internet and pull a few stories from TMZ or grab a few magazines at the grocery store.

Share a few current stories of celebrities making outrageous demands or expecting special treatment. Ask your students if they have any others to share.

If you are in a community where you have a relationship with someone who is or has lived on the street, ask him or her if they would be willing to come and share a few of their experiences with your youth group. Be certain this will be a safe place for them to share and not an experience of humiliation.

Does anyone deserve special treatment? If yes, who?

We give special treatment to famous people, actors, musicians, athletes, and the wealthy. On a different level research has shown that those who are good-looking, thin, and tall receive better treatment.

What is the criteria for special treatment? Do you actually follow this yourselves? How can you make a difference right now in your lives and your world?

Have you ever thought about Jesus as having been from a working-class family, at times wandering with no home or even a bed of His own? This is the King of kings, Lord of lords, Creator of the universe! This is a far different perspective than most of us consider when we think of a baby receiving gold!

# Discovery

Tape three large sheets of butcher paper on the wall. Title each with one of the following: things we are to do, things we are not to do, things Jesus did.

Separate your students into groups of three and have them read Philippians 2:1–11, keeping in mind the three categories on the butcher papers. After they have read through the passage once, ask them to read it again, writing their responses on the appropriate butcher paper.

Look over the lists. What are we called to do and not to do?

Even more, what did Jesus do?

## Life Application

No one wants to be treated poorly. This is not what this lesson is about.

Rather, it is about humility. It is about not thinking of yourself as any better than anyone else. This means that you do not ask of others anything that you would not be willing to give or do yourself. This is the flip side of not being arrogant. It is not low esteem or self hate. It is simply knowing that you are a child of the King but not rubbing it in anyone's face.

Lead a discussion on humility and arrogance using the following questions:

- How would life be different if we all wanted to serve others instead of being served?
- What would change at your school if everyone treated everyone else well?
- What causes someone to become arrogant?
- How can we learn or relearn humility?
- What does Jesus' position of humility have to teach us today?

## Memory Verse Activity

Candy canes are a part of the tradition of Christmas. While there is much controversy as to what is truth and what is an urban legend, the candy cane can be a great illustration of Christian truths.

It is shaped like a shepherd's cane reminding us of the shepherds in the field hearing of the birth of Christ. The cane is striped, representing purity and death for which Jesus came. While it is a sweet treat, it falls short of the sweetness of salvation offered by Jesus.

Type out the memory verse, make copies, and tie it to the candy canes to be handed out to each student. Offer a short explanation of how these Christmas candies can remind us of the real meaning of Christmas.

# Upside-Down Kingdom

*By Rick Bennett and Amy Jacober*

## In this lesson, students will:
- ✔ Consider the messages in the *Magnificat*.
- ✔ Discuss what it means to be a true leader.
- ✔ Recognize God's heart for the poor and powerless.
- ✔ Consider how concern for those with no power plays out in our world today.

## Stuff you'll need:
- ❑ Guest speaker and script (see Focus)

## Memory Verse
Therefore be imitators of God as dear children.—Ephesians 5:1

## Scripture
Luke 1:46–55

## Lesson in a Sentence
The social structure of the world was changed by Jesus' birth when He placed the least powerful above the most powerful in society.

## The Big Picture
When Jesus was born, He brought with Him a new kingdom, one diametrically opposed to the kingdom of the world. As the new King, He would take care of those who could not care for themselves and give a voice to those with no voice. As His followers, we must take up our cross and bear the same responsibilities that Jesus bore when He gave voices to the voiceless. We have been given the task of caring for our fellow men and women who are in need of help and support. God's love for us empowers us to be more and do more. During this Christmas season, we are to focus on the real meaning of Jesus' birth and share this message with others in whatever way we can.

# Focus

You will need to arrange this ahead of time.

While this is certain to be controversial for some, it is a great discussion starter. Ask one of your leaders to introduce a *guest speaker* for your group. Note to the group that he or she will be offering some unique thoughts on Christmas. Be certain to give no hint as to what is coming.

## Script for the Guest Speaker

Christmas has not always been a popular holiday celebration for Christians or society in general. In fact, Puritans even outlawed celebrations in some places. According to Stephen Nissenbaum (*The Battle for Christmas,* Knopf, 1996), Puritans objected to Christmas celebrations because, "Most fundamentally, Christmas was an occasion when the social hierarchy itself was symbolically turned upside down, in a gesture that inverted designated roles of gender, age, and class."

The modern American celebration of Christmas with gift buying and family times was started by rich New Yorkers wanting to change the very meaning of the holiday (which they saw as dangerous to the social order).

This dramatic shift in the way to celebrate Christmas led to the holiday commercialism we see today. This means that the modern "religion of consumer capitalism" is only a couple hundred years old.

As the group "Buy Nothing Christmas" points out, we still emphasize the over-consumption aspect of Christmas while we've lost the upside-down dimensions of Jesus' message. Quoted on their Web site is this statement from Leigh Schmidt: "Feasts celebrating affluence and indulgence are seen as standing the liberating message of Christianity—good news for the poor and the downtrodden—on its head. Santa Claus and the promise of material reward, not the Christ Child and the divine humility of the manger, become the ultimate symbolic measure of American time."

Think about it. We complain about children being bratty and wanting stuff all the time, but we take them to a mall and sit them on the lap of a stranger. We then have our kids tell this guy to give them exactly what they want. We have them make a list of what they want for Christmas and wonder why they are brats when they don't get everything on their list. We have set up a system that will cause parents and children to fail. The only ones who succeed are the makers of the products we buy and their advertising geniuses.

How have we chosen to celebrate the most subversive message the world has ever seen? By buying into the most overarching themes the world gives us: guilt, compulsion, spending more money than we have, listening to those in power and doing what they say, and eating too much while celebrating the birth of a homeless Man.

If your guest is able to stay in character, invite your students to give any comments or questions they may have. If your guest is not able to maintain this character, conduct the discussion yourself.

The details in this scenario are not fictional. Let your students know there really is a group proposing to buy nothing for Christmas. While this may seem extreme to some, they are serious about shifting the focus back to the birth of Christ. They are willing to turn the world's current perspective on Christmas upside down.

# Discovery

Even before Christ was born, God was at work on this upside-down kingdom. Mary, Jesus' own mother, understood this.

Read Luke 1:46–55. Be certain to set this in context for your students. Mary knows that she is pregnant and has gone to Judah to visit her cousin, Elizabeth.

In this passage, Mary praises God and then lists what He has done.

On a dry-erase board, ask your students to list, in their own words, what God has done in these passages. There are at least twelve different actions.

Now ask your students how Mary responds to these actions she has listed.

## Life Application

Bring in newspapers, magazines, and other materials for your students to use. Bring in construction paper for the foundation and glue sticks, glue, or tape for their use.

You've heard about a radical movement regarding Christmas and you've read what Mary had to say while pregnant with Jesus.

In pairs, ask your students to make a collage of all the places they believe God is or should be at work in the world. It may be a specific picture or headline or it may be that they form their own words by cutting out the letters for what they want to communicate.

Give a specific time limit for this project. It can be done in as little as ten minutes or take up to thirty. Once complete, ask each group to share what they created.

Tape each of these on a wall for easy reference.

## Making It Personal

This week the Memory Verse is integral to the lesson. Hand out a 3x5 card to each of your students. Ask them to write Ephesians 5:1 legibly on the card. Once it is written, ask them to pass their card to someone else until everyone has traded. The reason for trading is to remind your students when they see this verse in someone else's handwriting, it means they are not alone in this endeavor.

Invite each student to look to the wall. Several examples of where God is or could be at work have been offered. If we are to imitate Christ, in what ways can we join Him as He is at work in the world? Ask each student to consider what it would be like to be a part of bringing about an upside-down kingdom.

## TEACHER'S NOTE:

Don't be surprised if you have some students who really take you up on this! Often, teenagers are willing to go where adults are not. Adults often reason why this kind of radical move is unrealistic. Teenagers can serve as the greatest challenges to adult faith and not because they are rebelling. The opposite is true. When a teenager decides to follow Christ with his or her whole life, the adults around often realize how anemic their own faith has been. Be aware of this danger, reminding your students that they are not to judge others who do not join them. Rather, just like last week's lesson, this is to be done with humility.

## Song Connect

"A King and a Kingdom" by Derek Webb

"Crumbs from Your Table" by U2

## Web Connect

www.buynothingchristmas.org

# Upside-Down Kingdom

*By Rick Bennett and Amy Jacober*

## Memory Verse

Therefore be imitators of God as dear children.—Ephesians 5:1

## Scripture

Matthew 20:20–28

## Lesson in a Sentence

The social structure of the world was changed by Jesus' birth when He placed the least powerful above the most powerful in society.

# Focus

Let your students line up shoulder to shoulder on a masking tape line in order of height, shortest to the tallest. Once they are in place, tell them to reverse the line completely without talking and without stepping off the line. They may step around one another or play a form of leapfrog to try to switch places.

This is not a difficult activity but it is a life-sized example of order shifting. Ask your students what changed. Why did they change? (The answer is as simple as, you asked.)

Jesus asks us to change the world—in essence to turn it on its head. What the world considers important, Jesus does not. What Jesus names as important, the world does not. This is a hard concept to get but one that is repeated throughout Scripture.

# Discovery

Ask your students to pay attention to what this passage says about the kingdom and their role in it.

Read Matthew 20:20–28.

First things first. The mother of the sons of Zebedee asked something very specific for her children. What did Jesus mean in verse 22? (When Jesus was crucified, there was a thief on His right and left. Essentially, she was asking for her sons to be crucified with Christ.)

What does Jesus say He came to do?

## Life Application

- What comes to mind when you hear that you are not to be first, but last?
- How does the world view this kind of thinking?

- What about your family or friends?
- How do you talk about doing well in school yet place yourself as a servant helping others? Can these things happen at the same time?
- What about pulling more than your weight in a group project?
- What about on a sports team?
- At home?
- In the arts?
- As a leader in your school?

Choose examples to talk about that fit the activities and roles your students hold.

Most of us are taught that we need to be the best at something in order to get recognition and get ahead. God is not against being the best at something. After all, He was the Creator of the world! What He is against is using the gifts and skills He has bestowed upon us for our own personal gain, instead of the good of others and the kingdom. Translation, God is not for those who want to be first. They don't know what they are asking!

Christmas is a time for celebration! What gift or skill do you have that you can use to help others? If you like to play basketball, offer to play with some younger children and teach them a few things. If you are good at cooking, make some treats for others. If you are a good listener, consider going to a retirement home where so many people are lonely and looking for someone to listen. There is no gift or skill too big or too small. If you can't think of anything yourself, work as a group to help one another.

## Quotable Quote

*Serving God is doing good to man, but praying is thought an easier service and therefore more generally chosen.*—Benjamin Franklin

# Good News, Great Joy!

*By Amy Jacober*

In this lesson, students will:
- ✔ Hear the story of the birth of Christ.
- ✔ Be reminded of the real reason for Christmas.
- ✔ Be given opportunity and time to praise the Lord.
- ✔ Celebrate the Incarnation with the community.

Stuff you'll need:
- ❑ Decorations and lighting for ambiance, this may vary (see Focus)
- ❑ Three copies of the reading for the Discovery section

## Memory Verse

Then the angel said to them, "Do not be afraid, for behold, I bring you good tidings of great joy which will be to all people. For there is born to you this day in the city of David a Savior, who is Christ the Lord."—Luke 2:10–11

## Scripture

Luke 2

## Lesson in a Sentence

God sends the best news for everyone who will listen!!

## The Big Picture

Jesus came to the world for a specific purpose. His birth, the Incarnation was no accident. He longs to be in a relationship with us. What better news could there be? For too many of us, Christmas is about presents, parties, spending, eating, and other things that produce stress in the family. We miss the sheer joy that is intended for this time of year. Slow down, take a deep breath, and let the true meaning of Christmas really sink in. This may mean being a little misunderstood by others but what better gift could anyone receive than to experience Christmas in the presence of God?

# Focus

As students arrive, have the room lit with low-wattage lights and candles. Ideally the area should have hay spread around as if they are entering a barn. If you are in a part of the country where weather permits, this may even be a time spent outside experiencing a little of what Mary and Joseph did on the night Jesus was born.

Invite one of your students or an adult to lead in a series of worship and Christmas songs. Be certain to give plenty of time to enjoy, to make requests, and to slow down the pace of life in general.

You may want to have hot chocolate or cider on hand to serve to your students to create a more relaxed atmosphere.

# Discovery

After a season of singing and praising, ask a few of your leaders to offer a dramatic reading of the passage as follows.

**READER 1:** And it came to pass in those days *that* a decree went out from Caesar Augustus that all the world should be registered. This census first took place while Quirinius was governing Syria. So all went to be registered, everyone to his own city.

**READER 2:** Joseph also went up from Galilee, out of the city of Nazareth, into Judea, to the city of David, which is called Bethlehem, because he was of the house and lineage of David, to be registered with Mary, his betrothed wife, who was with child.

**READER 3:** So it was, that while they were there, the days were completed for her to be delivered. And she brought forth her firstborn Son, and wrapped Him in swaddling cloths, and laid Him in a manger, because there was no room for them in the inn.

**READER 1:** Now there were in the same country shepherds living out in the fields, keeping watch over their flock by night. And behold, an angel of the Lord stood before them, and the glory of the Lord shone around them, and they were greatly afraid. Then the angel said to them,

**READER 2:** "Do not be afraid, for behold, I bring you good tidings of great joy which will be to all people. For there is born to you this day in the city of David a Savior, who is Christ the Lord. And this *will be* the sign to you: You will find a Babe wrapped in swaddling cloths, lying in a manger."

**READER 3:** And suddenly there was with the angel a multitude of the heavenly host praising God and saying:

**READER 2:** "Glory to God in the highest, and on earth peace, goodwill toward men!"

**READER 1:** So it was, when the angels had gone away from them into heaven, that the shepherds said to one another,

**READER 3:** "Let us now go to Bethlehem and see this thing that has come to pass, which the Lord has made known to us."

**READER 1:** And they came with haste and found Mary and Joseph, and the Babe lying in a manger. Now when they had seen *Him*, they made widely known the saying which was told them concerning this Child.

**Reader 2:** And all those who heard *it* marveled at those things which were told them by the shepherds. But Mary kept all these things and pondered *them* in her heart. Then the shepherds returned, glorifying and praising God for all the things that they had heard and seen, as it was told them.

## Life Application

In small groups, ask your students to discuss why this is such good news. Do they feel the importance of this occasion today?

Give your students time to ask questions. You may need to encourage them to do so if this has not been a part of your pattern.

This passage is intended as good news for all the world. The good news is not that the world is suddenly going to be perfect. In fact, when you look at the bigger picture, for many people life gets more difficult when they choose to follow Jesus. The good news is that you are not alone—there is someone who deeply loves you and longs to have a relationship with you. The good news is that God almighty is stepping out of heaven to ensure that you and I may be able to be with Him in heaven for all eternity.

Ask your students to offer up praises just as the people did on the night of Jesus' birth. This is a wonderful time to teach the difference between thanking and praising the Lord. We thank Him for what He has given to us or done for us. We praise Him for who He is. The angels praised Him saying, "Glory to God in the Highest." Ask your students to offer popcorn praise expressing who He is to them. (*Popcorn praise* is simply a term stating there is no specific order of how things are done or what is said. As someone feels moved or led, they simply say it out loud.) If this is new for your students, ask your leaders to take the lead by offering examples.

## Making It Personal

Preprint some small business-card-sized cards with the Memory Verse on it. You can use actual business card templates or copy on cardstock and cut them out. Be certain to have at least three to four cards for each person present. Invite them to keep one card for themselves and to give the others away to anyone they believe needs to hear the Good News. It could be a neighbor, a parent, or a friend at school.

Close with a few more songs celebrating the season and most importantly, the birth of the Christ Child!

# Good News, Great Joy!

*By Amy Jacober*

Christmas Eve and Christmas Day are part of this week. This is a great time to encourage greater connection with the church family. If your church has not planned a Christmas Eve or Christmas Day service, consider a meeting with your pastor to suggest such a time. Youth group is great but not to the exclusion of the church as a whole.

*Merry Christmas!!*

# Jeremiah: Concern for How Believers Treat Those in Need

*By Scott and Carina Schubert*

In this lesson, students will:
- ✔ Learn that righteousness is about caring for other people and being obedient to God's commandments.
- ✔ See that God provides for His people despite circumstances.
- ✔ Understand that every Christian has a responsibility to act no matter what the consequences.
- ✔ Adopt their role as a believer for defending the oppressed.

Stuff you'll need:
- ❏ Identity Cards
- ❏ Bibles in different versions (different one for every small group)
- ❏ Whiteboard
- ❏ Dry-erase markers
- ❏ Paper and pencils
- ❏ Current newspapers and news magazines
- ❏ Scissors
- ❏ Glue
- ❏ Poster board (one piece for each group)
- ❏ *Invisible Children* DVD

## Memory Verse

Pure and undefiled religion before God and the Father is this: to visit orphans and widows in their trouble, and to keep oneself unspotted from the world.—James 1:27

## Scripture

Jeremiah 22:1–30

## Lesson in a Sentence

As Jesus' followers, we are to see the world as God sees it, compelling us to live a life of compassion and service.

# Focus

This activity is designed to bring awareness to a new level for your students. There are examples of oppression and unfair treatment of people as individuals and also as groups that take place every day. Students are sometimes in positions to see this happening. We have put together some names of people or groups and listed them on identity cards.

Divide the students into smaller groups of four to six. Make sure you have a volunteer leader or a responsible student in each group. Each group should get an identity card. As a group, discuss the following questions:

1. Put yourself in the position of a member of the community where this person lives. What do you think your role is—active or passive? What can you do to help?
2. Next, this person is now a member of your church? What is the responsibility of the church as a whole? What is your individual responsibility?
3. Finally, put yourself in the place of this person. What are you going to do? Would you want help? Is there a solution to your problem?

After each group spends fifteen to twenty minutes discussing, invite each of the groups to share with the big group about their discussion.

Do you feel more prepared to stand up for others who may be oppressed? Do you have ideas on how you can help someone this week?

# Discovery

Ask the students to stay in the same small groups. Each group should have a Bible of a different version. The group should read the Scripture passage together and come up with three key words, phrases, or themes. After each group is done (give them fifteen minutes), have them share their findings and record them on the whiteboard together.

Has anyone ever had an experience where a leader abused his or her power? Can you think of any current examples in today's society of leaders abusing their power? How does power affect you? What does this passage say about the abuse of power and resources?


## Life Application

Read the following intro for the movie *Invisible Children*:

**Invisible Children: Rough Cut** is a documentary recorded in 2003 based on the experiences of three college students in Northern Uganda. The filmers are from San Diego, California. They went to Uganda to see what they could film, and they found thousands of people affected by the insurgency of the Lord's Resistance Army (LRA). The resulting story focuses on the war's effects on children, particularly child soldiers.

They found that thousands of children flee their homes nightly in order to escape being abducted. Children in Uganda are regularly abducted by the LRA to be trained as child soldiers. The children who run from their homes walk miles to find shelter in hospitals or bus parks—virtually anywhere far away from rebel camps.

Show the trailer for *Invisible Children*.

## Making It Personal

After the trailer ends, lead the groups into discussion of the abuse of power that is happening in this tragedy. Hand out the pens and paper. Instruct the students to write hypothetical letters to the leaders of the LRA, just like the words that Jeremiah wrote to the kings of Judah. What do you say on behalf of these children who are trapped in oppression? How would you "plead the cause" of the afflicted and needy?

Before the students leave, challenge them to take notice of modern-day oppression around them.

# Jeremiah: Concern for How Believers Treat Those in Need

*By Scott and Carina Schubert*

## Memory Verse

Pure and undefiled religion before God and the Father is this: to visit orphans and widows in their trouble, and to keep oneself unspotted from the world.—James 1:27

## Scripture

Various Scriptures (see Discovery section)

## Lesson in a Sentence

We must act on behalf of the oppressed in our society, noticing and caring for the widows and orphans with the love of Christ.

# Focus

Bring in national newspapers and news magazines and let the students look through them in groups. Their goal is to find examples of modern-day oppression. Give them fifteen minutes to come up with examples. Ask them to share in small groups of four to six their findings and any observations from the week that they witnessed themselves.

# Discovery

Give each group one of the following verses:

- Exodus 3:7–8
- Deuteronomy 14:28–29
- Psalm 146:7–8
- Jeremiah 22:15–16
- Isaiah 32:16–17
- Luke 4:18–19
- 2 Corinthians 8:9

Give each group a large piece of poster board. With their verse and their news stories, ask them to make an art collage. Give them fifteen minutes to work on this in their group. After they have finished, display the art around the church in an effort to inform the congregation about oppression around the world.

## Life Application

For the remaining time, show the movie *Invisible Children.* After the forty-minute movie, lead a short time of discussion in small groups about practical ways of responding to this tragedy. Challenge the students as individuals and as a group to make significant steps to better the lives of the children in Uganda.

## Song Connect

"Made to Love" by tobyMac on *Portable Sounds*

## Quotable Quote

*Charity sees the need not the cause.*—German Proverb

# APPENDIX

# For Further Research

# Youth Ministry Web Resources

## Curriculum Resources

These are the Web addresses for publishers who offer dated and undated curriculum.

www.abingdon.com

www.augsburgfortress.org

www.Cokesbury.com

www.cookministries.com

www.grouppublishing.com

www.helwys.com

www.lifeway.com

www.standardpub.com

www.studentlife.net

www.thomasnelson.com

www.tyndale.com

www.upperroom.org

www.urbanministries.com

www.wjkbooks.com

www.youthspecialties.com

www.zondervan.com

## Games

www.egadideas.com—Offers a directory of indoor and outdoor games for your youth group to play.

www.funattic.com—A Web site dedicated to games of all sorts, for all age groups.

www.ferryhalim.com/orisinal—A whole host of silly Internet games.

www.gameskidsplay.net—Recreational activities for all ages of youth.

www.thesource4ym.com—Provides a huge collection of games for youth groups, ranging from mixers to swimming pool games.

www.theultimatecampresource.com—A Web site that is not Christian-camp specific but offers a variety of games, skits, activity, and other recreational ideas.

www.youthministry.com—Offers games that are just for fun, for large and small groups, noncompetitive, and that illustrate a point.

## Human/Social Resources

www.adopting.org—Adopting is a Web site designed to offer assistance, information, and support for adoption.

www.amnesty.org—A worldwide group seeking to end human rights violations.

www.aspenyouth.com—This is a Web site that provides information about Aspen Youth Ranches, which provide education, treatment, and rehabilitation to at-risk youth.

www.bread.org—Bread for the World. A lobbying group to Congress which provides study materials for high schoolers.

www.breakawayoutreach.com—Breakaway Youth is a ministry that reaches troubled youth through juvenile justice ministries, sports, and multimedia productions.

www.childrensdefense.org—Children's Defense Fund. They offer materials on the needs of American children, in particular the poor, for use in churches.

www.faithtrustinstitute.org—Formerly the Center for the Prevention of Sexual and Domestic Violence, now the FaithTrust Institute. This organization seeks to educate and prevent sexual and domestic violence and is the only one of its kind in the country looking at this from a faith perspective.

www.esa-online.org—Evangelicals for Social Action. Publishers of a wide array of Bible-based materials on social justice.

www.jmpf.org—John Perkins Foundation. Social justice and service.

www.mcc.org—Mennonite Central Committee. The relief and development agency of the Mennonite and Brethren in Christ churches.

www.newdream.org—A look at Sweatshop free clothing and links to look at some of the most popular brands and their company practices.

www.renfrew.org—The Renfrew Center Foundation, one of the nation's leading foundations in the battle against eating disorders. They have several in- and out-patient centers in the eastern half of the US with connections all over the country.

www.rainn.org—Rainn is the Web site to a confidential 24-hour rape hotline.

www.rockies.net/~spirit/grief/grief.html and http://www.griefworksbc.com/About.asp—Web sites offering insight and information surrounding the developmental issues of adolescence and grief including resources and support.

www.stopthetraffik.org—Stop the Traffik, a Web site seeking to raise awareness about human trafficking and the impact on ministry and adolescents worldwide.

www.teenchallengeusa.com—Resources, references, and treatment centers focused on drug and alcohol abuse.

www.vpp.com/teenhelp—VPP provides a national toll-free hotline designed to assist parents, childcare professionals, and others in finding resources for the treatment of struggling youth.

## Magazines

www.briomag.com—*Brio* is a magazine for teenage girls that strives to teach, entertain, and challenge girls while encouraging them to grow in a closer relationship with Christ.

www.sweet16mag.com—*Guideposts for Teens* is similar to the original *Guideposts* magazine for adults. *Guideposts for Teens* tackles real issues such as sex, dating, faith, and spirituality.

www.marshillforum.org—Mars Hill Forum looks at Christianity within a post modern context looking at Scripture and culture.

www.theotherjournal.com—An online journal looking at the intersection of theology and culture. It is only in an online formula with updates during the month of the initial release. There are also interactive portions.

www.pluggedinonline.com—Plugged In is designed to help parents, youth leaders, ministers, and teens to both understand and impact the culture they live in. Plugged In offers reviews and discussions regarding entertainment and its effects on youth and families.

www.relevantmagazine.com—A magazine for considering God and progressive culture.

www.sojo.net—*Soujourners,* a magazine and online source for faith, culture, and politics.

www.youthspecialties.com—*Journal of Student Ministries*

www.thejournalofstudentministries.com—A thematic magazine aimed bimonthly at youth workers seeking to be a connection point for practitioners and researchers. A focused value is on underrepresented voices, both veteran and novice. Practical articles, devotional articles, resources and a whole host of information regarding thoughts and trends within youth ministry.

## Missions and Service

www.amor.org—A missions agency specializing in trips to northern Mexico.

www.apu.edu/iom/mexout—Mexico Outreach. A ministry based out of Azusa Pacific University taking high school and young adult groups into northern Mexico for service.

www.agrm.org—Association of Gospel Rescue Missions. An associational Web site that links to local missions. Missions typically provide shelter, kitchens, community development, and community centers.

www.asphome.org—Appalachia Service Project, a ministry that takes other groups on week-long mission trips to Kentucky and Tennessee to repair homes for the poor.

www.calebproject.org—An organization offering information and resources for global missions.

www.christiansurfers.net—An organization that helps students form a Christian organization of surfers or to offer the possibility of missions in the surfing community.

www.compassion.com—Compassion International. World Relief organization with programs that can educate and involve junior and senior high students.

www.crm.org—Church Resources Ministries—CRM exists to develop leaders in the church and to provide resources worldwide.

www.empoweringlives.org—An organization seeking to address spiritual and physical needs in struggling countries primarily in Africa. They seek outreach and leadership development and child sponsorship opportunities.

www.gospelcom.net/csm—Center for Student Missions. A ministry offering customized mission trips to large cities for junior and senior high students.

www.habitat.org—Habitat for Humanity. Provides housing for low-income families with many service opportunities.

www.joniandfriends.org—An excellent (and one of the only) resource for ministry with those with disabilities.

www.larche.org, www.larcheusa.org, www.larche.org.uk, www.larchecanada.org— L'Arche is an organization begun in France which has spread to much of the world. They provide communities for those with and without physical or mental disabilities. Henri Nouwen is probably the best-known participant associated with the organization.

www.newadventures.org—Missions organization providing trips for junior and senior high school students.

www.oneliferevolution.org—A focused ministry encouraging youth groups to not only raise awareness regarding the AIDS pandemic as well as a way for your group to fight this problem.

www.servlife.org—A missions organization which seeks to develop and empower indigenous workers in difficult areas. This is an organization that has taken innovation and heart to share Christ in places others were not going.

www.worldvision.org—World Vision is an organization that provides relief to third world countries by reaching out to the poor, and staying aware of current worldwide events.

## Music Resources

www.acaza.com—Offers current news on Christian artists.

www.ccmcom.com—Provides up-to-date news on today's hottest contemporary Christian musicians.

www.christianfestivals.com—A resource listing Christian festivals and concerts all over the country.

www.christianitytoday.com/music/—Reviews new Christian music and provides interviews with the artists.

www.cmcentral.com—Christian Music Central offers visitors the chance to view editorials on music and artists, shows album and artist reviews, lists tour dates, and offers MP3 downloads.

www.christianradio.com—Christian Radio gives a list of over 2,000 Christian radio stations as well as over 500 Christian artists.

www.christianrock.net—Christian Rock is a 24-hour radio show broadcast on the Internet. Christian Rock has two sister stations:

http://www.christianhardrock.net/

http://www.christian-hiphop.net/

www.tollbooth.org—The Phantom Tollbooth. A Look at music, concerts, and movies all with a Christian eye to review.

www.rockrebel.com/—Christianity and Spirituality in Secular Music (articles).

www.wellwatermusic.com—A resource for and about new artists.

www.worshiptogether.com—Provides a great overview of what is hot in Christian music by offering top ten lists, free song downloads, and more.

www.youthfire.com—Youth Fire is a great Web site to refer to when looking for Christian music that is comparable to what is played daily on mainstream radio.

## Pop Culture

www.christianitytoday.com—Provides a good way to identify with Christian youth and their beliefs, by giving current detailed reviews on movies and music, and provides discussion questions.

www.cpyu.org—Center for Parent and Youth Understanding. A comprehensive Web site with constant updates covering youth culture from many angles.

www.dickstaub.com—Pop culture review from a Christian perspective.

www.commonsensemedia.org—Family oriented media reviews (philosophy is sanity not censorship).

www.gracehillmedia.com—This is a company which holds major Hollywood studios as clients to find points of connection with the Christian community.

www.hollywoodjesus.com—A source that offers Christian perspectives of today's pop culture. You'll find reviews for today's newest movies, music, and much more.

www.medialit.org/focus/rel_articles.html—Center for Media Literacy (has some faith based articles on media discernment.

www.mrfh.cjb.net—(Screen It Entertainment Reviews) Offers a detailed description of what viewers will see, i.e. violence, sex, bad language in current movies, and why the MPAA rated the movie they way they did.

www.planetwisdom.com—Reviews of movies and music with insights on culture and faith.

www.rollingstone.com—Update yourself on what youth are watching and hearing in today s secular media. This source reviews movies and particularly secular music, providing CD reviews, photos, and videos of today's pop stars.

www.screenit.com—Screen It offers reviews on all sorts of entertainment.

www.textweek.com—Gives sermon topics stemming from current and past movies.

www.tollbooth.org—An online magazine that provides reviews of Christian music, concerts, and books. Also provides reviews of past movies.

www.wikipedia.org—An open source encyclopedia (online and built by its users).

## Spiritual Disciplines

www.contemplativeoutreach.org—An offering of both information as well as connection with other sites and groups interested in exploring the contemplative side of faith.

www.labyrinth.org.uk—An adaptation of the cathedral labyrinth, the most commonly known labyrinth among youth workers.

http://www.princeofpeaceonline.org/psalms/lectio.html—A Web site offering articles and explanations into the practice of *lectio devina.*

www.sdiworld.org—The directory of Spiritual Directors International.

www.sfts.edu—San Francisco Theological Seminary has a Lilly-endowed program called the Youth Ministry and Spirituality Project. Many insights and resources are available.

www.taize.fr—Web site for the Taize community in France.

www.tddm.org—Daily devotionals, poems, stories, and chat rooms all geared toward teens.

## T-Shirts, etc.

www.mcduck.com—A company familiar with youth ministry offering embroidery and screen printing on a variety of items.

www.zazzle.com—A Web site that allows for you to create your design and have it printed on multiple variations of shirts at a relatively low cost.

# Worship Resources

www.audiblefaith.com—Audible Faith offers downloadable worship music and sheet music can be ordered from this Web site in any key.

www.ccli.com—CCLI is a strong communication network that allows the dispensing of comprehensive and valuable informational resources about worship.

www.christianguitar.org—Christian Guitar is a fantastic Christian guitar resource page with over 7,000 tabs. Christian Guitar also offers lessons, PowerPoint slides, and message boards.

www.integritymusic.com—Integrity Music offers a number of different worship resources that include information on artists, albums, and much more.

www.maranathamusic.com—Maranatha Music offers a number of resources for worship and worship leaders.

www.pastornet.net.au/inside—Inside Out offers free downloadable contemporary and evangelical worship music for noncommercial use.

www.songs4worship.com—Songs 4 Worship offers numerous worship resources including music, community, freebies, and more.

www.worshipmusic.com—Worship Music is a Christian music resource with CDs, cassettes, sheet/print music, videos, software, and more for sale.

# Youth Activities

www.30hourfamine.org—30 Hour Famine is a movement led by World Vision that fights world hunger with the help of youth and churches all around the world.

www.adventures.org—Adventures in Missions is an interdenominational short-term missions organization that offers programs for youth, college, and adults.

www.bigworld.org—Big World Ventures offers customized short-term mission trips for youth, adults, individuals, groups, church networks, and Christian organizations. This Web site provides information regarding all trips and destinations.

www.jeremiahproject.org—The Jeremiah Project offers missions trips that are planned specifically for junior high youth.

www.noahsark.com—Noah's Ark is located in Colorado, offering a uniquely Christian perspective on whitewater rafting, rock climbing, rappelling, and a whole lot more!

www.syatp.org—See You at the Pole. Once a year in September it has become a youth ministry tradition in the United States and around the world for students to gather around the flag pole at school to pray.

www.ywam.org—YWAM Urban Ministries is an organization that attempts to bring safe and exciting events to communities in need through innovative ministries and living with the people in the community.

## Youth Pastor-Emergent

http://emergingchurch.info/—A sort of primer and advanced conversation Web site for the movement of the emerging church.

www.emergentvillage.com—Resources and links for missional Christians across generations.

www.theooze.com—Online magazine that looks to any and all issues, bringing them into a conversation within a Christian community.

## Youth Pastor Resources

www.americanapparel.net—A Los Angeles-based company that ensures fair wages and good working conditions from production to distribution. This is a socially responsible resource for those plain shirts you want printed for camp or your retreat.

www.bgu.edu—Bakke Graduate University of Ministry. A unique accredited school offering a global perspective and experience to theological education. Because those attending are in ministry, the classes are offered in intensives and through cohorts allowing the person to remain in ministry while training.

www.biblegateway.com—A collection of several translations of the Bible online.

www.buwc.ca/youthline—Youthline is a youth ministry resource page with events located primarily in Canada.

www.younglife.org/Capernaum/—A division of Young Life which focuses on ministry for adolescents with special needs.

www.crosswalk.com—Many different resources, from articles and advice to online translations of the Bible.

www.discipleshipresources.org/downloads.asp—Free discipleship downloads from the United Methodist Church.

www.family.org—Provides articles that help parents know how to better deal with their growing children and changing families. Offers advice and wisdom for the ups and downs of family life.

www.highwayvideo.com—Highway video offers culturally relevant videos to be used in ministry and worship.

www.ileadyouth.com—A Web site offering articles, trainings, resources, and events for youth workers.

www.notboring.com—Free comics, jokes, e-cards etc. These are updated three times each week.

www.familybuilders.net—Provides youth workers with articles that help build a stronger family-based ministry, and offers parents helpful articles for understanding their adolescent children.

www.persecution.com—A Web site offering updates and prayer requests regarding the persecuted church around the world.

www.reach-out.org—A resource for youth leaders that presents, finds books, articles, Bible studies, illustrations, ideas for training volunteers, and insight into leading a successful missions trip.

www.teamce.com—A Web site from Christian Endeavor, often credited with founding youth ministry in the U.S. An offering of philosophy and training for simplified youth ministry.

www.uywi.org—A ministry offering trainings for those specifically working in urban settings.

www.yfc.org—Provides current information on youth ministries for youth pastors, youth, and parents.

www.ymwomen.com—A networking resource for women in youth ministry including free articles, resources and an e-mail newsletter.

www.younglife.org—Offers information about Young life and its work with today's youth.

www.youthbuilders.com—A resource for parents and youth leaders offering articles, answered questions that help parents and youth leaders better understand how to work with and relate to the youth in their lives.

www.youth-ministry.info—Great Web site with tons of information, both practical and philosophical and links to just about everything connected with youth ministry you can imagine.

www.youthpastor.com—Provides youth pastors with articles, games, youth group names, recommended reading, topical music resource, and more.

www.youthspecialties.com/links—This Web site offers thousands of links to Web sites on leadership, missions, skit ideas, crisis hotlines, and much more.

www.youthworkers.net—A resource that allows youth workers to be able to connect with each other by region. Also provides links to activities in which youth nationwide participate. In particular, check out the link to the *Youth Ministry Yellow Pages* which contains hundreds of phone numbers and connections to resources.

## END USER LICENSE AGREEMENT

CAREFULLY READ THE FOLLOWING LICENSE AGREEMENT. BY CLICKING ON THE "I ACCEPT THE TERMS OF THE LICENSE AGREEMENT" BUTTON AND CLICKING THE NEXT BUTTON, YOU ARE CONSENTING TO BE BOUND BY AND ARE BECOMING A PARTY TO THIS AGREEMENT. THIS PRODUCT REQUIRES USER REGISTRATION AND WILL CEASE TO FUNCTION IF USER REGISTRATION IS NOT CONFIRMED. IF YOU DO NOT AGREE TO ALL OF THE TERMS OF THIS AGREEMENT, CLICK THE "CANCEL" BUTTON, AND, IF APPLICABLE, RETURN THIS PRODUCT TO THE PLACE OF PURCHASE FOR A FULL REFUND.

### LICENSE GRANT
The package contains software ("Software") and may contain electronic text, graphics, audio, or other resources ("Content") and related explanatory written materials ("Documentation"). "Software" includes any upgrades, modified versions, updates, additions and copies of the Software. "You" means the person or company who is being licensed to use the Software, Content and Documentation. "We" and "us" means Libronix Corporation and its parent company, Logos Research Systems, Inc.

We hereby grant you a nonexclusive license to use one copy of the Software and "unlocked" Content on any single computer, provided the Software and Content are in use on only one computer at any time. The Software is "in use" on a computer when it is loaded into temporary memory (RAM) or installed into the permanent memory of a computer—for example, a hard disk, CD-ROM or other storage device.

If the Software and Content are permanently installed on the hard disk or other storage device of a computer (other than a network server) and one person uses that computer more than 80% of the time, then that person may also use the Software and Content on a portable or home computer.

The package may contain Content that is NOT licensed to you. This Content is "locked" in electronic form and is included for your convenience should you desire to "unlock" it by purchasing a license for it. Content that you "unlock" is covered by this agreement.

### TITLE
We remain the owner of all right, title and interest in the Software and Documentation. Ownership of the Content remains with Copyright holders.

### ARCHIVAL OR BACKUP COPIES
You may either:
— make one copy of the Software solely for backup or archival purposes, or
— transfer the Software to a single hard disk, provided you keep the original solely for backup or archival purposes.

### THINGS YOU MAY NOT DO
The Software, Content, and Documentation are protected by United States copyright laws and international treaties. You must treat the Software, Content, and Documentation like any other copyrighted material—for example a book. You may not:
— copy the Documentation,
— copy the Software or Content except to make archival or backup copies as provided above,
— modify or adapt the Software or merge it into another program,
— reverse engineer, disassemble, decompile or make any attempt to discover the source code of the Software,
— place the Software or Content onto a server so that it is accessible via a public network such as the Internet,
— sublicense, rent, lease or lend any portion of the Software, Content, or Documentation, or
— reverse engineer, disassemble, decompile or make any attempt to "unlock" or circumvent the digital copyright protection of the Content.

### TRANSFERS
You may transfer all your rights to use the Software, Content, and Documentation to another person or legal entity provided you transfer this Agreement, the Software, Content, and Documentation, including all copies, update and prior versions to such person or entity and that you retain no copies, including copies stored on computer.

### LIMITED WARRANTY
We warrant that for a period of 90 days after delivery of this copy of the Software to you:
— if provided, the physical media on which this copy of the Software is distributed will be free from defects in materials and workmanship under normal use, and
— the Software will perform in substantial accordance with the Documentation.
To the extent permitted by applicable law, THE FOREGOING LIMITED WARRANTY IS IN LIEU OF ALL OTHER WARRANTIES OR CONDITIONS, EXPRESS OR IMPLIED, AND WE DISCLAIM ANY AND ALL IMPLIED WARRANTIES OR CONDITIONS, INCLUDING ANY IMPLIED WARRANTY OF TITLE, NONINFRINGEMENT, MERCHANTABILITY OR FITNESS FOR A PARTICULAR PURPOSE, regardless of whether we know or had reason to know of your particular needs. No employee, agent, dealer or distributor of ours is authorized to modify this limited warranty, nor to make any additional warranties.

SOME STATES DO NOT ALLOW THE EXCLUSION OF IMPLIED WARRANTIES, SO THE ABOVE EXCLUSION MAY NOT APPLY TO YOU. THIS WARRANTY GIVES YOU SPECIFIC LEGAL RIGHTS, AND YOU MAY ALSO HAVE OTHER RIGHTS WHICH VARY FROM STATE TO STATE.

### LIMITED REMEDY
Our entire liability and your exclusive remedy shall be:
— the replacement of any diskette(s) or other media not meeting our Limited Warranty which is returned to us or to an authorized Dealer or Distributor with a copy of your receipt, or
— If we or an authorized Dealer or Distributor are unable to deliver a replacement diskette(s) or other media that is free of defects in materials or workmanship, you may terminate this Agreement by returning the Software and Documentation and your money will be refunded.
IN NO EVENT WILL WE BE LIABLE TO YOU FOR ANY DAMAGES, INCLUDING ANY LOST PROFITS, LOST SAVINGS, OR OTHER INCIDENTAL OR CONSEQUENTIAL DAMAGES ARISING FROM THE USE OR THE INABILITY TO USE THE SOFTWARE (EVEN IF WE OR AN AUTHORIZED DEALER OR DISTRIBUTOR HAS BEEN ADVISED OF THE POSSIBILITY OF THESE DAMAGES), OR FOR ANY CLAIM BY ANY OTHER PARTY.

SOME STATES DO NOT ALLOW THE LIMITATION OR EXCLUSION OF LIABILITY FOR INCIDENTAL OR CONSEQUENTIAL DAMAGES, SO THE ABOVE LIMITATION MAY NOT APPLY TO YOU.

### TERM AND TERMINATION
This license agreement takes effect upon your use of the software and remains effective until terminated. You may terminate it at any time by destroying all copies of the Software and Documentation in your possession. It will also automatically terminate if you fail to comply with any term or condition of this license agreement. You agree on termination of this license to either return to us or destroy all copies of the Software and Documentation in your possession.

### CONFIDENTIALITY
The Software contains trade secrets and proprietary know-how that belong to us and it is being made available to you in strict confidence. ANY USE OR DISCLOSURE OF THE SOFTWARE, OR OF ITS ALGORITHMS, PROTOCOLS OR INTERFACES, OTHER THAN IN STRICT ACCORDANCE WITH THIS LICENSE AGREEMENT, MAY BE ACTIONABLE AS A VIOLATION OF OUR TRADE SECRET RIGHTS.

### GENERAL PROVISIONS
1. This written license agreement is the exclusive agreement between you and us concerning the Software, Content, and Documentation and supersedes any and all prior oral or written agreements, negotiations or other dealings between us concerning the Software.
2. This license agreement may be modified only by a writing signed by you and us.
3. In the event of litigation between you and us concerning the Software or Documentation, the prevailing party in the litigation will be entitled to recover attorney fees and expenses from the other party.
4. You agree to register this product with Libronix Corporation within 30 days. (Registration may be accomplished via the Internet or by mail. Registration helps protect the owners and publishers of copyrighted Content and encourages more publishers to release their Content electronically.) You may register anonymously but we may not provide certain types of support or opportunities to participate in certain online features if you choose to do so. After 30 days the software may cease to function until it receives confirmation of registration.
5. You represent that if you choose to provide name, address, credit card, or any other information that it will be your true information. You may choose or be assigned a user name, confirmation code, and/or password in connection with your use of the Software. You agree to keep your confirmation code and password confidential. We disclaim responsibility for unauthorized use of your credit card or password.
6. Registration with Libronix Corporation implies registration with the Content owners whose Content you have licensed for use with the Software. We may share your registration information with the owners of Content you have licensed. We will honor your indication that you do not want registration information shared with any other third party. (You may indicate this during registration if you choose to provide name, address, etc.)
7. You agree that the Software may detect the presence of a connection to the Internet and communicate with servers controlled by Libronix in order to submit anonymous statistical information on use of the Software and Content and to detect and download updates to the Software and Content and new Software and Content for which you may have chosen to purchase licenses. You agree that new and updated Software and Content downloaded by the Software from the Internet are covered by this license.
8. This license agreement is governed by the laws of the State of Washington, USA.
9. You agree that the Software will not be shipped, transferred or exported into any country or used in any manner prohibited by the United States Export Administration Act or any other export laws, restrictions or regulations.
10. The controlling language of this agreement is English. Any translation of this agreement that you may have received is provided only for your convenience.